STUDIES ON THE TEXT OF SUETONIUS
DE GRAMMATICIS ET RHETORIBUS

AMERICAN PHILOLOGICAL ASSOCIATION
American Classical Studies

Series Editor

Matthew S. Santirocco

Number 28

Studies on the Text of Suetonius
De Grammaticis et Rhetoribus

by
Robert A. Kaster

Robert A. Kaster

STUDIES ON THE TEXT OF SUETONIUS
DE GRAMMATICIS ET RHETORIBUS

Scholars Press
Atlanta, Georgia

STUDIES ON THE TEXT OF SUETONIUS
DE GRAMMATICIS ET RHETORIBUS

Robert A. Kaster

© 1992
The American Philological Association

Library of Congress Cataloging in Publication Data

Kaster, Robert A.
  Studies on the text of Suetonius De grammaticis et rhetoribus /
Robert A. Kaster.
  Includes bibliographical references and index.
  ISBN 1-55540-720-X (alk. paper). — ISBN 1-55540-721-8 (pbk. :
alk. paper)
  1. Suetonius, ca. 69-ca. 122. De grammaticis et rhetoribus—
Criticism, Textual. 2. Philologists—Rome—Biography—Criticism,
Textual. 3. Latin prose literature—Criticism, Textual.
4. Manuscripts, Latin. I. Title. II. Series.
PA6700.D9K37 1992
470'.92'2—dc20   92-5797
[B]   CIP

Printed in the United States of America
on acid-free paper

TABLE OF CONTENTS

Preface vii

Conspectus codicum et siglorum ix

Chapter 1: The Stemma 1
    The Familiies α β γ 12
    The Manuscripts **V** and **L** 14
    Conclusion 31

Chapter 2: The Text 35
    Loci sanandi, deliquandi, conclamandi 38

Appendix 1: Robinson and della Corte 131

Appendix 2: **O** and **W** 135

Appendix 3: Biblioteca Riccardiana 3595 147

Bibliography 157

Index locorum 163

PREFACE

These *Studies* present the *prolegomena* to a critical edition of Suetonius *De grammaticis et rhetoribus* that is to appear, with a translation and full commentary, in the not-too-distant future. Chapter 1 takes up the transmission of the text following the discovery of the codex Hersfeldensis and--as a kind of appendix to the splendid work of R. P. Robinson--modifies the latter's analysis of one of the tradition's two main branches. Chapter 2 offers discussions of a number of passages in the poorly preserved text.

In addition to Bibl. Ricc. 3595, which is reported here for the first time (App. 3), I have collated afresh eight of the most important manuscripts (**OWNGVBLH**); attempts to obtain a film of a ninth (**M**) unfortunately proved unsuccessful. For this and the remaining manuscript and incunabular witnesses I have relied on the reports of Robinson and (especially for codd. **TE**) G. Brugnoli (see also Chap. 1, n. 8).

I am indebted to the John Simon Guggenheim Memorial Foundation for the fellowship that facilitated the final revisions of this monograph. For making photographs of manuscripts available to me I wish to thank: the Biblioteca Apostolica Vaticana; the Biblioteca Nazionale Vittorio Emanuele III, Naples; the Biblioteca Riccardiana, Florence; the British Library, London; the Bodleian Library, Oxford; the Oesterreichische Nationalbibliothek, Vienna; and the Herzog-August-Bibliothek, Wolfenbüttel. I am very grateful also to M. D. Reeve, who alerted me to the existence of Bibl. Ricc. 3595; to Matthew S. Santirocco, editor of the series American Classical Studies, and Dennis Ford, of Scholars Press, for their patient technical advice; to B. C. Barker-Benfield (Bodleian Library) and M. Prunai Falciani (Biblioteca Riccardiana), who kindly answered questions concerning manuscripts in their collections; to K. R. Bradley, E. Courtney, and W. Braxton Ross, for helpful comments on individual problems; and especially to C. E. Murgia, R. Renehan, and J. E. G. Zetzel, who generously and candidly commented on the whole typescript. It should not be assumed that any of those just mentioned agrees with all that follows: I can say for certain that several of them do not, and that I alone am responsible for the errors that remain.

R. A. K.
Hyde Park
January 1992

CONSPECTUS CODICUM ET SIGLORUM

X O   Vat. Ottob. lat. 1455
     O^1 codex eadem manu correctus
     O^m lectio eadem manu in margine notata   ⎫ W^1, W^m, W^2, etc.
     O^2 codex altera manu correctus   ⎭
  W   Vindob. lat. s. n. 2960 (olim 711) (an. 1466)

α N   Neap. IV. C. 21
  G   Guelf. Gud. lat. 93
  I   Vat. lat. 1518
       Vat. Ottob. lat. 1434 (apographon codicis I)
       Vat. Ottob. lat. 3015

β B   Bodl. Canon. Class. Lat. 151
  V   Vat. lat. 1862
  D   Haun. Gl. Kgl. s. 1629 4º
  L   Leid. Periz. Q. 21 (an. 1460)

γ M   Marc. Lat. XIV. 1. (4266) (an. 1464)
  K   Ambros. H. 29 sup.
  H   Lond. Harl. 2639 (ante an. 1465 script., fort. 1462)
  P   Paris. lat. 7773 (apographon codicis H)
  U   Vat. Urb. lat. 1194 (post an. 1482 script.)
  S   Neap. IV. B. 4. bis
  C   Berol. lat. 8º 197
  F   Laurent. plut. (Gadd.) 89. inf. 8.1 (apographon codicis C)
  Δ   Vat. lat. 4498
  Q   Berol. lat. 2º 28 (an. 1477)
  T   Vat. lat. 7190
  E   Vat. Borg. lat. 413
       Univ. Notre Dame 58
       Colker ms. 11
       Ricc. 3595 (vide pp. 147-56)

CHAPTER 1

THE STEMMA

Early in the second century Suetonius composed his work *De viris illustribus*, comprising the biographies of distinguished men of Latin letters--poets, historians, orators, philosophers, and teachers--who flourished during the late Republic and early Empire. From the greater part of this work only scattered excerpts have come down to us, most notably the lives of Terence, Horace, and (substantially) Vergil. But one major segment, *De grammaticis et rhetoribus (DGR)*, chanced to be transmitted independently: rediscovered in the 15th century, it survives as a precious source both for the history of Roman education and for the literary and cultural history of Rome more generally.[1]

The *DGR* survives because of a single 9th-century MS, the codex Hersfeldensis, to which we also owe our texts of Tacitus' minor works (*Agricola, Germania, Dialogus de oratoribus*). The story of this MS's discovery has often been told, and some details remain controversial; the main outlines of the story are nonetheless clear, and can be recounted briefly here.[2] Though the presence

---

[1] The best modern edition is still that of R. P. Robinson (Paris, 1925)--though relatively few copies remain available, and those that remain are rapidly disintegrating because of the poor quality of the paper; for Robinson's fundamental work on the paradosis, see at n. 7 below. Editions have more recently been published by C. Bione (Palermo, 1939; 2nd ed. 1941); F. della Corte (Genoa, 1947; 2nd ed. Rome, 1954; 3rd ed. Turin, 1968); and G. Brugnoli (Leipzig, 1960; 2nd ed. 1963; 3rd ed. 1972). Robinson's edition is cited hereafter as "ed."; the 2nd ed. of Bione and the 3rd ed. of Brugnoli are cited throughout, with reference only to the editor's name; and the "2nd ed." and "3rd ed." of della Corte, which differ significantly from each other, are distinguished thus.

[2] For a clear, detailed, and sober review, with full bibliography, see now F. Römer, "Kritischer Problem- und Forschungsbericht zur Ueberlieferung

of the MS in Germany was reported as early as 1425 by Poggio Bracciolini, the book remained beyond the reach of the learned world until it was brought to Rome, probably by Enoch of Ascoli, in the autumn of 1455. There it was soon examined by the papal secretary Pier Candido Decembrio, whose extant description shows that the MS presented the works in the order *Germ., Agr., Dial., DGR*.[3] Yet it seems that sometime between the beginning of 1456 and Enoch's death in December 1457, the MS was broken up and the *Agr.* was disposed of (perhaps sold) separately.[4] As a result of this dismemberment, the subsequent transmission of the *Agr.* stands apart from that of the *Germ., Dial.,* and *DGR*; from among the latter works, the paradosis of the *Germ.* partly overlaps with, partly diverges from, that of the other two, while it

---

der taciteischen Schriften," *ANRW* 2:33.3 (Berlin and New York, 1991), pp. 2324ff.; also interesting, in the same volume, is H. Merklin, "'Dialogus'-Probleme in der neuren Forschung: Ueberlieferungsgeschichte, Echtheitsbeweis und Umfang der Lücke," pp. 2255ff. (largely recapitulating and modifying the arguments of his earlier article, "Probleme des 'Dialogus de oratoribus,'" *A&A* 34 [1988]: 170ff.). The textual histories of the *DGR* and Tacitus' *minora* are also briefly sketched, with further refs., by M. Winterbottom in L. D. Reynolds, ed., *Texts and Transmission: A Survey of the Latin Classics* (Oxford, 1983), pp. 404f., 410f.

[3] For Decembrio's description, often reproduced, see, e.g., R. P. Robinson, *De fragmenti Suetoniani "De grammaticis et rhetoribus" codicum nexu et fide* (Urbana, 1920), pp. 15f., id., *The "Germania" of Tacitus* (Middletown, Conn., 1935), pp. 8f. The text of the MS Decembrio described gave out after *DGR* 30. 6 *abstinuit cibo* (i.e., after the fifth of the original sixteen biographies of *rhetores*), as does the text of all surviving MSS.

[4] On the chronology, see esp. B. L. Ullman, "Pontano's Handwriting and the Leiden Manuscript of Tacitus and Suetonius," *IMU* 2 (1959): 322-23; cf. G. Brugnoli, *Studi Suetoniani* (Lecce, 1968), pp. 89ff., F. Stok, "Le vicende dei codici Hersfeldensi," *MAL* 28 (1984-86): 304ff., Römer, "Kritischer . . . Forschungsbericht," pp. 2324ff., Merklin, "'Dialogus'-Probleme," pp. 2263ff. It is not clear that the *Germ., Dial.,* and *DGR* were in general circulation before Enoch's death: after Decembrio's description, the earliest certain reference to any of these works occurs in a letter of Enea Silvio de' Piccolomini dated 1 Feb. 1458 (citing the *Germ.*: see Brugnoli, ed., p. xiii, Merklin, "'Dialogus'-Probleme," p. 2259); among the extant MSS, the earliest dated copy is Pontano's autograph of 1460 (which contains all three works: Leid. Periz. Q. 21 = **L** for *DGR*, **b** for *Germ. / Dial.*), though at least Vat. lat. 1862 (= **V** for *DGR*, **B** for *Germ. / Dial.*) must be earlier: see at n. 54, below.

has long been remarked that the *Dial.* and *DGR* followed very similar paths of descent.⁵ The Hersfeldensis itself has vanished, save for a fragment of the *Agr.* that was incorporated in codex Aesinas lat. 8.⁶

Modern understanding of the *DGR*'s tradition was put on a sure footing by the excellent dissertation of R. P. Robinson, who examined the relations among all nineteen MSS of the work then known, together with the three incunabular editions (**ed. Inc.** [1471?], **ed. Ven.** [1474], **ed. Flor.** [1478]).⁷ The essential points of Robinson's findings are presented here in Figure 1 (p. 4), which reproduces the stemma from his dissertation (p. 186, cf. ed., p. ix), with a few minor adjustments: the relations within family α have been slightly redrawn (the better to represent the relations that Robinson actually described at diss., p. 114), and some of the lost intermediaries that Robinson posited in sub-family ζ are omitted for the sake of clarity; also omitted are the seven additional MSS

---

5 On the distribution and ordering of the *Germ., Dial.,* and *DGR* in the MSS, cf. Brugnoli, *Studi Suetoniani,* pp. 79ff.; on the MSS of the *Dial.* and *DGR,* see Robinson, *De fragmenti Suetoniani . . . codicum nexu et fide,* pp. 187ff.

6 The fragment consists of a quaternion (fol. 56-63) and a unio, the latter erased and overwritten by Stefano Guarnieri; as Winterbottom remarks (*Texts,* p. 410 n. 3), "the manuscript has disappeared again, but a facsimile is available in R. Till, *Handschriftliche Untersuchungen zu Tacitus Agricola und Germania* (Berlin-Dahlem, 1943)." The identity of the Aesinas-fragment is still contested: its origin in the Hersfeldensis was most recently denied, on codicological grounds, by D. Schaps, "The Found and Lost Manuscripts of Tacitus' *Agricola,*" *CP* 74 (1979): 28ff.; for a critical response see esp. C. E. Murgia and R. H. Rodgers, "A Tale of Two Manuscripts," *CP* 79 (1984): 145ff.; for a defense of Schaps see Merklin, "Probleme," pp. 178ff.; and note that Merklin has now somewhat modified his own position in "'Dialogus'-Probleme" (esp. pp. 2268f.). The debate is likely to continue; for a dispassionate overview, see Römer, "Kritischer . . . Forschungsbericht," pp. 2328ff.

7 Robinson, *De fragmenti Suetoniani . . . codicum nexu et fide,* hereafter "diss."; the 15th-cent. witnesses are described on pp. 29-37; for a survey of printed editions down to the time of his own, see Robinson, ed., pp. 53ff.

Figure 1: Suetonius *De grammaticis et rhetoribus* (Robinson)

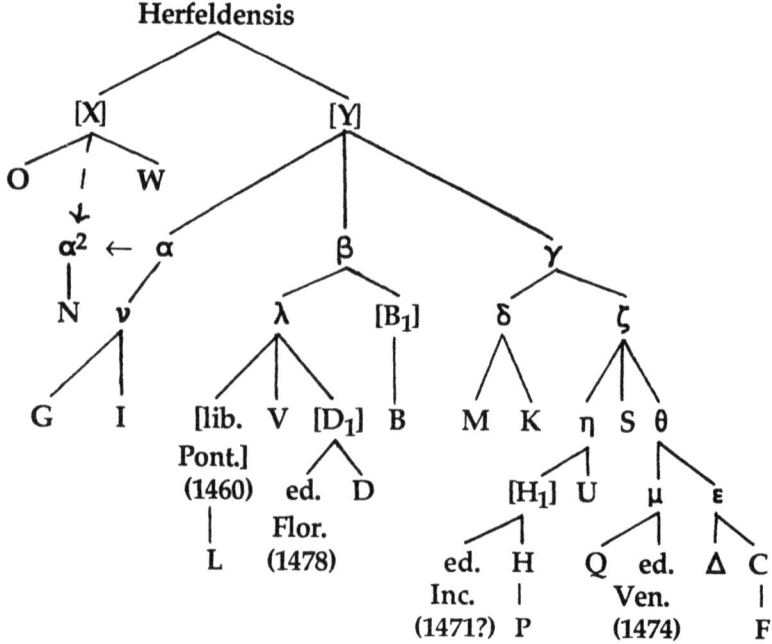

discovered after Robinson's work, since these bring nothing new to the text and nothing important to the analysis of the stemma.[8]

---

[8] These MSS are: Vat. lat. 7190 (= Brugnoli's T); Vat. Borg. lat. 413 (= Brugnoli's E, also containing *Dial.*); Vat. Ottob. 1434 (also containing *Dial.* and *Germ.*); Vat. Ottob. 3015; Univ. Notre Dame 58; Colker ms. 11 (privately owned); Ricc. 3595 (also containing the *Dial.*). The first four are described by G. Brugnoli, "De IV codicibus . . . nuperrime adinventis," *GIF* 13 (1960): 346-50 (with ed., pp. xx-xxvii; Ottob. 1434 was first described by D. Robathan, "Another Fifteenth-Century Manuscript of the *Germania*," *AJP* 71 [1950]: 225-38); the fifth and sixth by M. L. Colker, "Two Manuscripts of Suetonius' *De grammaticis et rhetoribus*," *Manuscripta* 27 (1983): 165-69; the last in App. 3, below. None of these is of the slightest value for an editor of the *DGR*: T and E, though included by Brugnoli in his apparatus, are undistinguished MSS of the ζ-family that offer no worthwhile conjectures and reveal nothing about the tradition that is of consequence for an editor (cf. already H. Dahlmann, rev. of Brugnoli, *Gnomon* 33 [1961]: 797); Ottob. 1434 is an apograph of I (for both *DGR* and *Dial.*; cf. M. Winterbottom, "The Transmission of Tacitus' *Dialogus*," *Philol.* 116 [1972]:

The stemma shown in Figure 1 depicts a tradition composed of two branches descending from the lost hyparchetypes X and Y, which are assumed to have been copied directly from the Hersfeldensis. X is represented by its two extant descendants, the *gemelli* O and W; Y is represented by three families, each descended independently from the hyparchetype *via* a lost copy, α or β or γ. The most densely populated of these families--and the family that offers the poorest testimony overall--is γ, whose descendants constitute two main sub-families, δ (=MK) and ζ (=η[=HPU ed. Inc.] S θ[=CFΔQ ed.Ven.]); in practice, since S is a generally negligible witness (offering only an epitome of *DGR* 1-11 and a wretchedly corrupt text for the rest of the work), the text of γ can usually be reconstructed from the agreement of δ (or M or K) with either ζ or η (against θ) or θ (against η; divisions of the sort Mθ vs. Kη are in fact rather rare). The text of β, the second lost copy of Y, can be reconstructed from the agreement of B and λ (=VLD ed.Flor.); concerning these witnesses much more will be said below. Finally, the text of the lost MS α is usually evident from the consensus of NGI; but since N was derived from α after the latter had received some variants from an X-source (either X itself or a copy of X), N sometimes reflects this contamination, offering the α-reading in the text and the X-reading as a variant, or the X-reading in the text and the α-reading as the variant, all in the first scribal hand (a smaller number of X-readings also occur as variants or corrections entered by a second hand in G: see Robinson, diss., pp. 113ff.). In principle, then, when the texts of α β γ have been reconstructed from their descendants, the agreement of any two against the third should (absent coincidental agreement in error) reveal the reading of Y, for each descends independently from the hyparchetype; and since both X and Y are assumed to have been copied directly from the Hersfeldensis, the agreement of X (or O or W) with Y (i.e., α β γ, or α β vs. γ, or α γ vs. β, or β γ vs. α) should in principle represent the reading of the lost 9th-century MS (divisions of the sort O α β vs. W γ, which would *prima facie* suggest the presence of contamination or archetypal variants, are very uncommon).

120f.); Ottob. 3015 is another α-MS contaminated from X; Colker ms. 11 is clearly a copy of ed. Inc.; Univ. Notre Dame 58 and Ricc. 3595 are equally clearly two more undistinguished ζ-MSS (the latter closely related to Brugnoli's T). None will be reported in my edition.

Subsequent editors of the *DGR* have for the most part based themselves entirely on Robinson's analysis, with good reason: his two major contributions--the description of an essentially bipartite tradition, and the appreciation of **X**'s importance within that tradition--are firm and enduring.⁹ Yet it is possible to say more about the tradition's second branch, derived from **Y**, in part because of the light that has been thrown indirectly on the tradition of the *DGR* by recent work on the history of Tacitus' *minora*, especially the *Dial*. Sixteen of the twenty-six known MSS of the *DGR* also contain the *Dial*.; and as noted above, it has long been recognized that the early transmission of these two texts, in the generation or so after the discovery of the Hersfeldensis, followed very similar lines. It should be instructive, then, to compare Robinson's stemma for the *DGR* with an up-to-date stemma of the *Dial*.

Figure 2 (p. 7) provides such a stemma, based on the analysis of Michael Winterbottom and incorporating an important adjustment made by C. E. Murgia; since many of the same MSS are involved, I have retained for the *Dial*. the sigla used in editions of the *DGR* (where Winterbottom uses different sigla for the *Dial*., I indicate the latter in parentheses).¹⁰ One can quickly see that the tradition depicted here closely resembles that described by Robinson for the *DGR* (Fig. 1), both in its general outlines and in the relations among the individual MSS. Thus, both traditions are basically bipartite, with two main branches descending from the

---

⁹ For the editions of Bione and Brugnoli, see n. 1 above. Della Corte's first two editions were based explicitly on Robinson (cf. 2nd ed., p. 20); on his departures from Robinson in the 3rd ed., see n. 26 below and App. 1.

¹⁰ See Winterbottom, "Transmission," with refs. to earlier discussions; and C. E. Murgia, "The Minor Works of Tacitus," *CP* 72 (1977): 336f., who demonstrated that the two strands Γ and **Bb** (= **VL** for the *DGR*) do not descend from the archetype independently of one another but derive from the same hyparchetype, [**Y**] (a comparable, bipartite tradition is likely for the *Germ*, as well: see Robinson, *Germania*, pp. 91ff., with Murgia, ibid., pp. 327ff., and cf. Winterbottom, *Texts*, p. 411). It should be noted that Murgia's demonstration is contested *obiter* (and with some confusion) by Merklin, "Probleme," p. 174 n. 10. Note too that H. Heubner, in his recent Teubner edition (Stuttgart, 1983), recognizes the same three basic families as Winterbottom (ζ Γ β) but declines to draw a stemma (pp. vi-viii), while D. Bo, in his Paravia text (Turin, 1974), declines to place much faith even in families (p. lxxxi).

Figure 2: Tacitus *Dialogus* (Winterbottom-Murgia)

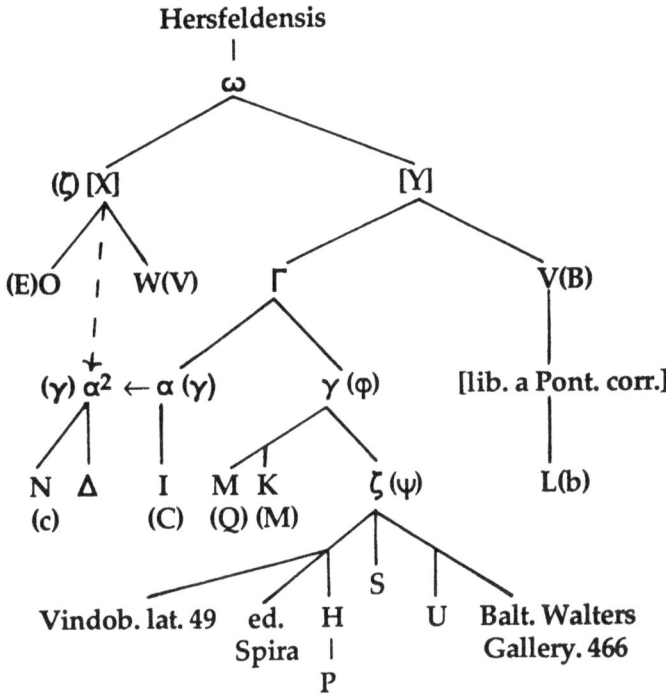

hyparchetypes **X** and **Y**. In both cases the two MSS **OW** (=**EV**) have the same relation to each other and to the rest of the tradition, as *gemelli* descended from **X**.[11] In both cases, too, the *deteriores*--family **γ** (=**φ**), and especially the sub-family **ζ** (=**ψ**)--line up in much the same way.[12] More significantly still, Robinson and

---

[11] On the argument of D. Bo that O (=E) is a descendant of W (=V) in the *Dial.* see App. 2.

[12] Robinson's **θ** has no counterpart in the stemma of the *Dial.*: from among the descendants of **θ**, QCF and ed. Ven. do not have the *Dial.* at all (but see now App. 3, on Ricc. 3595); and as Robinson recognized (diss., pp. 189f.), Δ, a MS with very miscellaneous contents, must have drawn its text of the *DGR* and its texts of Tacitus from quite different sources--hence its appearance among the *deteriores* for the *DGR* but among the somewhat better MSS of the **α** (=**γ**)-family for the *Dial*. Δ is also unique among the MSS of the *DGR* in preserving the *Agr.*--a fact that should signal its

Winterbottom independently described the same distinctive set of relations among the members of the α (=γ)-family: while some of these MSS (GI in *DGR*, I [=C] in *Dial.*) reproduce the text of α (=γ) before it received readings from an X-source, others (N in *DGR*, N[=c]Δ in *Dial.*) reflect the results of this contamination.[13]

There are in fact only three noteworthy differences between the traditions described by these stemmata. Two of these differences concern members of the Y-branch: where Robinson took V and L to be independent witnesses (to λ and thence to β), Winterbottom regarded L (=b) as a descendant of V (=B); and where α and γ stand as independent witnesses to the hyparchetype Y in the stemma of the *DGR*, they share a descent from Γ, a lost intermediary between themselves and Y, in the stemma of the *Dial.* The third difference concerns the relation between the hyparchetypes XY and the Hersfeldensis itself. We can consider these differences in turn, starting with the last.

Robinson (followed by subsequent editors) assumed that X and Y in the *DGR* were copied directly from the Hersfeldensis. In the case of the *Dial.*, however, it seems clear that at least one 15th-century copy--and more likely, at least two such copies--intervened between the Hersfeldensis and the hyparchetypes: for there are places at which all the extant MSS share an error that most probably derives from the use of abbreviations; and the abbreviations at issue would not have occurred in the Hersfeldensis or any earlier MS, but were common in the 15th century.[14] So, for example, at *Dial.* 31. 7 *comitem* Vahlen : *civitatem* **codd.**, the false reading most probably arose, not from the confusion of multiple

---

relative lateness, in view of the history of the *Agr.* after the dismemberment of the Hersfeldensis.

[13] On the presence of Δ here, see the preceding n. G does not exist for the *Dial.* (the MS contains only the *DGR*), and Winterbottom had no reason to posit an intermediary--a counterpart to Robinson's v--between his C and γ.

[14] On the likelihood of a 15th-cent. archeytpe for the *Dial.*, see esp. Murgia, "The Minor Works of Tacitus," p. 336, noting the errors at 31. 7 *comitem* Vahlen : *cîtem* V (=B, *artem* L = b), *civitatem* cett. (L^m = b^m) and 37. 4 *civibus* Put. : *comitibus* ω. See also ibid., on the corruption of *illi* to *isti* at 41. 5, in conjunction with p. 337, on the confusion of *illae* /*regulae* at 21. 4; and cf. id., "The Length of the Lacuna in Tacitus' *Dialogus*," *CSCA* 12 (1979): 222f., Winterbottom, "Transmission," pp. 127f., and n. 17 below.

letter-forms, but from the mistake of a single letter: *côitem* (= *comitem*) > *cîtem* (= *civitatem*). That is, the shared error *civitatem*, which appears thus spelled out in most of the MSS, is merely the expanded version of the abbreviation *cîtem*, which we find as such in **V** (= **B**): this is a common 15th-century abbreviation for *civitas* and its oblique forms (see Capelli, *Dizionario di abbreviature*6, p. 52), but one that certainly would not have appeared in the Hersfeldensis or any earlier MS. Accordingly, since *civitatem* is the reading in both branches, the error must already have stood in the hyparchetypes **X** and **Y**; and since the error was shared by both hyparchetypes, it must already have been present in their common parent--which cannot, therefore, have been the Hersfeldensis: at least one 15th-century MS, with *cîtem*, must have intervened. Yet *cîtem* itself is probably not an error generated directly from *comitem*: it is more likely to be a miscopying of *côitem*--again, a common humanist suspension for forms of *comes* (see Capelli, p. 58), but one that would not have occurred in the Hersfeldensis.[15] The probable genesis of the error therefore implies the presence of (at least) two 15th-century copies between the Hersfeldensis and the hyparchetypes from which the extant MSS descend: one with *côitem* (correctly) for *comitem*, another with the error *cîtem* (= *civitatem*). The same conclusion is suggested, no less clearly, by *Dial.* 25. 4 *nervosior* Meiser : *nûosior* **VL** (=**Bb**), *numerosior* **cett.**, which implies the sequence *ñuosior* (= *nervosior*) > *nûosior* (= *numerosior*). Again, the presence of the error in both branches establishes that *numerosior* itself, or the abbreviation *nûosior* (thus **VL** = **Bb**: for *nû-* = *numer-*, Capelli, p. 242), already stood both in the two hyparchetypes and in their common ancestor, a MS which was thus already infected with the error; but that error in turn simply represents the misreading of an exemplar in which the suspension

---

[15] Surveying abbreviations in MSS of the early Middle Ages (700-850), W. M. Lindsay remarks (*Notae Latinae*, p. 345): "the symbolism of prevocalic *m* is a feature of scripts at a later (generally much later) time. The few examples within our period may possibly all be unintentional blunders, although it is significant that most are found in two words (and their derivative), *animus*, rarely *numerus*." Thus, e.g., the Aesinas-fragment of the *Agr.* is thoroughly typical of its period: its 8 folia show over 140 uses of the suspension-stroke for *m*, almost all of them at word-end, none of them medially before a vowel (cf. Robinson, "Germania," p. 357).

ñ-, for ner-, was already used. That exemplar, therefore, must have been another 15th-century MS, not the Hersfeldensis.[16]

To explain either one of these examples differently, then, one must posit either a much less likely *ratio corruptelae* or a thoroughly unlikely use of abbreviations in the Hersfeldensis (or some earlier MS) or an equally unlikely amount of coincidental error. (Alternatively, one could decide that all recent editors have been wrong to accept the emendation, and deny that the error exists-- though in each of the present cases that would be more desperate still.) If one further wished to avoid the necessity of positing a 15th-century archetype by explaining *both* of these errors differently, the weight of improbability would only be compounded.[17]

---

[16] Again, the Aesinas-fragment is typical of its period, showing a suspenion for -*er* only with *t* (= *ter*). That compendium is very common in other Carolingian MSS, whereas the chance that any such MS would have used the suspension with *n* is vanishingly small: Lindsay, *Notae Latinae*, pp. 333ff. (cf. p. 498), cites no instance, while Bains' *Supplement* (for the period 850-1050) cites only one (p. 54), from a MS in Beneventan script, hardly relevant here. The generalized use of the suspension for *er* was by contrast very common in the 15th cent.: cf., e.g., below, p. 29, on the error *Nuncino*, for *Nucerino*, at *DGR* 28. 2.

Bo's report (ed., p. 77 app.) that *ñuosior* itself stands in **V**L (= **Bb**) is incorrect, as is his statement (p. 97 app.) that the abbreviation *cîtem* = *comitem* (cf. above); yet even if these statements were correct, the evidence of the other MSS would show that both abbreviations must already have stood in the archetype (as Bo also seems to believe: ed., p. lxiii), which could not then have been the Hersfeldensis. Cf. App. 2 at nn. 2 and 19.

[17] So, e.g., H. Merklin, who would prefer to regard **W** (=**V**) as a direct copy of the Hersfeldensis (cf. App. 2, n. 6), must try to dismiss Murgia's first two examples (*Dial.* 31. 7, 37. 4, in n. 14 above) by claiming that the readings in **W** can be explained "ebensogut durch eine nicht bzw. schwer entzifferbare Fassung der Hersfeldensis" ("Probleme," p. 174 n. 10, cf. "'Dialogus'-Probleme," p. 2271): this would imply that the scribe of **W** happened to be unable to read forms involving *comi-* and *civi-* at these two places, and no others, that the illegible state of the Hersfeldensis caused the scribe to make errors that happen, in effect, to be mirror images of one another, and that exactly the same errors happened to be made, at exactly the same places, and no others, by at least two other scribes working separately (i.e., the scribes of β and Γ, for Merklin also prefers the three-branch model of the *Dial.*'s tradition, cf. n. 10 above). A marvelous unanimity would thus emerge from multiple independent readings of an illegible MS (Merklin did not have the opportunity to add to this a special explanation for **W**'s *numerosior* at *Dial.* 25. 4, which Murgia did not cite).

By contrast, the presence of these telltale errors harmonizes easily with what we know and can reasonably conjecture about the crucial period when the Hersfeldensis seems to have passed out of Enoch of Ascoli's possession and its texts began to be read (see n. 4, above). The available evidence suggests that Enea Silvio de' Piccolomini (= Pope Pius II, after August 1458) was the key figure who knew of and had an interest in Enoch's holdings, and who perhaps first enjoyed use of the Hersfeldensis. If the MS came into his possession, it would very probably have been one of his first acts to have a clean, new copy made for himself (one, say, in which the abbreviations *côitem* and *ñuosior* appeared)--after which the old book may well have simply been discarded. However the latter event occurred, when the works were then made available for more general circulation, the likely medium would have been a copy (or more than one) taken from this new MS--at which stage, perhaps, the errors *cîtem* and *nûosior* made their first appearance, thence to be transmitted to the hyparchetypes of the extant MSS as the tradition branched out. This is, of course, only the simplest scenario.

As for the *DGR* itself, there is little that can be said on this matter. Since good, direct evidence for a 15th-century archetype, of the sort found in the *Dial.*, does not exist in the *DGR*, Robinson was in principle correct to posit the immediate descent of the hyparcheytpes from the Hersfeldensis. The absence of such evidence, however, does not guarantee that he was correct in fact. (I will return briefly to this matter at the end of the chapter).[18] More can be said about the two other points at which the two stemmata diverge, both of which concern the MSS descended from Y: the relations among families α β γ in the "generation" after Y; and

---

Note that a 15th-cent. archetype for the *Germ., Dial.,* and *DGR* was already posited by J. Perret, *Recherches sur la text de la "Germanie"* (Paris, 1950), pp. 111ff. Much of Perret's extended argument is only circumstantial, when not actually dependent on his mistaken view of the MS-families (cf. App. 1); but one item of direct evidence that he notes--the testimony for *inscientia* (Hersfeldensis, teste Decembrio) vs. *inscitia* (**codd.**) at *Germ.* 16. 1--is at least intriguing when compared with the passages from the *Dial.* noted above: see Perret's remarks, pp. 117f.; and cf. also Murgia, "The Length of the Lacuna," p. 229 n. 29 (on *Germ.* 16. 1 and a similar case at *Dial.* 36. 1).

[18] See at n. 57 below.

the relation between **V**(=**B**) and **L**(=**b**). In the sections that follow I will consider each of these divergences in turn.[19]

The Families α β γ

In Robinson's reconstruction, the lost MSS α β γ are all directly descended from **Y**, and the family of MSS derived from each is independent of the other two: α is no more closely related to β than it is to γ (and so on); the agreement of any two against the third will in principle reveal the reading of **Y**. In the stemma for the *Dial.*, however, only β (which, for the *Dial.*, = **VL**) is descended directly from **Y**:[20] α γ are descended from a common parent, Γ, derived from **Y**; accordingly, while the agreement of α β (against γ) or of β γ (against α) will in principle still reveal the reading of **Y**, the agreement of α γ (against β) obviously cannot be assumed to do so. In effect, the stemma for the *Dial.* attributes greater stature to β relative to either α or γ taken individually: whereas α β γ are all "brothers" of equal standing in the stemma of the *DGR*, for the *Dial.* only **V** (i.e., β) and Γ are "brothers," while α γ are the "nephews" of **V**.

Now it happens that Robinson himself considered just this latter alternative for the *DGR* as well (diss., pp. 182-85), noting a total of 15 possible conjunctive errors of α γ (8 instances where α γ agree in error against all the other MSS, 3 where the uncontaminated MSS of α--**GI**--agree with γ against the rest, and 4 more where **GI** agree with ζ). Robinson ended by discarding that alternative; but I believe that he was mistaken in doing so.

Removing the trivial or questionable items from Robinson's list (including, for rigor's sake, the instances where **GI** agree only with ζ), we have the following:

---

[19] I use only the Suetonian sigla from here on, with the chapter- and section-numbers that will appear in my edition; the section-numbers differ in some cases from those in Brugnoli's Teubner, but the differences are generally slight, and the passages cited should in each case be easily identifiable.

[20] Since the Suetonian MSS **BD** do not exist for the *Dial.*, editors of the latter have no reason to posit either Robinson's β or his λ in this branch of the *Dial.*'s stemma; cf. n. 13, on α (and **v**).

7. 2 *primum*] *prius* **GIγ** (praeter **Q**)
15. 2 *oris probi*] *oris improbi* **α γ**
15. 2 *lurc(h)onem* **XNλHU** (*surconem* **B**) : *curc(h)onem* **N¹GIγ** (praeter **HU**)
17. 2 *centena sestertia*] *sestertia* (vel *sex-*) *centena* **α γ**
24. 2 *omnes*] *se* **GIγB**

Robinson thought that all these agreements could and should be attributed to some cause other than inheritance from a common source: for example, he regarded 15. 2 *oris improbi* and 17. 2 *sestertia centena* as coincidental, 15. 2 *curconem* as due to a double reading already present in **Y** or the archetype (i.e., for Robinson, the Hersfeldensis). But (to take the last instance first) there is no stemmatic justification at all for referring *curc(h)onem* to the archetype, and very little reason to think a double reading stood in **Y**. The error occurs only in the MSS of **α** and **γ**, and the correct reading occurs, among the MSS of **α γ**, only in the heavily interpolated books **HU** (=η) and in **N**, which we know was contaminated from **X** (**N** has **X**'s *lurchonem* in the text, *curchonem* as a suprascript variant in the same hand): compare an instance that Robinson omitted from his list but almost certainly should have included, 7. 3 *ut hoc*] *ut hic* **N¹GIγ** (see the discussion ad loc. in Chap. 2). Among the other items, 15. 2 *oris improbi* is not readily explained away as coincidental, since the probable cause of the error is not mechanical but substantive and psychological: it results from a misunderstanding of the passage, and produces a reversal of the sense that seems correct at first glance but is in fact wrong. It is no doubt possible that the scribes of **α** and **γ** each independently misunderstood the passage in the same way and produced the same corruption as a result--but is it likely that the two scribes then independently produced the same transposition at 17. 2 and the same error, *omnes* (another substantive / psychological error), at 24. 2?

The cumulative unlikelihood of such coincidences increases geometrically as they are compounded: if we suppose that two scribes had, say, a one-in-five chance of independently making exactly the same error in any one of the latter three places (generous odds, I think, given the nature of the errors), then the chance that they would independently make the same mistake in all three places is .2 x .2 x .2, or less than 1 in 100. That by itself should be sufficient to suggest that Robinson was incorrect; the matter should be put beyond reasonable doubt if we note that no comparable list of conjunctive errors can be drawn up for βγ or αβ, and if we add the evidence of the manuscripts' relations in the *Dial*. Indeed, Robinson himself wrote (diss., p. 185): "Altior inquisitio de *Dialogi* codicum nexu, quam brevi me suscipere posse spero, huic obscuritati lumen diffundet." Though Robinson did not undertake that study of the *Dial.*, others have; and the results can be added to our weighing of the probabilities.[21] The families α and γ in the stemma of Suetonius should be referred to a common ancestor mediating between themselves and Y, as they are in the stemma of the *Dial*. To avoid the proliferation of sigla, I will call this hyparchetype Γ:

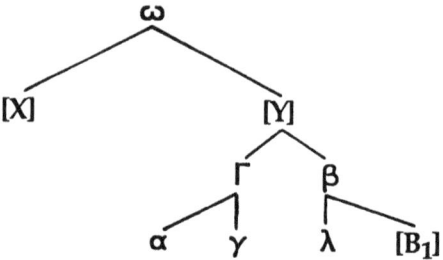

The Manuscripts V and L

These are both important witnesses, carefully written and offering texts of high quality. For the *Dial.*, they are also the only two surviving witnesses to one branch of the Y-tradition;[22] and Winterbottom argued that for the *Dial.* (and for the *Germ.* as well), L--a MS written by Giovanni Pontano in 1460--is descended directly from V, by way of a MS corrected by Pontano himself (i.e., Pontano corrected a MS descended from V and then wrote L as a fair copy of the corrected MS). On this view, L is to be taken into account for the *Dial.* (and the *Germ.*) only when it

---

[21] Cf. Winterbottom, *Texts*, p. 405.

[22] Winterbottom took this branch to represent a third independent line of descent from the archetype, though Murgia showed that it was descended from the same hyparchetype (= Y) as Γ; see n. 10 above.

offers interesting conjectures made by Pontano; it has no value as a witness independent of V.[23]

Robinson's description of this part of the tradition differs in two ways, one minor, one major. The minor discrepancy is due to an error on Robinson's part that can easily be removed; for following Wissowa, Robinson believed that L was not itself the MS written by Pontano in 1460, but a copy of that MS.[24] B. L. Ullman, however, showed that L is indeed in Pontano's hand, copied from a MS that Pontano must first have corrected;[25] as a result, Robinson's stemma for the β-family should show not:

but:

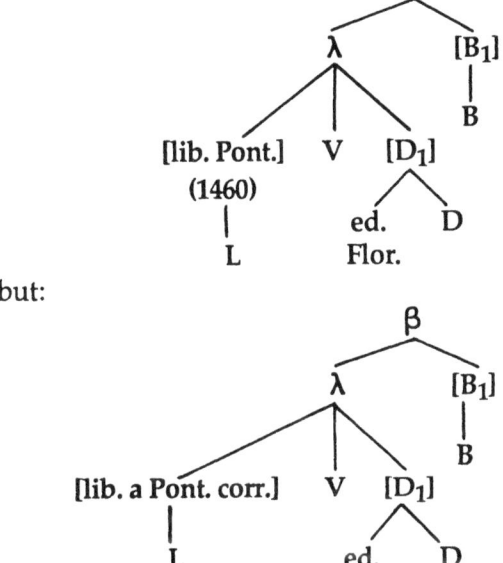

---

[23] For Winterbottom's discussion of VL in the *Dial.*, see his "Transmission," pp. 115f., and in the *Germ.*, "The Manuscript Tradition of Tacitus' *Germania*," *CP* 70 (1975): 2; accepted by Murgia, "The Minor Works of Tacitus," pp. 327 and 335; rejected for the *Dial.* by D. Bo, "Il codice Leidense Perizoniano XVIII Q. 21 in relazione al *Dialogus de oratoribus*," *RIL* 110 (1976): 22f., who follows Wissowa in regarding V and L as *gemelli*.

[24] Diss., p. 32, with G. Wissowa, *Taciti "Dialogus de Oratoribus" et "Germania," Suetoni "De Viris Illustribus" Fragmentum: Codex Leidensis Perizonianus phototypice editus* (Leiden, 1907), p. xviii.

[25] "Pontano's Handwriting," pp. 309ff., esp.. 313, 326ff.

That is, from the lost MS β two other MSS now lost, λ and B_1, were copied; B_1 was the exemplar of the surviving MS B; λ was the parent of three more MSS--the lost D_1 (the source of D and the Florentine printed edition of 1478), the lost MS corrected and copied by Pontano to produce L, and the surviving V. On this view, then, L is not a descendant of V; it is the fair copy of a corrected *gemellus* of V, with a stemmatic value equal to D's in reconstructing both λ and (with B) the "head of the family," β.[26]

Now it is hardly likely that both Winterbottom and Robinson are correct--i.e., that Pontano drew on a descendant of V for his texts of the *Dial.* and *Germ.* but then turned, for his text of the *DGR*, to a different MS, not descended from V but very closely related to it (for there is not the slightest doubt that V and L are very closely related indeed, whatever the relation may be). Either Robinson or Winterbottom must be mistaken--or they both are. It is worth considering the divergence between the two accounts,

---

[26] A slightly different situation was posited in the 3rd ed. of della Corte (p. xvii). Following Ullman, della Corte correctly held that L = the MS written by Pontano in 1460. But della Corte then assumed that the lost book corrected and copied by Pontano (the "liber Pontani deperditus," to which della Corte gave the siglum Π) was also the source of VD (or D_1, in Robinson's terms): that is, della Corte assumed that if L = the book Pontano wrote, then the lost MS that he corrected and copied must = Robinson's λ. The validity of this assumption is (at best) undemonstrated. If Π (λ) was Pontano's exemplar, it would also have carried the corrections that he made (including most of his conjectures) before he copied it to produce L (cf. Ullman, "Pontano's Handwriting," pp. 313, 335); since VD do not reflect these corrections, della Corte's equation of Π with λ can be correct only if one further assumes that Pontano corrected Π *after* V and D_1 were copied from it, thus:

$$\begin{array}{c} \Pi^2 \leftarrow \Pi \\ | \quad\quad \wedge \\ L \quad V \quad D_1 \end{array}$$

That is, we must assume a set of relations very similar to those in family α; but where α² is distinguished from α by contamination, Π² would be distinguished from Π by Pontano's corrections. Cf. below, at the conclusion of the present discussion; and on della Corte's other differences from Robinson, see App. 1.

both for an accurate appraisal of L's place in the two traditions and for the methodological questions that the divergence raises.[27]

We can begin with the stemmatic alternatives noted above:

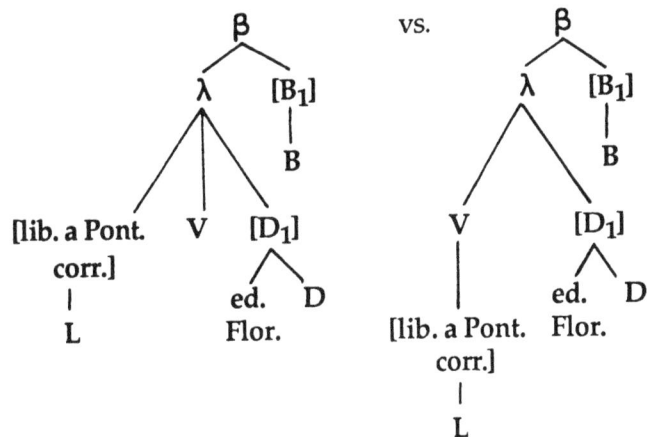

In a world wholly congenial to stemmatic analysis--one in which all scribes performed their work diligently, or at least with roughly equal skill and accuracy, and in which contamination or archetypal variants did not exist--we would know perfectly well what to expect from MSS in these two stemmata. If L is an independent witness to λ (so the stemma on the left), it should in general have a text very similar to VD (which of course it does). It should also sometimes agree with V against D, and sometimes with D against V--i.e., join with V or D in transmitting the reading of λ, against the error of the third, or (far less often) have the same error as V or D by accident. And it should sometimes

---

[27] Sepp, Reifferscheid, and Wissowa attempted to show that L was or was not descended from V, but as Robinson remarked (diss., p. 126), their discussions all lacked rigor. Robinson himself (diss., pp. 129f., cf. p. 140) considered the possibility that V and L were copied from a common exemplar that stood between them and λ, i. e.:

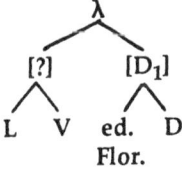

Cf. below, at the end of this discussion.

stand alone against the consensus of **VD**, where **VD** coincidentally agree in error, or (much more commonly) where **L** introduces an error of its own (i.e., either an error in the common sense of the word or a free conjecture: the two amount to the same thing in stemmatic terms, according to which an "error" is simply a failure to reproduce the exemplar, whether the failure leads to gibberish or recaptures the authentic text). Of course, we must expect the relationship to be somewhat attenuated, since neither **L** nor **D** (according to the stemma) is a *gemellus* of **V**, but each, in effect, is **V**'s "nephew": **L** and **D** will therefore be distinguished from **V** (and from each other) not only by their own errors but also by whatever errors each inherited from its exemplar (the book corrected by Pontano and D_1, respectively). Furthermore, even this small corner of the tradition is not wholly congenial to stemmatic analysis. Though there is no evidence that λ was contaminated from another family,[28] it is clear that the scribes of **V** and D_1 were of very different sorts, the former being as careful as the latter was slovenly.[29] In addition, the very fidelity of **V** reveals that there were suprascript variants in λ (some of these were certainly present in λ's parent, β, and some were almost certainly already in Y): these will have to be considered below as they become relevant.[30] Given these facts, then--especially the fact that **L** and

---

[28] Contrast the contamination of **N** from **X** (Robinson, diss., pp. 113ff.) or the contamination of **Q**, a MS of the γ-family, from **L** (or its corrected exemplar: ibid., pp. 180-82, where adjustment must be made for Robinson's belief that **L** was not written by Pontano).

[29] On the character of **V**, see below, n. 35; on **D** and D_1, see Robinson, diss., pp. 124ff. The fault is plainly to be laid at the door of D_1, since **ed. Flor.**--which Robinson showed was a *gemellus* of **D**, not based on it-- reproduces scores of the same errors (ibid.). The man responsible for **D**, by contrast, was far more careful, going so far (e.g.) as to correct the text before him by comparing it with the text of Cicero: see *DGR* 14. 2, where **D** uniquely records several correct readings in Suet.'s quotation from Cic. *Fam.* 9. 10. 1; cf. also at n. 33 below.

[30] The variants recorded in **V** are as follows (in several cases the same variants are similarly recorded by the first hand in **N**, the α-MS contaminated from **X**; these are indicated by "(N)"): 3. 5 *panosagacema* (*panosa gace-* [*l'sagāc*] *ma ul' panosa saga* **B**, cf. *-ansema* in **I**), 5.1 *ac*, 6.2 *divarum* [*l'at l'duarum e*], 9. 6 *palliati* (**N**; *l'est paleati ac palliati* **B**), 10.2 *notus* (**N**), 10.3 *hermam* (**N**), 11.2 *inscripsit* [*l'a haere l'is*]

D are not themselves *gemelli* of **V**, and that **V** and **D** testify to the work of very different scribes--we must qualify the expectations noted above: in particular, we should expect **L** to agree with **D** against **V** relatively infrequently. The expectations, however, are not fundamentally altered.

By contrast, the second stemma above does raise fundamentally different expectations, at least in one respect. If **L** is descended from **V**, it should follow **V** whenever **V** differs from **D**, save when those differences entail obvious corruptions in **V** easily corrected by conjecture; and it should have peculiar readings (errors in the common sense of the word, or conjectures) of its own--peculiar readings either derived from its exemplar, the book corrected by Pontano, or produced when **L** itself was copied. *But it should never agree with **D** against **V***, save where that agreement is the result of easy, coincidental error or is attributable to the correction of an obvious error made by **V**.

I. Now plainly, in either case, **VL** are going to agree very frequently against **D**, if only because of the depravity of D_1: for the most part, these agreements will prove nothing about the precise relation of **VL**. Therefore, in deciding which of our alternatives is correct (if either one is), we should first ask whether, or how often, **L** agrees with **D** against **V**.[31]

---

l'lycida
(**N**; **B** has *l'is lydia* in the next line, clearly displaced), 11. 2 *Lydia* (**N**), 13.1
l'eros nametra   *i*   *l'hanc*   *l'pro*
hero suo Metre, 14. 3 *non possit*] *possem*, 18. 2 *hoc* (**N**), 19.1 *Aphrodisius*
                l'phryginus   *l's*
(*aprodisius* **B**), 20. 1 *Hyginus*, 23. 4 *parcisse*. At 3. 5, 9. 6, and 11. 2 the reading of **B** shows that the variants were already in β; those in **N** suggest their presence in **Y**, the common ancestor of βΓ. In most of the places listed, **L** has the reading of **V**'s main text; it twice has the variant reading (11. 2 *is scripsit*; 18. 2 *hanc*--the correct reading, also in **D**), it twice has both readings (13. 1, 20. 1--in both cases the relation between text and variant is the same as in **V**), and it once goes its own way (23. 4 *pepercisse*, see below). **V** does not record suprascript variants after 23. 4, though it is clear that there were other such variants in λ after that point: see at n. 44 below.

[31] Here, as throughout, I ignore merely orthographical divergences and agreements--e.g., the presence or absence of *h, ph* vs. *f*, the doubling of consonants, *e* vs. *ae, y* vs. *u* or *i*; I also ignore other matters--e.g., the expansion of abbreviations, the writing of numbers in words vs. Roman numerals--in which individual scribes followed their own lead. In

I have seen only 6 instances of such agreement that are even remotely worth noting. The number is small, even given the circumstances described above and the brevity of the text; more important, the character of these agreements is quite unimpressive:

4. 6 *grammatici* **BV** (I) : *-ticae* **G** : *-ticis* **DL** (cett.)
10. 4 *vindicavit* **V** (Xγ) : *vendicavit* **BDL** (αQ)
17. 3 *(h)emicy(-ci-)clium* **BV** (cett., *-cidium* I) : *-clum* **DL** (USQ, *-culum* Δ)
22. 2 *futurum certe iam inde. mentitur*] post *inde* punx. **V** (ONI), post *futurum* **DL** (om. *inde* D; post *certe* CΔ)
24. 3 *cum plurimum* Δ : *cum plurimos* **DL** (OKUCS) : *cum plurimis* **V** (NGMQ; *plurimis* [om. *cum*] W, *cum plurim'* I, *cum plurimi* H) : *complures* **B**
25. 4 *exoluerunt* **L** (HUS), *exsoluerunt* **D** : *-oluerint* **BV** (cett.) : *-oleverunt* **S**

All of these can reasonably be attributed to coincidence, either of error or of correction. The instances at 10. 4, 17. 3, and 22. 2 are probably just trivial: 10. 4 could easily be no more than an example of the common confusion of *e* and *i*;[32] at 17.3 the succession of minims in the ending *-ium* could independently have produced the corruption to *-um* found in **DL** and several unrelated MSS; and at 22. 2 the agreement in incorrect punctuation is probably no more significant than coincidences in orthography, since in both matters scribes, though no doubt influenced by their exemplars, felt free to make their own choices (here the mispunctuation produces an awkwardness--mitigated in **D** by the omission of *inde*--but the cause of the mistake is obvious: one expects the *sententia* to end with the verb *futurum*, one does not expect the adverbial phrase to follow). 24. 3 and 25. 4, where **L** and **D** agree on a true (or at least plausible) reading against **V**, probably involve independent corrections of an obviously corrupt text (*cum plurimis* and *-oluerint* are impossible in their contexts), both of them easy even for a

---

reporting the readings I give the MSS of the β-family first, then the rest in parentheses; "cett." = "all those not specifically reported."

[32] To take just one example: at 26. 2 *hordearium* we find the *e* confused with *i* in both descendants of X (*hordiarium* **W**, *ordiarium* **O**); in the β-family, the same confusion led to the *(h)ordinarium* found in **DVL** (**B** has *horditarium*). Cf. also section IV below.

scholar less talented than Pontano.[33] At 4. 6, by contrast, L agrees with D against V in the incorrect reading; but the agreement is again probably accidental. The context--*quosdam e grammatici statim ludo transisse*--virtually insures the corruption of *-tici* to *-ticis*, with the preceding preposition leading one to expect the ablative and the following *statim* readily providing the *s*;[34] Pontano dealt with the passage by writing *e grammaticis statim e ludo*. It is difficult to see in these instances any good evidence of L's independence from V as a witness to λ.

II. The instances at 24. 3 and 25. 4 do, however, suggest the next question to be asked: how often is V wrong where L is right? The answer is, simply, *not at all*--except (to borrow from Winterbottom, "Transmission," p. 115) "in cases where the support of the rest of the tradition for [V's] error demonstrates that [L's] truth is due to emendation." This is not surprising, given what we already know about V's habits, and Pontano's.[35] To concentrate

---

[33] Nor should the readings in D surprise: see n. 29 ad fin. At 24. 3 *cum plurimos* is at least intelligible Latin (it has been printed by some editors), though Δ's conjecture *cum plurimum* is probably what Suet. wrote; note that this is perhaps the place where the divisions among the MSS are most pronounced, so that other very closely related books--OW, MK, HU--go their separate ways. I would also attribute to independent correction 3. 5 *Catulo* L¹D (WᵐαMCU), *capulo* X : *Catullo* BVL (KHΔQ), where Pontano, as corrector (= L¹), placed a mark of deletion under the first *-l-* of the inherited *Catullo*.

[34] The nesting of *statim* in the midst of the prepositional phrase is a mannerism of Suetonius: cf. *Aug.* 28. 1 *post oppressum statim Antonium* (i.e., *statim post . . .*), *Galb.* 1 *post Augusti statim nuptias, Tit.* 10. 1 *ad primam statim mansionem, Dom.* 17. 2 *ad primum statim vulnus*.

[35] Robinson, a careful collator and a sober judge, went so far as to state that--orthographical idiosyncracies aside--V "vitiis sui ipsius propriis adeo caret" (diss., p. 130), and that "errores quos librarii inconsulto vulgo facerent, in hoc codice tantum non videbis" (p. 132). Those familiar with scribal habits may be skeptical; but I can confirm Robinson's judgment. Robinson was able to instance only the following (all but the first immediately corrected by the text-hand): index *Flabius* (in Quintilian's name, where L has the correct *Fabius*), 9. 5 *stestimonium*, 21. 1 *datus est muneri*, 25. 2 *facieundum*, 26. 2 *quadam* (for *quam*)--and Robinson was probably partly wrong to include 21. 1, since the text of λ was evidently already disturbed there (see n. 44 below). To Robinson's list I can add only 11. 3 *Crateris* (see section III, below).

on the latter: I have noted forty-one places where L's reading differs from that of all its close kin, BVD; twenty-four of these readings occur in no other MS (or no MS other than the contaminated Q: see n. 28 above), and they are all clearly either free conjectures or singular errors of Pontano.[36] In the other seventeen places L stands apart from the other β-MSS, though its reading occurs in one or more of the other MSS (again, besides the contaminated Q): these are the only places, that is, where there is even a *prima facie* reason to think that L has inherited its reading independently of V.

In three of these seventeen places, the reading is clearly wrong, the result of an easy coincidental error.[37] The remaining fourteen are as follows (L = the text-hand, L¹ = suprascript readings entered in the same hand; * = a reading commonly accepted by modern editors):

1. 2 *adnotatum*] *notum* L¹ (UΔ; *atnotum* L, *adnotum* VD [Xγ])
1. 2 *praelegebant** L¹ (cett., *per-* B) : *pr(a)eal(l)egabant* λ

---

[36] In these lists I do not distinguish between readings found in the text and those written suprascript by the same hand (either while copying the text or while reviewing it and comparing it with the exemplar). Conjectures (* = a reading commonly accepted by modern editors): 1. 2 *ac nihil*, 2. 2 *retrectarent*, 2. 2 *Vectius et Q.*, 3. 4 *post hos*, 4. 2 *Ticida**, 4. 6 *reputo*, 4. 6 *e ludo* (cf. above on this passage), 11. 3 *custodis**, 11. 3 *cauliculi**, 14. 2 *magister*, 17. 3 *publicaverat*, 25. 2 *censores ita**, 29. 2 *salsum** (incert. man.), 30. 2 *tamen non* (cf. also 3. 5 *Catulo** in n. 33 above). Simple errors (or very unhappy conjectures): 4. 1 *valuit* (pro *invaluit*, post *consuetudINe*), 4. 5 *apparandam*, 7. 1 *Dionis*, 7. 2 *pueri* (om. *adhuc*), 9. 1 *moxque equo*, 9. 2 *leviter* (om. *non*), 15. 3 *et doctrina* (corr. ead. man.), 23. 1 *comitatus* (pro *dum comitatur*, corr. ead. man., ut vid.), 23. 7 om. *qui eum*, 30. 5 *redigerent* (corr. L²). The hand designated as L² (= Robinson's L³ = Wissowa's B²) was once thought to be that of a different, later reader; but Ullman ("Pontano's Handwriting," pp. 329ff.) has shown that this is also the hand of Pontano, writing later and in a different ink. The readings of this hand (other MSS with the same reading are noted in parentheses): 3. 1 *generque** (X), 11. 3 *miretur*, 15. 3 *surreptis* (X, probably correct), 18. 3 *nobiles et in*, 23. 1 *textrinus*, 25. 2 *et iis* (1º)* (γ), 25. 3 *profluxit** (corr. *profluit*, error. commun. VDL), 25. 4 *anascenas . . . catascenas* (-*enas* BMCΔ . . . -*enas* M), 28. 1 *Epidii** (αCΔ), 30. 2 *tum*] *ut*, 30. 5 *excanduisse* (αS).

[37] These are: 4. 2 *nec cum* (pro *ne cum*) L¹ (O [corr. O¹]ζ); 4. 4 *rhetoricam* (om. *et*) L (CΔQ); 17. 1 *claruit* (pro *inclaruit*, post *maxiMe*) L (HQ; corr. L¹).

The Stemma

3. 5 *Gaius* conieci (*Caiius* iam Vahlen) : *Laeneus* L (*Len(a)eus* γ
 [praeter Q]), *Levius* BV (Xα, *Livius* G¹), L. D
 L L
 L
6. 1 *Opillus* Schulze : *opimius* L¹ (*Opillius* WK), *Opilius* BVD (cett.)
6. 2 *simul** L (QU) : *simulque* BVD (cett.)
9. 6 *marmorea** L¹ (G²) : -*reo* LBVD (G cett.)
11. 3 *sit sapientiam** L (QHPF) : *sapientiam sit* BVD (cett.)
21. 4 *inscribuntur** L (GU) : *scribuntur* BVD (cett.)
22. 3 *Gallus** L (αHUQ) : *gallius* BVD (cett.)
 l's
23. 4 *pepercisse** L (OUS; *percisse* W) : *parsisse* D (HΔ), *parcisse* V,
 parcisse B (cett.)
25. 2 *Messalla** L (S) : *Sala* BVD (cett.)
25. 2 *consuerunt* VD (Xζ [praeter H]) : -*sueverunt* L (αMKH), -*erant*
 B
25. 5 ὑποθέσεις Wolf : *synthesis* L (HE; -*tesis* K, συνθέσεις S), -*taxis*
 L¹VD (WαM), -*tasis* B (O; -*thasis* QUC)
27. 1 *Otacilius* L (E) : *Olta-* VB (X), *Octa-* D (α; *Volta-* γ)

There is no need to review these instances individually: in the cases where L is certainly or probably right (1. 2 [2°], 6. 2, 9. 6, 11. 3, 21. 4, 22. 3, 23. 4, 25. 2) or nearly right (6. 1), the correction would be evident to any knowledgeable reader who attended to grammar, meter, or context. The man who produced 11. 3 *cauliculi* would not need the assistance of a manuscript to arrive at any of these readings. Of the rest, 1. 2 *notum* was an obvious correction for the text in Pontano's exemplar; 25. 2 *consueverunt* is merely the introduction of the more common form; 25. 5 *synthesis* produces a kind of sense in this corrupt context, whereas the *syntaxis* transmitted by λ (preserved in L with the suprascript letters *ax*, see n. 47 below) does not; and at 27. 1, where *Otacilius* was at least on the right track, we happen to know that Pontano made the identical emendation in another, very similar context, at Macrob. *Sat.* 2. 2. 13.[38] Only one reading--3. 5 *Laeneus*, for *Levius*--gives the slightest pause, because the alteration of the name, which is also found in most MSS of the γ-family,[39] appears to be arbitrary and, hence, unlikely to be a free conjecture:

---

[38] On 27. 1 and its relations to the passage in Macrobius, see the discussion in Chap. 2.

[39] Except, interestingly, Q, the MS that so consistently gives evidence of contamination from L or its exemplar: on this place cf. Robinson, diss., p. 181.

perhaps here, one might think, we have evidence of an error inherited (*via* a variant in λ?) independently of **V**. The change, however, is in fact easily explained, either mechanically--as a simple misreading of *Levius* (*n* for *u*, *e* for *i*)--or psychologically--as a conscious or unconscious recollection of the name *L(a)eneus* that appeared shortly before (2. 2, only 18 lines earlier in **L**)--or as some combination of the two. For this reason, and because the evidence for other such inheritances is so insubstantial (see section IV, below), the agreement between **L** and **γ** here should most probably be attributed to coincidence.

III. We have so far seen that the agreements of **LD** against **V** give no ground for thinking that **L** descends from λ independently of **V**, and that **L** nowhere inherits the truth independently of **V**: **V** is wrong, **L** correct, only when **L** has reached the correct reading by conjecture. This certainly looks like the description of one book's descent from the other. Furthermore, there are several other places that--though incapable *per se* of proving **L**'s descent from **V** (for they can be otherwise explained)--do seem to corroborate the picture we have seen:

> 4. 1 *aliquid diligenter*] *diligenter aliquid* **VL** : *diligenter* (om. *aliquid*) **BD**
> 7. 1 *Scytobrachionis* **U** : *Scytobachionis* **B**, *scitabachionis* **D**, *Scythabachionis* **VL**, alii alia
> 11. 3 *Cratetis* **BD** (**X** [*eratetis* **W**] α**H**Δ) : *-teris* **V** (**MKUQ**), *-teri* **L**
> 25. 5 *res cognita est* **D** (**X** [*rec-* **W**] **NG**²) : *rescogniti sunt* **VL** (*res cogniti sunt* **Q**), *recogniti sunt* **BL**² (cett.)
> 30. 5 *excanduisset* **BD** (**X**) : *excanduisse et* **VL** (**γ**) : *excanduisse* **L**² (α**S**)

11. 3 is the least substantial of these, or at any rate the most ambiguous. The variation *-tet-* / *-ter-* that divides the β-MSS could be attributed, for example, to the presence of a variant in β; but since the confusion of *t* and *r* is so common (*Crateris* also appears in some γ-MSS, I assume independently), it is at least equally possible that *Crateris* is **V**'s peculiar error. If that is the case, then **L**'s *Crateri* looks very much like the further corruption (after *Zenodoti* in the same line) of the reading *Crateris* already present in its ancestry: note also 18. 3 *compararetur*, written as *comparetur* in **V** (with p̱ = *par*, as not infrequently in 15th-cent. MSS), where **L** has *comperaretur*, a reading that appears to be derived

from the form of the word found in **V**.⁴⁰ 7. 1 *Scythabachionis* also looks insubstantial, but it just might be more solid than it looks. Poor Scytobrachion's name was roughly handled by the scribes, who produced many variations on it; but only **BVDL** offer the variation *-bachionis,* which I take to be the reading of β. The combined testimony of **BVDL** further suggests that *-obachionis* became *-abachionis* in λ. Whether λ had *Scyth-* or *Scith-* or *Scyt-* or *Scit-* it is obviously impossible to say--nor would the answer, or **VL**'s agreement in *Scyth-,* ordinarily be of the slightest interest, were it not for a pair of facts: **V**'s scribe was extraordinarily fond of *y,* inserting it for *i* even in places where it did not conceivably belong;⁴¹ **L**, by contrast, shows a distinct preference for avoiding *y*.⁴² It may be, therefore, that *Scyth-* represents the legacy of **V**'s scribe to **L**.

With 4. 1 we are on very different ground: here the transposition clearly seems to bind **VL** together at the same time that the omission of *diligenter* (the root cause of the transposition) separates **BD** from them. I take it that *diligenter* had already been omitted in β; it presumably was also already written above *aliquid* as a correction, else λ would probably not have recaptured it. It was certainly written suprascript in λ, whence **V**'s scribe copied it, but in the wrong order, while **D₁**'s careless scribe omitted it by simply writing what was under his nose in the main text: the question is, did the scribe of **L**'s exemplar get his version from λ, independently repeating **V**'s mistake (that is the necessary implication of Robinson's stemma), or is that version derived from **V**? Coincidental error plainly cannot be ruled out, especially if a caret was misplaced in λ to indicate the (wrong) place of insertion--or perhaps *only* if a caret was misplaced: for the context is such ("eos qui aliquid diligenter et acute scienterque possint aut dicere aut scribere") that a moment's thought makes it plain where the displaced adverb belongs.⁴³ Two scribes could have

---

⁴⁰ For p̄ = *per* and *par,* see the discussion of 23. 4 *pepercisse* in Chap. 2.

⁴¹ E.g., 23. 7 *ablygurire;* cf. Robinson's list, diss., p. 131.

⁴² Cf., e.g., 20. 1 *Hyginus* **V** vs. *higinus* **L**. (with superscript *l'phryginus* over Hyginus and *fri* over higinus)

⁴³ Reifferscheid did print *diligenter aliquid*--but only because he was all but prepared to follow **V** through a brick wall.

independently made the same blunder, but to assume so without hesitation may be pushing faith in coincidence to the limit.

The last two instances perhaps take us past that limit. With 25. 5 and 30. 5 we are again clearly confronted with variants passed on to λ from β.[44] I assume that the readings in λ looked something like this:

>   *cogniti sunt*   *excanduisse et*
> 25. 5 *res cognita est*   30. 5 *excanduisset*

I base this assumption on the fact that in both cases D has the correct reading--a circumstance most readily explained, given the habits of D_1, if those were the readings available for copying in the text itself (cf. just above, on 4. 1 *diligenter aliquid*). Whatever the relation between text and variant, V made the wrong choice in both places, copying a reading that made no sense in the context and that-- in the case of the first--did not even consist of a Latin phrase; and as at 4. 1, we find the same readings in L (in the case of *rescogniti sunt*, the agreement of VL is singular, since Q's *res cogniti sunt* is the result of contamination from L or its exemplar). So again the questions arise: did the scribe of L's exemplar coincidentally make these same two inept choices by drawing independently on λ? Or are these readings part of V's legacy to L ?

IV.   After the preceding discussion, the answer to those questions seem obvious: L is descended from V. Or it would seem obvious, were it not for four readings adduced by Robinson to demonstrate that "L nullo modo ex V derivari potuisse":[45]

---

[44] As remarked above (n. 30), V does not reproduce the variants found in its exemplar after 23. 4, though there must have been others to reproduce: beyond 25. 5 and 30. 5, note also 21. 1 *muneri datus est* BV^1L (**cett.**) : *datus est muneri* VD (*datus est* W, om. *muneri*; another case of omission and transposition, this time miscopied by V but immediately corrected), 25. 1 *paululo* VL (XMC) : *paulo* BD (**cett.**), 25. 3 *declamitavit* VL (XMKHU) : *declamavit* BD (αCΔS). Robinson, diss., p. 129, noted the readings of VL at 25. 5 and 30. 5 but dismissed them as irrelevant to the question of the MSS' relation, "cum his locis VL codicis Y lectiones servare putem": the MSS may do so, but that does not quite address the question of their relation, which depends on how VL came to have those readings.

[45] Diss., pp. 128f.; Robinson also adduced 4. 6 *grammatici* /-*cis* and 10. 4 *vindicavit* / *ven*-, already noted in section I above. These are consistent with his argument, but of no weight *per se*.

14. 2 *criticus* **VB** (cett.) : *creticus* **D**, *criticus* **L** ($\overset{e}{creticus}$ **S**, $\overset{i}{Craticus}$ **NI**)
16. 1 *Attici* Beroaldus : *Attici Satti* (vel sim.) **CΔQ** : *Satti* **V** (**OGMK**, alii alia sim.), *Sattr* **W**, $\overset{r}{Satti}$ **L**, *Sarti* **D** (*satyri* **S**)
16. 3 *versiculus* **V** (i.e., -*l'*) **DL**¹ (cett.) : -*lis* **BL** (**Q**)
28. 2 *Nucerino* **B** (**X**) : *Nuncino* **DV** (-*cino* vel -*tino* **cett.**) : *Mancino* **L** (**MK**, *minemo* **Q**)

In arguing for the descent of **L** from **V** in the *Dial.*, Winterbottom remarked that he was "not impressed by the counter-evidence of Robinson";[46] but these *loci* seem at least to merit inspection.

In the first two passages we face the same situation: while (or soon after) writing the text of **L**, Pontano noted a variant reading (there is no mark of deletion in either case). Neither reading occurs in **V**, which shows no sign of the variant and whose text is perfectly legible in each case; in both places the reading does appear in other MSS, including **D**, and so could have appeared in **λ**, the common parent of **DVL**, as text or variant.

At 14. 2 the reading involves the common confusion of *e* and *i*. The form of the reading in **L** could mean that Pontano found *creticus* in his exemplar, emended it to *criticus*, but decided to preserve the memory of the transmitted text and so wrote the suprascript *e* (we find him doing precisely that elsewhere):[47] in that case Pontano's exemplar may simply have introduced *creticus* as a misreading of **V**. Alternatively, Pontano's exemplar may itself have read *criticus*, while Pontano chose to venture *creticus*, in the belief--fostered by his experience with early MSS--that that was the correct spelling.[48] In any case, it is certainly not necessary to suppose that this place gives evidence of **L**'s independence from **V**.

---

[46] "Transmission," p. 116 n. 8, citing Robinson, ibid., and id., "Germania," pp. 194ff.

[47] E.g., 25. 5 *synthesis*, where *syntaxis* was the reading of **λ** (so **DV**; -*tasis* **B**), *synthesis* Pontano's conjecture (Brugnoli was incorrect to write "corr. syntaxis" in his apparatus here, for it is not a correction; better Robinson's "$\overset{ax}{}$ *add. eadem manu*").

[48] I owe this suggestion to C. E. Murgia, who notes that "*creticus* is the standard spelling of *criticus* in the early manuscripts of Servius, and . . . *criticus*, where it exists, is a medieval correction."

The second passage is more interesting on several counts. The correct text at 16. 1 is *libertus Attici* ("Q. Caecilius Epirota . . ., libertus Atti<ci> equitis Romani ad quem sunt Ciceronis epistulae"): the reading of the archetype was *Satti* (*Attici* appears only in CΔQ = θ, as a conjecture); the corruption was produced by the addition of *s* (from *-tus*) to the beginning of *Attici* and the loss of *-ci* by haplography. *Sattr* in W arose from the confusion of *i* and *r* that is possible in certain humanist hands.[49] The readings of L and D (not to mention *satyri* in the wretched S) can plausibly be attributed to one of two causes: either they result from the common confusion of *t* and *r* (*Satti* > *Sarti* or *Satri*); or the reading of L (perhaps, too, that of D) reflects an attempt to emend *Satti* to an actual Roman name (*Satri* < *Satrius*: a Satrius is mentioned in-- but is not the recipient of--a letter of Cic., *ad Brut.* 1. 6. 3).[50] Whichever of these alternatives is correct (there is not much to choose between them), we can infer that L's exemplar read either

Satti or *Satti* (with *r* superscript) (it could not have read *Satri*, for that would mean Pontano introduced the meaningless *Satti* by conjecture). If that exemplar had the latter reading, it obviously could not have been V, though it could have been a copy of V in which the *r* was added by conjecture; if L's exemplar read *Satti*, then *Satri* plainly is Pontano's own conjecture. In either case, we are left to find an independent explanation for D's *Sarti*--perhaps no more than the common confusion of *r* and *t*.

The two other passages can be treated more briefly. At 16. 2 BL (with L's shadow, Q) have the impossible reading *versiculis*.[51]

---

[49] The same confusion is also found, interestingly enough, in this pair of readings in VL at *Germ.* 40. 5 (noted by Robinson, "Germania," p. 198):

Nuithones V vs. *Nurtones* L (with *i* superscript).

Robinson remarked: "In V the letter *i* bears a close resemblance to a type of *r* frequent in late manuscripts, though not the form of *r* [normally] used by the scribe of V."

[50] In L the *r* is squarely over the second *t*, and there is no question but that *Satri* is meant: correct Brugnoli's app. crit. ad loc. ("*littera r suprascr. quasi* Sarti").

[51] The reading is impossible, that is, with the verb *indicat*, which both MSS also have; Robinson, followed by Brugnoli, emended to *indicatur* and printed *versiculis*--but that is another story: see the discussion in Chap. 2.

Because it is impossible in its context, it cannot be Pontano's conjecture (Pontano, in fact, corrected it himself): it must either have stood in his exemplar or be an error made by Pontano while copying from his exemplar; but if it stood in his exemplar, it cannot have been taken from **V**, which has *versicul'*--unless we suppose that the stroke of abbreviation was misunderstood (the supposition is unlikely, but cf. the reading of **I**, *cum plurim'*, at 24. 3, where its close kin, **NG**, both have *cum plurimis*). In the last of Robinson's passages, the paradosis is essentially divided between *Nucerino* (*C. Epidio Nucerino*, i.e., of Nuceria Alfaterna) and *Nuncino* (i.e., *Nuc(er)ino*, written with a suspension-stroke above the -*c*-, > *Nûcino*): the former was the reading of **X**, the latter of **Y** (since **B** is the only Y-MS to have *Nucerino*, it is more likely that **B**, or **B₁**, acquired that reading by contamination than that **Y** had *Nucerino* / *Nuncino* as a double reading). But two Y-MSS--**L** and **δ** (= **MK**)--show a third reading, *Mancino*: this must be a conjecture based on *Nuncino*, an attempt to make sense of the already-corrupted word by replacing it with an actual Roman cognomen.[52] Moreover, since it is the sort of learned conjecture that seems unlikely to have been made independently twice, it probably originated in either **L** or **δ** and then passed to the other by contamination--or else both **L** and **δ** acquired it from a common source. (Since **L** was written in 1460, **M** in 1464, it plainly cannot have passed from the latter to the former; we do not know the dates of **δ** and **K**.) That the conjecture arose in **δ** is improbable, since there is no evidence elsewhere of striking conjecture originating in that MS (**δ**, in fact, contributes not a single good or interesting reading of its own);[53] and given Pontano's habits--not least, his willingness to tinker with unusual names (see above, at n. 38, on 27. 1 *Otacilius*)--there is good reason to find the conjecture's source in **L**. I cannot, however, point to another case where **δ** acquired one of **L**'s conjectures; a common source, therefore, cannot entirely be ruled out.

---

[52] An informed reader of the 15th century would have known of the Hostilii Mancini from, e.g., Livy 22. 15. 4, 9, 40. 35. 2, Cic. *De or.* 1. 181, 238, 2. 137, *Off.* 3. 109, or Quint. *Inst.* 7. 4. 12. **Q**'s *minemo* must be a garbling of the *Mancino* acquired from **L** by contamination.

[53] The one certainly conjectural reading attributable to **δ** is 14. 1 *Memmius* (for the archetype's *Memmia*), which makes sense, but the wrong sense; 4. 1 *accurate* (for *acute*) may be another.

Taken together, these places certainly do not show that "L nullo modo ex V derivari potuisse." 14. 2 *criticus / creticus* seems to me to be trivial; and on balance, I think it most likely that 16. 3 *versiculis* is a casual error in L (as its immediate correction suggests) and that 28. 2 *Mancino* is a conjecture by Pontano. That leaves only 16. 1 *Satti / Satri*, which is too ambiguous to serve as the basis of argument one way or the other.

In all strictness, of course, nothing in this discussion has *proved* either that L descends from V or that it does not. But given all the evidence reviewed above--especially the absence of significant agreements between L and D against V, and the absence of truth inherited by L independently of V--the following view of the MSS' relations seems to me most likely to be correct:

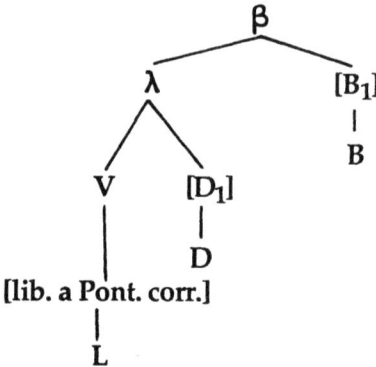

I can add three points by way of a coda to the discussion. First, those who prefer not to accept that L descends from V should not assume that Robinson's stemma for λ is therefore necessarily correct. There are in fact three possibilities:

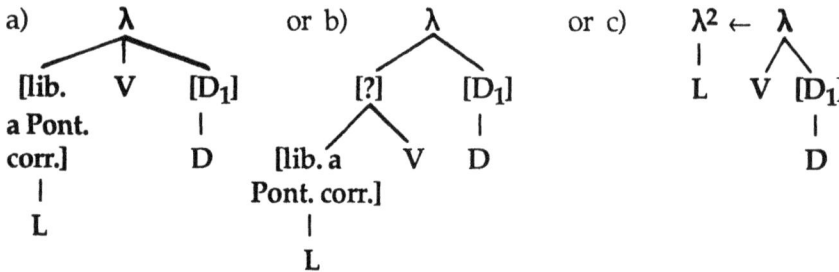

(a) is the alternative presented by Robinson's stemma; (b) is an option also considered by Robinson--viz., that V and L descend independently from a common source intermediate between themselves and λ (see n. 27 above); and (c), in effect, is the modified assumption of della Corte (see n. 26 above)--viz., that λ itself was the book corrected and copied by Pontano, but only after V and D_1 had already been copied from it. All three are consistent with the evidence, which (it hardly needs saying) does not allow us to prove that any one is certainly correct. If I were going to choose among them, I would prefer (b), since it would most economically explain the passages considered in section III (esp. 4. 1 *diligenter aliquid*, 25. 5 *rescogniti sunt*, and 30. 5 *excanduisse et*).

Second, if L descends from V, then L--written in March 1460--is no longer the earliest datable extant MS of the *DGR* (or Tac. *Dial.* and *Germ.*): V must obviously be earlier; and if L is (at least) one copy removed from V, the latter is perhaps most safely dated no later than the end of 1459. Of course, that is still nearly two years after the time when the Hersfeldensis (minus the *Agr.*) seems to have passed out of Enoch's possession and the works it contained began to be read and copied[54]--more than enough time for the three further stages of copying (in ascending order: λ, β, γ) that separate V from the archetype in Robinson's stemma.[55]

Third, and finally, whether or not one believes that L descends from V, it should be clear that L provides nothing to an editor that V does not provide--except Pontano's corrections. As in the case of the *Dial.* (and *Germ.*), so in the case of the *DGR* the MS "should appear in an apparatus only when it offers worthwhile conjectures."[56]

Conclusion

Robinson's stemma for the *DGR* should be redrawn as shown in Figure 3 (p. 32), to reflect the discussions of αγ (=Γ) and VL above. In all relevant particulars, this revised stemma is identical to the stemma of the *Dial.* (Fig. 2); and that is no more than we should expect, given that so many of the same MSS transmit both texts. Only one important question must be left open: was the ar-

---

54 On the chronology see n. 4 above.

55 Contrast Robinson, diss., p. 130, on a similar point.

56 Winterbottom, "Manuscript Tradition," p. 2.

Figure 3: Suetonius *De grammaticis et rhetoribus*

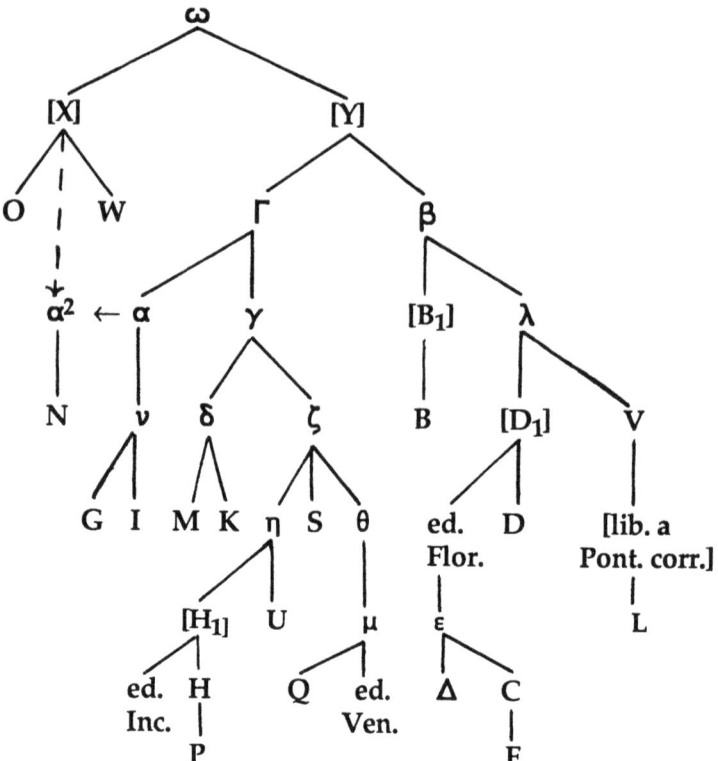

chetype--ω, the antecedent of the hyparchetypes X and Y--the Hersfeldensis itself or a 15th-century copy descended from the Hersfeldensis? Since a Renaissance archetype existed for the *Dial.*, and since the transmission of the *Dial.* is in all other relevant respects identical to that of the *DGR*, the presumption plainly must be very strong that a Renaissance archetype existed for the *DGR* as well; but there is, strictly speaking, no direct evidence that would allow us to prove its existence.[57] Be that as it may: using this stemma we can reconstruct the archetype's text,

---

[57] On the Renaissance archetype of the *Dial.*, see above at n. 14. It is possible, but not probable, that one *crux* in the *DGR* involves a corruption derived from such a MS: see the discussion of 13. 1 †nametra† in Chap. 2.

with certainty or a high degree of probability, for nearly all of the
DGR. As we shall see in the next chapter, however, reconstructing that text often leaves us well short of the truth, since the
archetype itself--whether of the 9th century or the 15th--was a
very poor witness indeed.[58]

For the apparatus criticus in my edition I will use a simplified
form of the revised stemma:

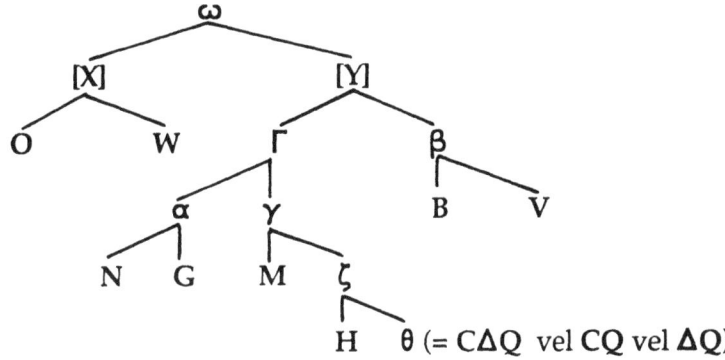

That is:

$$X = \text{the agreement of OW}$$

$$Y \begin{cases} \beta = \text{the agreement of VB} \\ \Gamma \begin{cases} \alpha = \text{the agreement of NG} \\ \gamma = \text{the agreement of M}\zeta \text{ (or MH [vs. }\theta\text{] or M}\theta \text{ [vs. H])} \end{cases} \end{cases}$$

From among these witnesses, γ is by far the least important:
though independent both of β (as a descendant of Γ) and of α (in
its descent from Γ), γ preserves no archetypal readings not also
found in α and/or β; it offers only one good correction of its own
(25. 2 *iis* [1º]), and it has only two other peculiar readings worth
reporting in a limited apparatus (18. 3 *edoceret*, 27. 1 *L. Voltacilius
Pilutus*). Beyond the last three places its individual readings can be

---

[58] On the general character of the archetype, see esp. the introduction to
Chap. 2.

ignored.⁵⁹ Of the twenty-six extant MSS, only **OW VB NG** need be reported individually throughout (among themselves these six account for all archetypal readings). Eight other MSS--**LDMHU SQΔ**--require individual report only for the conjectures and other corrections of the archetypal text that they occasionally offer. The remaining twelve MSS--Robinson's **IKPCF**, plus all seven MSS more recently discovered (see n. 8)--provide no such assistance and need not be cited individually at all.⁶⁰

---

⁵⁹ One of **γ**'s descendants, **ζ**, offers two more good corrections (14. 1 *Memm(i)i*, 16. 3 *Epirota* [del. *et*]) and three other noteworthy variants (4. 5 *etimologias*, 13. 1 *L. Taberius*, 28. 2 *ab Epidio*); η (=HU) has two good corrections (4. 6 *vero mane*, also in D; 25. 4 *exoluerunt*, also in L); θ has one unique reading worth reporting (16. 1 *Attici Sati*).

⁶⁰ On the desirability (and feasibility) of a more economical apparatus, see already P. Wessner, rev. of Robinson's diss., *PhW* 43 (1923): 537-38, and id., rev. of Robinson's ed., *PhW* 46 (1926): 1225-26.

CHAPTER 2

THE TEXT

Thanks to the efforts of R. P. Robinson above all, we can reconstruct the text of the *DGR*'s archetype, the common parent of the lost hyparchetypes **X** and **Y**; that archetype was either the 9th-century Hersfeldensis itself (as all recent editors assume) or a 15th-century MS descended from the Hersfeldensis (as I think more likely).[1] But what sort of witness--how generally trustworthy a witness--are we reconstructing when we use the tools that Robinson has given us? Before we begin to examine individual passages, a few words on the general quality of the archetype are perhaps in order. For the sake of the next few paragraphs, let us assume with recent editors that the archetype was in fact the Hersfeldensis; obviously, if one or more Renaissance MSS stood between the Hersfeldensis and the hyparchetypes **X** and **Y**, the following remarks will be directly relevant not to the 9th-century MS but to a 15th-century descendant of it. The central point here--the degree of corruption that marked the book from which all extant MSS descend--remains the same in either case.

Every editor--every reader--of the *DGR* must bear in mind Robinson's warning, ". . . ne nimiam bonitatem libro Hersfeldensi attribuamus" (diss., p. 60). In fact, we can gauge just how deficient a witness the archetype was, at least in rough and relative terms, from a comparison with three other ninth-century MSS: Bern. 165 (**b**), Oxon. Auct. F. 2. 8 (**f**), and Vat. lat. 1570 (**v**). These are all MSS of Vergil, of quite distinct qualities: **b** is an excellent MS--the best of the early Carolingian books--carefully written and carefully corrected, with an original text clearly supe-

---

[1] On the latter possibility, see the discussion of the *DGR*'s transmission, and its relation to that of Tac. *Dial.*, in Chap. 1, with the comments below on 13. 1 †nametrat†.

rior to at least one of the ancient capital MSS (the codex Romanus [R]); f belongs to a group of MSS of somewhat lower quality overall; and v belongs to the poorest class, a group of MSS (aeuv) derived ultimately from R.[2]

Now in the first 600 lines of *Aeneid* 4--a sample chosen at random, comparable in length to the *DGR*--b contains 28 significant errors, f contains 38, and v contains 55; these figures accurately reflect the relative quality of the three MSS overall, and they are much the same as the figures that I found when I tested other 600-line samples as a control. (For our present purposes, an error is defined as a deviation from Mynors' OCT.)[3] Omitted from the count are orthographical differences and other trivialities: the errors of which I speak range from incorrect forms, through omitted or added or transposed or substituted words, to interpolated verses (273 and/or 528). They are not the only errors that the scribes copied or committed in these 600 lines, but they are *the errors that would have been transmitted to later copies*--that is, uncorrected errors, or errors introduced by early correction where the original reading would not have been visible to a later scribe. If we imagine for a moment, then, that one of these MSS was for the text of Vergil what the Hersfeldensis was for the *DGR*--the sole surviving witness, discovered and copied in the 15th century--we can see that there would be from 28 to 55 places in *Aen.* 4. 1-600 where Vergil's text could be recaptured only by emendation: some of these corrections would be obvious; some would have to await their Bentley; and *some would certainly never be made at all,* because the transmitted error is apparently correct--unobjectionable *per se* and, absent other testimony, undetectable--in every respect.

How does the *DGR*'s archetype match up with these MSS? By my count there are nearly *80* places in the *DGR* where all (or virtually all) modern editors agree that it was corrupt--places,

---

[2] On these MSS, and the groups to which they belong, see my *Tradition of the Text of the "Aeneid" in the Ninth Century* (New York, 1990).

[3] As a further check I tested the same passages against Ribbeck's edition, with very similar results: e.g., in *Aen.* 4. 1-600, b showed 33 errors, f showed 43, and v showed 60; this does not include the many lines or half-lines that Ribbeck ejected (53, 126, 236, 256-58, 280, 286, 343, 375, 395) or transposed (486 *post* 517, 548-49 *post* 418), decisions in which few if any more recent editors have followed him.

that is, where they accept, as a correction from one of the 15th-century MSS (or MS-families), a reading that would not have stood in the archetype, or print a conjecture made by an early editor or later scholar. (Again, this count leaves orthographical and similar errors to one side.) This comparison suggests two conclusions. First, Robinson was clearly correct: the archetype was--to say the least--not a witness of *nimia bonitas*. In fact, it appears to have been for its text a much poorer witness than even a third-rate MS like v is for Vergil: by these standards, then, our archetype was a *codex deterrimo deterior*. (This may appear to be a harsh judgment, but it errs, if at all, on the side of generosity: where we *do* have independent testimony--for example, in Suetonius' quotations from Cicero--the record of the archetype is even more wretched than this comparison suggests.)[4] Second, and no less important, we should not for a moment suppose that all the archetype's errors have been--or will be--detected and corrected.

The discussions that follow address more than forty places where the archetypal text is, or has been thought to be, problematic. In the majority of these discussions I argue either for a fresh restoration of the text or for the return to an older reading (usually, an earlier emendation) that has been ignored in most or all editions produced in this century.[5] Several more discussions concern passages where the archetypal text has mistakenly been questioned (16. 3 *versiculus indicat*, 23. 7 *in mulieres*, 24. 2 *repetere*), or where (by contrast) the obelus--too little used in recent editions--should be adopted (5. 1 †*posthus idem ac*†, 10. 3 †*haeret*,

---

[4] In the excerpts from Cicero's letters given in chap. 14 and the excerpt from *Phil*. 2 in chap. 29--a total of 18 Teubner lines--the archetype offered 12 major errors, including 7 omissions. For other omissions see esp. the discussions of 9. 5 *Varrone* <*Murena*>, 23. 6 *CCCLXV* <*dies quotannis*> *uvas*, 24. 2 *legerat* <*enim*>, and 28. 1 <*Servili*> *Isaurici . . . consularis Isaurici*.

[5] See 3. 3 *tantus*, 3. 5 *Guius*, 4. 6 *vero mane*, 6. 2 *quae*, 7. 3 [*ut hoc*], 9. 3 Περὶ ἀλογίας, 9. 4 *omni occasione*, 9. 5 <*Murena*>, 10. 2 *praetextatis nobis*, 11. 3 *deficere*, 14. 1 <*ad*>*haesit*, 14. 3 *ego*, 15. 2 *Catonis[que]*, 15. 3 *catenis subreptis*, 22. 1 *Porcellus*, 22. 2 *verbis*, 23. 4 *praesagiente*, 23. 6 <*dies quotannis*>, 24. 1 <*enim*>, 25. 4 <*versare*>, 25. 5 [*liber*], 25. 5 *appellatione Graeca*, 25. 5 ὑποθέσεις, 27. 1 *M'. Otacilius Pitholaus*, 28. 1 <*Servili*> . . . *consularis*, 30. 2 *declamabat*, 30. 2 *ornate*.

13. 1 †nametra†).⁶ In the remaining places I have tried to augment or clarify previous discussions that the passages have attracted.⁷

Loci sanandi, deliquandi, conclamandi

1.3 nam quod nonnulli tradunt duos libros--de litteris syllabisque, item de metris--ab eodem Ennio editos, iure arguit L. **Cotta** non poetae sed posterioris Enni esse, cuius etiam de augurali disciplina volumina ferantur.

C. Cotta *della Corte*

Following the tentative suggestions in Teuffel⁶ (1:303) and Schanz-Hosius (1:97), Bione firmly identified this L. Cotta with L. Aurunculeius Cotta, a legate of Caesar in Gaul (died 54: see "Aurunculeius (6)," *RE* 2 [1896]: 2555-56; *MRR* 2:204, 219, 225, 3:33), said by Athenaeus (6. 273B) to have composed a work περὶ τῆς Ῥωμαίων πολιτείας. Perhaps. But the connection between such a σύγγραμμα and the question at issue here seems slight; and in any case the man referred to here simply as L. Cotta ought to be a bearer of that name better known than the relatively obscure lieutenant of Caesar: note that Suetonius refers to the latter as *Aurunculeio* at *Jul.* 25. 2; and each time Caesar himself introduces the man into a book of the *BCiv.*, he first uses the *tria nomina* Lucius Aurunculeius Cotta--so at 2. 11. 3, 4. 22. 5, 5. 24. 5-- and only thereafter refers to him as Lucius Cotta (4. 38. 3, 5. 35. 8, 37. 4) or simply Cotta (9 times). If the text is sound, a better candidate is L. Aurelius Cotta, cos. 65, cens. 64, XVvir sac. fac. 44 ("Aurelius (102)," *RE* 2 [1896]: 2485-87; *MRR* 2:127, 157, 161, 333, cf. 3:30), commonly called simply "L. Cotta" in the sources (see the

---

⁶ In the texts of Robinson, della Corte, and Brugnoli the obelus appears a total of four times: Robinson and Brugnoli each use it twice (respectively, 25. 5 †appellatione†, 28. 2 †aureis†, and 16 fin., 23. 6 †CCCLX uvas†: in the first three cases the use is mistaken, in the last a better solution can now be proposed, see the notes ad locc.); della Corte makes it a matter of editorial principle not to use the obelus at all (3rd ed., p. xxxvii).

⁷ See 1. 3 *L. Cotta*, 3. 3. *Metellum*, 3. 5 *conductum ut Oscae doceret*, 3. 6 *Sescenius*, 6. 2 *simul*, 6. 2 *<in>scripsisse*, 8. 3 *opusculum*, 10. 1 *<L.>*, 10. 6 *rerum omnium Romanarum*, 21. 4 *inscribuntur*, 23. 4 *pepercisse*, 28. 2 *aureis*, 29. 1 *extrisse*.

references in *RE* and *MRR* and note that Suetonius refers to him as Lucius Cotta at *Jul.* 79. 3 and in the consular formula--*L. Cotta et L. Torquato consulibus*--at *Vit. Hor.* p. 48 Reiff.).

The suggestion of della Corte, to read *C. Cotta*, is tempting.[8] This would be one of the older brothers of Lucius: cos. 75 (died late 74 or early 73: "Aurelius (96)," *RE* 2 [1896]: 2482-84, *MRR* 2:96, 103, 111, 3:31, and add C. F. Konrad, *CP* 84 [1989]: 119-29), he was one of the most distinguished orators of his age (see esp. Cic. *Brut.* 183, 201-5, and cf. *De or.* 1. 25ff.). Della Corte based his suggestion primarily on the connection between C. Cotta and Aelius Stilo, who is said to have written at least one speech for him (*Brut.* 205 "Cottae pro se lege Varia quae inscribitur, eam L. Aelius scripsit Cottae rogatu," generalized to *oratiunculas* at ibid. 207; cf. *DGR* 3.2 "Aelius . . . vocabatur et Stilo, quod orationes nobilissimo cuique scribere solebat"); and Stilo is known to have interested himself in questions of authenticity (esp. regarding Plautus) of the sort at issue here. One could even add a further consideration in favor of the proposal: the Cotta who attributed the grammatical works in question to a *posterior Ennius* evidently knew of the latter as an authority on augural lore (thus the subjunctive *ferantur*, which implies that the clause is not an addition by Suetonius but was part of Cotta's judgment, in whatever source Suetonius found it); and since C. Cotta was a pontifex (see *MRR* 2:23, 113: he was succeeded by Caesar on his death), he could be thought to have had an interest in the subject.

Still, these considerations are not decisive. The connection with Stilo, though to the point, is not crucial: note that C. Cotta--and so, presumably, both of his brothers, Lucius and Marcus--were nephews of P. Rutilius Rufus (Cic. *De or.* 1. 229, *ND* 3. 80, cf. *Att.* 12. 20. 2), who enjoyed an especially close connection with another grammarian, Aurelius Opillus (*DGR* 6. 2, discussed below); and Opillus was also concerned with questions of authenticity as they touched on the plays of Plautus (see Gell. *NA* 3. 3. 1).[9] Note, too, that an interest in *auguralis disciplina* would not be utterly alien to L. Cotta, who was a XVvir (see above). I intend to retain the

---

[8] See his rev. of Bione, *RFIC* 20 (1942): 137, and his 3rd ed., p. 73.

[9] L. Cotta appears to have been about 10 years younger than his brother Gaius (b. 124 B.C.): the former would have been of an age to receive instruction from Opillus in the early 90s, before Opillus accompanied Rufus into exile.

transmitted reading in my text, while noting della Corte's suggestion in the apparatus.

3.3 nam et Praeconinus . . . vocabatur et Stilo, quod orationes nobilissimo cuique scribere solebat, **tantus** optimatium fautor ut **Metellum** Numidicum in exilium comitatus sit.

    tantus Q : tantum ω   Metellum W : M. Metellum O Y, Q.
    Metellum *Aldus*

"Lectionem *tantus* ab Aldo ex editione Veneta 1474 vulgatam Statius neglegenter duobus Vaticanis (**VI**) attribuit, cuius errore inductus Roth eam resuscitavit, quamquam Tross et Osann veram scripturam [sc. *tantum*] iam restituerant." So Robinson (ed., p. 5), after whom the archetype's *tantum* has become the modern vulgate; only Bione prints *tantus*, which occurs as a conjecture in Q.

    Tantus is surely correct. Tross (1841) "restored" *tantum* because that is the reading of L, the MS that he took as the sole basis of his text; Osann (1854) accepted *tantum* ("positum pro *in tantum*") because he found it in **LHP** and was content to compare Livy 37. 39. 6 "Antiochus . . . tantum progressus e castris est, ut dimicaturum appareret." But the usage of Suetonius himself is unequivocal. Adverbial *tantum* occurs in the *Caesares* and *DGR* 50 times, 24 times as part of a fixed phrase (*non tantum, tantum modo, tantum non, tantum quod*), 26 times by itself.[10] In all of the former places and all but four of the latter, it has the sense "only" (*vel sim.*); the four exceptions are all instances of the idiom *tantum abesse ut* . . . (*Aug.* 21. 2, *Tib.* 50. 1, *Ner.* 25. 3,*Vesp.* 14), which is thus the only environment in which Suetonius uses adverbial *tantum* in the sense "so far" / "to such an extent," with *ut* in a clause of result. This idiom is obviously irrelevant to the present passage, for which the only apt comparison is provided by the 35 places where Suetonius coordinates adjectival *tantus, -a, -um* with consecutive *ut* + subjunctive (including 4 other places in the *DGR*: 3. 5 *pretia* . . . *tanta* . . . *ut* . . .; 13. 2 *tanta* . . . *honestate* . . . *ut* . . .; 15. 3 *tanto amore* . . . *ut* . . .; 23. 4 *arrogantia* . . . *tanta ut* . . .).

---

[10] Here and throughout I have been much assisted by A. A. Howard and C. N. Jackson, *Index verborum C. Suetoni Tranquilli* (Cambridge, Mass., 1922).

Tantus here was corrupted to *tantUM* presumably in anticipation of the following *optimatiUM*.

We can note, too, that Roth was certainly correct to print *Metellum Numidicum*, though the archetype apparently read *M. Metellum Numidicum* (*M.* produced by dittography, then deleted by conjecture--or more likely, omitted through a lucky haplography--in **W**): Suetonius' habits make clear that we should neither replace *M.* with *Q.* (so Aldus, followed most recently by della Corte) nor suspect that Suetonius wrote *M.* in error (a possibility mooted by Robinson, ed., p. 6). When in the *DGR* (or, for that matter, the *Caesares*) Suetonius refers to a person in passing--as here, to Numidicus--he uses either a single name (in the *DGR*, mostly for a few famous literary or historical personages, e.g.: Livius [sc. Andronicus], Ennius, Horatius, Vergilius, Brutus, Cassius, Augustus), or the *tria nomina* (in fewer cases still: e.g., 2. 2 *C. Octavius Lampadio*, 12. 1 *L. Corneli Sullae*), or--by far the most common--*two* names, in one of these combinations: praenomen + nomen (e.g., 2. 2 *Q. Vargunteius*, 14. 1 *Cn. Pompeio et C. Memmio*); praenomen + cognomen (e.g., 1. 3 *L. Cotta*, 3. 5 *Q. Catulo*, 7. 2 *M. Ciceronem*); and, most frequently, without praenomen, either nomen + cognomen (e.g., 2. 2 *Laelius Archelaus Vettiusque Philocomus*, 3. 5 *Lutatium Daphnidem . . . Aeficio Calvino*) or two cognomina (*Metellum Numidicum*, 4. 2 *Messalla Corvinus*). For a name of the sort Q. Caecilius Metellus Numidicus, therefore, we might find either Q. Metellus (cf. *Jul. 55. 3 Quinto Metello, Aug. 89. 2 Q. Metelli*) or Caecilius Metellus (cf. *Jul. 16. 1 Caecilio Metello tribuno plebis*) or Metellus Numidicus; Suetonius' habits do not lead us to expect Q. (or, even in error, M.) Metellus Numidicus, any more than we should expect M. Messalla Corvinus for the man whom Suetonius regularly names as either Valerius Messalla (*Aug. 58. 1, 74*) or (as in the *DGR*) Messalla Corvinus (*Tib. 70. 1 Corvinum Messallam*, cf. *Claud. 13. 2 Gallus Asinius et Statilius Corvinus, Pollionis ac Messallae oratorum nepotes*). See also the discussions of 9. 5 *Varrone <Murena>* and 28. 1 *Ti. Cannutius*.

3.5 . . . pretia vero grammaticorum tanta mercedesque tam magnae, ut constet Lutatium Daphnidem, quem **Gaius** Melissus per cavillationem nominis Πανὸς ἀγάπημα dicit, septingentis milibus nummum a Q. Catulo emptum ac brevi manumissum . . .

Gaius *conieci* (Caiius *iam Vahlen*) : Levius Xα (Livius G¹) β (L. D), Laeneus L, Len(a)eus γ, Cilnius *Heinsius*, Maecenas *Osann*, Laevius *Roth*, Laevius in Melissis *Lammert*, Aelius *Hillscher*, saepius Doergens, lepide *Wessner*   Πανὸς ἀγάπημα *Toup* (Πανὸς ἄγασμα *Salmasius, alii alia*) : panosagacema ω

Cf. Pliny *HN* 7. 128 "pretium hominis in servitio geniti maximum ad hanc diem, quod equidem conpererim, fuit grammaticae artis, Daphnin Attio [Accio *Detlefsen*] Pisaurense vendente et M. Scauro principe civitatis HS D̄C̄C̄ licente." The same *grammaticus* Daphnis must be the subject of both reports: either the name of the purchaser is mistakenly recorded in one of the passages, or-- perhaps more likely--Daphnis was first purchased at auction by Scaurus (d. ca. 90/89) and was then sold for the same price to Catulus (d. 86), whose nomen he gained upon manumission (so, e.g., Münzer, "Lutatius (15)," *RE* 13 [1927]: 2095). In either case, Daphnis' *floruit* should be put early in the first century B.C., a date that fits the general chronological framework with which Suetonius has presented us.[11] That date in turn appears to rule out the identification of the Melissus here named with C. Melissus, the freedman of Maecenas whom Suetonius treats in chapter 21:[12] for as Robinson argued (ed., pp. 6-7), the *cavillatio* in question should have originated in the time of Daphnis himself, as a joke made by a contemporary for the amusement of contemporaries; and C. Melissus can hardly have been Daphnis' contemporary. Robinson therefore accepted Roth's *Laevius* for the archetype's *Levius*,[13] and followed Buecheler in identifying

---

[11] Thus 3. 1 "instruxerunt auxeruntque ab omni parte grammaticam L. Aelius Lanuvinus generque Aeli Ser. Clodius . . .," with 3. 4 "posthac magis ac magis et gratia et cura artis increvit . . .," leading to the present passage. The next example that Suetonius offers cannot be dated securely but is almost certainly not earlier; see below on L. Appuleius and Aeficius Calvinus.

[12] That identification, common among earlier editors, motivated the conjectures *Cilnius, Maecenas,* and *Caiius* noted above. Hillscher conjectured *Aelius* on the basis of Gell. *NA* 18. 6; but the Aelius Melissus mentioned there was a contemporary of Gellius (ibid. 1 "*in nostra memoria* fuit Romae summi quidem loci inter grammaticos id temporis") and so too late to be intended here.

[13] The reading of γ, *Len(a)eus* (cf. L's *Laeneus*), is an importation from 2. 2, just above, where Pompeius Lenaeus is mentioned.

"Laevius Melissus" with the poet Laevius, author of the *Erotopaegnia*.[14]

But there are difficulties, at least as far as the latter identification is concerned. First, the cognomen Melissus is nowhere attested for the poet, who is always cited--dozens of times--simply as Laevius.[15] Second, there is the matter of the poet's date. Though "conventionally dated to early 1st cent. B.C." (as the *Cambridge History of Classical Literature* puts it, 2:830), there is in fact very little external evidence that can be used to date him.[16] Moreover, the one firm piece of internal evidence we have points to a date considerably earlier than the conventional one: for fragment 23. 1 *lex Licinia introducitur* (*FPL*, p. 74 B.) refers, in the present tense, to the introduction of the *lex Licinia*, a sumptuary law that should be dated to ca. 141 B.C. (after the *lex Didia* of 143 and before the retariffing of the *as*).[17] If Laevius was writing at the time of that law--as we should conclude in the absence of evidence to the contrary--then he is quite unlikely to have been a contemporary of Lutatius Daphnis.

If the identification of the *cavillator* with the poet Laevius is made doubtful by the questionable name and the questionable date, we have two alternatives: either Roth's *Laevius* should be

---

[14] F. Buecheler, "Coniectanea," *RhM* 41 (1886): 11-12--an identification based on the mistaken premise that Laevius is a rare name.

[15] Emphasized by F. Lammert, "Laevius Melissus?" *Hermes* 62 (1927): 251-53, who accepted the identification but proposed "Laevius in *Melissis*," interpreting the latter noun as a title of one of Laevius' works.

[16] Porph. ad Hor. *Carm.* 3. 1. 2 says merely "Laevius lyrica ante Horatium scripsit"; the present passage is also sometimes used, though the danger of circularity--establishing the text by assuming the identification, then using the text to date the poet identified--is obvious.

[17] On the date and its significance for Laevius: L. Holford-Strevens, *Select Commentary on Aulus Gellius Book 2* (D.Phil. diss., Oxford, 1971), pp. 278, 284 (n. 1), with P. G. McC. Brown, "The Date of Laevius," *LCM* 5 (1980): 213, and further elaboration by Holford-Strevens, "Laevius and Melissus," *LCM* 6 (1981): 181-82. As Brown points out, the law was independently dated to 134 B.C. by I. Sauerwein, *Die leges sumptuariae als römische Massnahme gegen den Sittenverfall* (Diss. Hamburg, 1970), pp. 94-104, and (on better grounds) to "142 or 141 (or just conceivably 140)" by M. H. Crawford, *Roman Republican Coinage*, vol. 2 (Cambridge, 1974), pp. 624-25.

retained--in which case we have a Laevius Melissus otherwise unknown to history; or that correction should be rejected--in which case we should re-examine Robinson's argument against identification of Melissus with C. Melissus. The former alternative is possible; but there is good reason to prefer the latter.

Robinson's argument--that the *cavillatio* was produced by a contemporary of Daphnis--is at least reasonable.[18] The point to be stressed, however, is that even if it is correct, it does not rule out C. Melissus as Suetonius' source. Suetonius tells us (21. 4) that Melissus produced "libellos *Ineptiarum*, qui nunc *Iocorum* inscribuntur," books that Suetonius clearly knew first hand (see below, at the discussion of 21. 4 *inscribuntur*); as Suetonius also tells us, Melissus himself reported (*ipse tradit*) that he began to compose these books (*componere instituit*) in his sixtieth year (*sexagesimum aetatis annum agens*) and that he completed 150 of them, to which he subsequently added other, different works ("absolvitque centum et quinquaginta, quibus et alios diversi operis postea addidit"). These 150 *libelli* of *Ineptiae / Ioci* produced by the sexagenarian Melissus were plainly not original compositions, but were the product of compilation--collections of witticisms and amusing anecdotes of the sort represented by the sources of much of Macrob. *Sat.* 2. 2ff. and by the Greek collection *Philogelos*.[19] As a compilation, Melissus' work (like the *Philogelos*) will have incorporated material from earlier times as well as his own: it is therefore not at all strange if Daphnis is to be dated closer to the century's beginning, while Melissus himself belongs closer to its end. The play on Daphnis' name is just the sort of thing that would appeal to a collector of "trifles" (cf., e.g,

---

[18] For doubts, see Holford-Strevens, "Laevius and Melissus."

[19] Melissus' collection is itself often identified as one of Macrobius' main sources, see esp. E. Bickel, *Diatribe in Senecae philosophi fragmenta*, vol. 1 (Leipzig, 1905), pp. 309ff. Note that at least one of the compilers of the *Philogelos* was also, coincidentally, a *grammaticus*: see my *Guardians of Language: The Grammarian and Society in Late Antiquity* (Berkeley and Los Angeles, 1988), pp. 333-34 (s.v. Philagrius, no. 117). For Roman compilations before Melissus, cf. the *dicta* gathered by Caesar (*Fam.* 9. 16. 4, cf. Suet. *Iul.* 56. 7), the collections of Cicero's witticisms made by C. Trebonius (*Fam.* 15. 21. 2) and (perhaps) Tiro (Quint. *Inst.* 6. 3. 5, cf. Macrob. *Sat.* 2. 1. 12), and the *liber bene dictorum* of the jurist A. Cascellius (*Dig.* 1. 2. 2. 45 [Pompon.]); note also the books of jokes alluded to at Plaut. *Stich.* 400, 454f., *Pers.* 392-95.

Macrob. *Sat.* 2. 2. 5 and 6).²⁰ It is reasonable to believe, then, that Suetonius found the *cavillatio* in Melissus' collection and reported it here: if *quem . . . Melissus . . . dicit* seems a bit inexact (since Melissus himself did not, strictly speaking, make the joke), the imprecision is venial, and should be attributed not only to Suetonius but also to the nature of such compilations, which (to judge, again, from the *Philogelos* and the sources transcribed by Macrobius) do not footnote the source of each joke they collect. We should remember, too, that twice elsewhere in these introductory chapters Suetonius draws on the written works of *grammatici* whose lives he later sketches (2. 2 ". . . Lucili saturas . . ., quas legisse se apud Archelaum Pompeius Lenaeus, apud Philocomum Valerius Cato praedicant," 4. 3 "quorum opinionem Orbilius etiam exemplis confirmat: namque . . . ait . . ."): when the presence of Melissus' name here (+ pres. indic. *dicit*) makes it appear that Suetonius is doing the same thing yet again, we should conclude that that in fact is what he is doing.

We do not want Roth's *Laevius*, therefore; neither do we want the archetype's *Levius* (or *levius*).²¹ Given Suetonius' habits, we *should* expect more of Melissus' name (cf. above, on 3. 3): read *Gaius* (after Vahlen's *Caiius*).²² The corruption will have proceeded from confusion of capital *G* and capital *L*. It is appropriate to note here that though the praenomina in the *DGR* are sometimes abbreviated, sometimes spelled out in the 15th-cent. MSS, and are regularly abbreviated in modern editions (as they will be in my own), all praenomina are spelled out in the fragment of the Hersfeldensis that survived in the codex Aesinas.²³

---

20 The play would have been all the more appealing if it involved sexual innuendo: Buecheler suggested that Catulus was "Pan" ("Coniectanea," p. 12); if that is correct, "the joke may follow from his having paid so high a price for Daphnis. . . . Catulus' proclivities are made clear enough by Cicero, *ND* 1. 79" (Holford-Strevens, "Laevius and Melissus," p. 182).

21 Holford-Strevens, ibid., rightly says that *levius*, as an adverb, would be "otiose and awkward," even if it could be taken to mean something like "rather flippantly." Wessner's *lepide* would offer better sense--if an adverb were wanted.

22 *De Verrio Flacco et Suetonii libello de Grammaticis* (Berlin, 1877), p. 8 n. = *Opuscula Academica*, vol. 1 (Leipzig, 1907), p. 48 n.

23 Remarked by Robinson, diss., p. 64.

We can now turn to the *cavillatio* itself, beginning with the readings presented by the MSS:

X	α	β	γ
	sacis	panosa gacema ul'	
panosagacema O	panasagacema N	panosa/sagâ B	panosagacema M T
	sâs		.i.sagacê
panosagecema W	pansa gacema G	panosagacema DL	pasiosagatema K
	c	l'sagâc	
	pansagasansema I	Panosagacema V	panosagatema CΔ
			Panosagarema QE
			p (spat. 10 litt.) H
			panasagacicon U
			pannosagacenia S
			Panos agamata F

"Hersfeldensis lectio hoc loco vix restitui potest": so Robinson (diss., p. 76, n. 108), but this is surely too pessimistic. Of *panos-* there can be no doubt: the only significant variation is the *pans-* (or *panas-*) that appears to have been a peculiar error of α (a similar error occurred independently in U). Of *-agacema* there can be only slight doubt, and even then the question is really whether that was the *only* reading in the archetype. *-agacema* was the reading of X (W's *-agecema*, which gave Robinson pause [ibid.], is a casual error), and it certainly occurred in Y as well: the texts of GI and BV point to the double reading *-agacema / agâsema* (or *agâcema*) in α and β, and so to the presence of a double reading in Y (despite the peculiarities of some individual MSS, γ clearly read *-agacema*); but this "double reading" need be due merely to a correction in Y (*-agansema*, vel sim., cf. I) and certainly does not need to be referred to the archetype.

With archetypal *panosagacema*, the two emendations most worthy of consideration are Toup's Πανὸς ἀγάπημα and Salmasius' Πανὸς ἄγασμα (also suggested independently by Baumgarten-Crusius).[24] Each has found suporters, and each presumes an easy error.[25] I prefer ἀγάπημα, since ἄγασμα is an exceedingly

---

[24] Other proposals: Πανὸς ἄγημα *Aldus*, Πανὸς ἄγαλμα *Salmasius*, *Gronovius* (qui et Πανὸς ἄθυρμα). One could also suggest Πανὸς ἄγρευμα, cf. Theocr. *Epigr.* 3. 3 ἀγρεύει δέ τυ [viz., Δάφνιν] Πάν.

[25] For ἀγάπημα, Π (or π) misread as Τ (or τ), with the latter then confused with c (cf. the confusion in KCΔ); ἄγασμα = ΑΓΑCΜΑ > agacema.

rare word (only once in all of Greek literature: Soph. frag. 971 Radt ἀγάσματα) and would have a less appropriate sense than ἀγάπημα (the latter = "Pan's delight"; ἄγασμα would suggest "object of adoration").[26]

3.5 ... L. Appuleium ab Aeficio Calvino equite Romano praedivite quadringenis annuis **conductum ut Oscae doceret**. (6) nam in provincias quoque grammatica penetraverat ac nonnulli de notissimis doctoribus peregre docuerunt ...

> Appuleium *Rolfe* : Apuleium ω, Apulei W^m, Appuleius *Statius* (Apuleius *Vahlen*) conductum GQE : -tos XNIVD¹L, -tus BDγ ut Oscae doceret *Robinson* (*post* ut osce doceret *Buecheler*) : mutoscedo doceret X, multos edoceret α (ut *add*. G) β (m- doceret B, m-edocent D) γ (multos edocuisse QE), multos edocuit *Statius*, si multos edoceret *Oudendorp*, multos edocere *Osann*, ut Tolosae doceret *Madvig*, ut filios edoceret *Reifferscheid*, ut suos Coo (*vel* Cnido) doceret *Rawson*, Mutuscae doceret *Badian*, ut suae domi doceret *Watt*

Suetonius continues his notice of the elevated costs that followed on grammar's new popularity and prestige ("posthac magis ac magis et gratia et cura artis increvit. ... pretia vero grammaticorum tanta mercedesque tam magnae, ut ..."): having given an example of the high *pretium* paid for a slave *grammaticus* (Lutatius Daphnis, see above), he now instances the high fee for which the *eques* Aeficius Calvinus hired the (free) *grammaticus* L. Appuleius (reading *App-*, after Rolfe, the regular spelling of the *gentilicium* in the republican period).

The end of the sentence was clearly corrupt in the archetype.[27] The reading of X is unambiguous: *conductos mutoscedo doceret*.

---

[26] So LSJ s.v.; the ancient lexicographers glossed ἀγάσματα with σεβάσματα, see *TGF* 4:600, ad Soph. frag. 971. As R. Renehan points out to me, the lexicographic tradition, which has the plural lemma only, strongly suggests that ἀγάσματα was a true ἅπαξ εἰρημένον, coined by Sophocles and not in common use to provide the material for a pun.

[27] Beyond the conjectures recorded above, note: a lacuna was posited after *annuis* by Mommsen and Roth, after *praedivite* by Vahlen (*De Verrio Flacco*, p. 8 n. = *Opusc. Acad.* 1:48 n., with *conductos multos edocere* after the lacuna), and after *conductum* by Reifferscheid. Bione printed †*conductos multos edoceret* (cf. id., "Note critiche ed esegetiche a Suetonio De grammaticis et rhetoribus," *RFIC* 20 [1942]: 20-21), Rolfe *conductum multos edoceret*.

The evidence of the Y-family can best be grasped if it is presented in tabular form:

         α   β
conductos multos edoceret **N I**   *conductos multos edoceret* **V L**
conductum ut multos edoceret **G**   *conductus (-tos* **D¹***) multos edocent* **D**
                                          conductus multos doceret **B**
                                        γ
                           conductus multos edoceret **δ ζ**
                           conductum multos edocuisse **Q E**

Robinson put his finger on two crucial points concerning this testimony (diss., pp. 79-81). First, emendation should proceed from the reading of **X**, precisely because it is thoroughly unintelligible: the readings that occur in the Y-MSS--with the flat *multos* and the verb *edoceret* (vel sim.), which manages to be pointlessly emphatic and un-Suetonian at the same time--are merely attempts to make "scribe's sense" of the transmitted reading.[28] Second, the sentence that immediately follows--*NAM in provincias quoque grammatica penetraverat* . . .--shows that a provincial place-name should be lurking in the corruption (this was appreciated earlier by Madvig, who proposed *ut Tolosae doceret*). The latter point has sometimes been circumvented, by emending *nam* to *iam* (so Reifferscheid) or by taking *nam* as = "in fact," marking a transition to a new topic;[29] but this will not do. Though Suetonius occasionally uses the word in something like the latter sense in the *Caesares*,[30] it happens that he uses it elsewhere in the *DGR* (7 times) exclusively to introduce a statement that elaborates or explains the preceding statement.[31] That *nam*

---

[28] So E. Badian, "Coo for the Teacher?" *LCM* 4 (1979): 140. The reading of Y itself was probably *conductos multos edoceret*; among Y's descendants, **G** and **Q E** share the palm for fashioning versions that at least are construable.

[29] Thus, e.g., Rolfe in his translation, followed by T. E. Kinsey, "Should Appuleius be Sent to Cos? (Suetonius, *de gramm.* 3)," *LCM* 4 (1979): 79.

[30] Cf. Badian, "Coo?" p. 140.

[31] See 1. 3, 3. 2, 7. 3, 22. 1, 25. 4, 26. 2, 30. 4; *namque* is used three more times (4. 3, 9. 3, 17. 1). Badian, ibid., suggests that *nam* "is surprisingly rare altogether" in the *DGR*; but Suetonius uses *nam* relatively more often in the *DGR* than he does in the *Caesares*--8 times in just under 600 Teubner lines (= ca. 19-20 ordinary Teubner pages) vs. 109 times in 334 Teubner pages (it also occurs another 10 times in texts Suetonius quotes)--despite

has the same function here is further indicated by the tense of *penetraverat*. Were *nam* merely marking the transition to a new topic, the sentence it introduces would be parallel to the first two sentences of the paragraph (*posthac . . . increvit. . . . pretia vero . . . tam magnae . . .*), and we would expect *penetravit* (*penetraverat* would imply that grammar had reached the provinces before it gained status at Rome, a strange idea that Suetonius cannot have meant); here the pluperfect must denote an action that is antecedent to (and so, as often, causally connected with) another action in the immediate context--in this case, the hiring of Appuleius. That is of course how Suetonius uses the pluperfect elsewhere (see 3. 2 *fecerat*, 9. 2 *attigerat*, 11. 3 *cesserat*, 12. 2 *reliquerat*, 15. 1 *fuerat*, 19. 1 *fuerat*, 24. 2 *legerat*), and that use is consistent only with the regular, explanatory force of *nam*.[32]

Robinson himself printed "Apuleius . . . conductus <esse dicitur atque in Hispaniam deductus,> ut Oscae doceret," adopting the nominatives *Apuleius . . . conductus* and positing a lacuna. He drew the inspiration for *Oscae* from Buecheler's (bizarre) *osce*,[33] combined with Plut. *Sert.* 14. 2-3, describing the steps Sertorius took to secure this μεγάλη πόλις of Hispania Tarraconensis, which he took as his capital: these steps included the importation of teachers (τοὺς γὰρ εὐγενεστάτους ἀπὸ τῶν ἐθνῶν συναγαγὼν εἰς Ὄσκαν . . ., διδασκάλους ἐπιστήσας Ἑλληνικῶν τε καὶ Ῥωμαϊκῶν μαθημάτων ἔργῳ μὲν ἐξωμηρεύσατο, λόγῳ δὲ ἐπαίδευεν, ὡς ἀνδράσι γενομένοις πολιτείας τε

---

the fact that the *DGR* consists largely of very brief chapters, within which it is fairly uncommon for a given topic to be allotted more than a sentence or two.

[32] The emendations proposed with transitional *nam* = "in fact" are in any case not compelling. Badian (ibid., pp. 142-43) attempted *conductum Mutuscae doceret* (from the Sabine town Trebula Mutuesca); but this leaves the clause without the *ut* that it needs. The latter deficiency was noted by W. S. Watt, "Facessat Mutusca," *LCM* 4 (1979): 167, who suggested *conductum ut su(a)e do<mi> doceret*.

[33] Accepted, astonishingly, by Funaioli, *GRF* 1:328 (= M. Terentius Varro, frag. 320. 46), and by C. Nicolet, *L'ordre équestre à l'époque républicaine (312-43 av. J.-C.)*, vol. 2 (Paris, 1974), p. 760 (no. 8); see, *contra*, E. Rawson, "M. Aeficius Calvinus and His *Grammaticus* (Suetonius, *de gramm*. 3)," *LCM* 4 (1979): 54-55.

μεταδώσων καὶ ἀρχῆς κτλ.).³⁴ The nominatives can hardly be correct, since the construction should follow from *ut constet Lutatium Daphnidem* . . . (see above: Robinson was seduced primarily by *conductus* in **BDγ**, which represents--at best--nothing more than a short-sighted attempt to provide a nominative to go with *(e)doceret)*; and without the nominatives there is no need to posit a lacuna. But the same proposal, with the accusative, may nonetheless be right: in *scriptura continua* (of which **X**, especially, gives many signs) *-tuM UT OSCE* [= *-ae*] *DOceret* could easily pass to *-tos mutoscedo doceret*, with the ending of *conduct-* assimilated to the following *os*, and with dittography of *do*. Such (by implication, at least) must be the understanding of Brugnoli and della Corte, who print . . . *conductum ut Oscae doceret*.

Robinson's *Oscae* was, however, vigorously criticized by Elizabeth Rawson, who stressed that "nothing whatever ties Aeficius Calvinus to Spain. . . . No Aeficii at all appear in any of the western provinces, as far as one can tell."³⁵ Rawson preferred to identify the Aeficius Calvinus in question with M. Aeficius Calvinus, a prefect (ἔπαρχος) of some sort mentioned on several inscriptions--from Samos, Athens, and Pergamum--honoring himself, his wife, or his daughter; the inscriptions from Samos, at least, can be dated to the second half of the 1st cent. B.C. (from the letter-forms).³⁶ Accordingly, she proposed *ut suos Cnido doceret*

---

34 On these measures, see most recently P. O. Spann, *Quintus Sertorius and the Legacy of Sulla* (Fayetteville, 1987), pp. 167-68, dating them tentatively to summer 77 B.C.

35 "M. Aeficius Calvinus," p. 54; for the attestations of the name, see pp. 54-56. By "western provinces" Rawson meant areas outside Italy (Aeficii are attested on inscriptions from Minturnae, Brundisium, Praeneste, Rome, and Ostia).

36 Ibid., p. 53. The Samian inscriptions are *SEG* 1. 388 (honoring Aeficius' wife, Magilia) and P. Herrman, *MDAI(A)* 75 (1960): 139 (Μάρκου Καλ[ουίνου τοῦ ἐπάρχου], without the *gentilicium*; the name of Aeficius' daughter, Aeficia Calvina, lies wholly within Herrman's restoration); Pergamum, H. Hepding, *MDAI(A)* 32 (1907): 324 (the restoration of Aeficius' name seems secure); Athens, *IG* 2².4243 (honoring the daughter), dated in *IG* to the 2nd half of the 1st cent. A.D., after P. Graindor, *Athènes de Tibère à Trajan* (Cairo, 1931), p. 42 (on the form of the Φ), though Rawson argues (pp. 57-58) that the date is not post-Augustan. The title ἔπαρχος appears securely in the inscription from Pergamum and in *SEG* 1. 388; on the range of possible meanings, see Rawson, p. 57.

(a M. Aeficius Apollonius is associated with Cnidos) or *ut suos Coo doceret* (some Aeficiae are attested there, "perhaps descended from freedmen"), with a preference for the latter.[37] But this does not inspire confidence either. The Greek East in the latter part of the 1st century B.C. is not impossible, but neither is it really what one expects in this chapter, where Suetonius *seems* to be talking about the Latin West, earlier in the century.[38] The identification itself is also not impossible--but neither is it certain: as Rawson acknowledged (p. 58), Suetonius' Aeficius could have been the father of the man known from the inscriptions; and in that case, the fact that the latter spent some portion of his life in the East (as an Italian *negotiator* abroad, Rawson suggested) need tell us nothing about the course of his father's life. Furthermore, the connection between Aeficius Calvinus and either Cos or Cnidos is rather attenuated. And unlikely above all is the form of Rawson's proposal--*Coo* (or *Cnido*)--which contradicts the rules of Latin morphology and Suetonius' own usage: both call for *Coi* (or *Cnidi*).[39]

To be sure, one would prefer to have hard evidence placing an Aeficius in Spain in the early 1st century B.C.; but it is not quite reasonable to demand or expect such evidence, especially in the case of a man who--wealthy though he may have been--was evidently not a person of much political consequence. (In Rawson's objection quoted above, the qualifying phrase, "as far as one can tell," must be given full weight: it is uncertain how far one *can* tell in such a case. As C. E. Murgia points out to me, it is even conceivable that Aeficius himself was never at Osca, if (e.g.) he served as Sertorius' agent in hiring the *grammaticus*.) In the end, Robinson's emendation withstands the criticism: the paleographical evidence, the demands of the context (with *nam . . . penetrav-*

---

[37] In her *Intellectual Life in the Late Roman Republic* (Baltimore, 1985), p. 13, Rawson puts Aeficius and his hireling grammarian more generally "in the region" (viz., the Aegean).

[38] Kinsey, "Should Appuleius be Sent to Cos?," gave too much weight to this consideration, in supposing that the location simply ruled Rawson's suggestion out of court; but Badian, in response ("Coo?" p. 141), gave it too little weight. On the chronological framework, see above, in the discussion of Lutatius Daphnis.

[39] So Badian, ibid., noting that *Coi* is attested at *ILLRP* 408; for loc. *Cnidi*, see Plin. *HN* 36. 83.

erat), and the attested presence of teachers at Osca combine to produce a fit that is too neat to be coincidental.

3.6 nonnulli de notissimis doctoribus peregre docuerunt, maxime in Gallia Togata, inter quos Octavius Teucer et **Sescenius** Iacchus et Oppius Chares . . .

> Sescenius D, Sescennius XαVL (Fescennius L²) : Siscenn- (*vel sim.*) γ, *om.* B

The *nomen* is spelled thus on *CIL* 6. 1058 (lat. 1. 108) (an. 210), 26458, 9. 815 (Luceria) (with an apex over the second -*e*-); it should be noted that all three inscriptions (the first obviously, the others probably) are a good deal later than the teacher in question. Be that as it may, the various conjectures that the passage has attracted--*Fescennius* (L² = Pontano),[40] *Sisinnius* (S, after γ's *Siscennius*), *Sisennius* (Wolf), *Caesennius* (Oudendorp), *Pescennius* (Osann)--are superfluous.

4.6 me quidem adulescentulo repeto quendam Principem nomine alternis diebus declamare, alternis disputare, nonnullis **vero mane** disserere, post meridiem remoto pulpito declamare solitum.

> vero mane DKHU : mane vero ω

The topic is *grammatici* who used to teach both grammar and rhetoric; Suetonius recalls an example from his youth: ". . . Princeps used to declaim on one day, hold discussions on the next"--that, in other words, was his regular regime--"but on some days he used to lecture in the morning, declaim in the afternoon."

Such seems to me to be the necessary structure of the passage: two co-ordinate and contrasting statements, articulated around *nonnullis*, with each statement consisting of an antithesis expressed by paired predicates in asyndeton. The first asyndetic pair--*alternis diebus declamare, alternis disputare*--states the typical pattern of the teacher's instruction; the second--*mane disserere, post meridiem . . . disputare*--notes an occasional variation in that pattern. Within each pair the antithesis is marked not only by the asyndetic juxtaposition--the sort of juxtaposition

---

[40] On the identification, L² = Pontano, see Chap. 1, n. 36

that in Latin is regularly the equivalent of Greek μέv ... δέ ...--but lexically as well (anaphoric *alternis* ..., *alternis* ..., or the opposition *mane* ..., *post meridiem* ...: with the latter J. E. G. Zetzel compares the phrasing of Pers. *Sat.* 1. 134, "his mane edictum, post prandia Callirhoen do").

Each of these antitheses, then, is more than sufficiently marked. On the other hand, some marking *is* required--but is not provided by the archetype's reading--at the main point of articulation, where the occasional variation is contrasted with the typical pattern. Indeed, mere *nonnullis*, as a third element in asyndeton (*alternis* ..., *alternis* ..., *nonnullis* ...), does not simply fail to provide what is needed; it actually obscures the structure of the sentence as a whole, since it gives the appearance of being the third member of a unified series--a rather nonsensical *tricolon crescens* ("on *one* day ..., on *the other* ..., [*and!*] on *some* ...")-- which is not at all its function: note the illogic of *nonnullis* as a third element after *alternis* ..., *alternis* ..., which properly imply that the phenomenon being described consists of two variables only (had Suetonius wanted to say what recent editors think he said, he would have written *aliis* ..., *aliis* ..., *nonnullis* ...).

Hence *nonnullis vero*, which occurs as an (apparently) independent conjecture in **D** (a MS of the β-family), **K** (descended, with **M**, from δ), and **HU** (i.e., η, the common ancestor of these two MSS within the γ-family). That was the vulgate reading in early printed editions, retained by Reifferscheid, Roth, and Rolfe, correctly. Tross and Osann printed *mane vero* and were followed by Robinson (followed in turn by Bione, della Corte, and Brugnoli), who offered the following reasons (ed., p. 10): "namque praeter id quod *mane vero* in Hersfeldensi codice erat hoc ordine servato *mane* vocibus *post meridiem* melius opponitur, et τῷ χιασμῷ (siquidem *disputare* et *disserere* ad grammatici officium, *declamare* autem ad rhetoris partes referendum est) plus leporis inest." The first two of these arguments carry no weight (the authority of the Hersfeldensis we know to be limited; the opposition between *mane* ... and *post meridiem* ... is already doubly marked, cf. above), whereas the third seems confused. Whatever one thinks of the *lepos* of the chiasmus, it exists regardless of the reading one chooses; but the order *mane vero* places on *mane* an emphasis that is wholly out of place in the context: it is the equivalent of saying "... on some days he used to hold discussions in the *morning* ..."-- a stress that would be appropriate only if Suetonius had previously said that Princeps ordinarily held discussions at some other time of the day, which of course he does not do.

5.1 fecitque [sc. Sevius Nicanor] praeter commentarios . . . saturam quoque, in qua libertinum se ac duplici cognomine esse per haec indicat:

> Sevius Nicanor Marci libertus negabit,
> Sevius †posthus idem ac† Marcus docebit.

Sevius (1º)] Servius α G² libertus] -tis X (W *ante corr.*, Oᵐ: *v. infra*) Sevius (2º)] Servius α Nicanor *om.* Y, *hab.* XNG² (Marci libertis: negabit sevius nicanor *om.* O, *add.* Oᵐ) posthus X (post his W¹) I, postli' B, post huius VLγ, post hoc G (*del.* hoc G²) *om.* N, Posthumius QE, ed. Inc., ed. Ven. (postmus D, postumus K), Postumeius *Casaubon*, Postumianus *Gronov.*, Postulenus *vel* Postumuleius *Oudendorp*, post tamen *Doergens*, qui fuit *Vahlen*, Pothus *Robinson* (Pothos *della Corte*), post huius <mortem *vel* obitum> *Morel* idem] is dem N, isdem G² (dem W, corr. W¹) ac ON¹ (ae N) βMᵐ : at V¹Γ (ut Δ), *om.* W, ast idem *Stat.*, quid id est? at *Scaliger*, idem sed *Casaubon*, idem ABC *Bergk*, (Posthumius) vero idem ac *Brewster*, idem, at idem atque hic *Beck*, idem tunc *Courtney*

The second verse evidently stood as "Sevius Nicanor posthus idem ac Marcus docebit" in X (= OW, with NG² contaminated from X here as elsewhere); the text of Y appears to have been "Sevius posth' idem ac Marcus docebit," without *Nicanor* (leaving the line at least three syllables short) and with the double reading ac / at where X had ac.[41] The archetypal text, which must have included the impossible *posthus* (or *posth'*), was obviously already corrupt. Further reconstruction of the archetype, however, largely depends on whether one assumes that *Nicanor* was correctly copied by X but accidentally omitted by Y (so Robinson, della Corte, Brugnoli) or that *Nicanor* was an intrusion in X, from the previous line, correctly omitted in Y (so, in effect, Reifferscheid, Roth, Bione, and Buechner in *FPL*, who print the line as "S(a)evius post huius idem ac Marcus docebit," with an obelus before and/or after *huius*). Since either the mistaken repetition or

---

[41] I's *posthus* and B's *postli'* (h misread as li) point in the same direction as X's *posthus*, as does the *post huius* of VL; other Y-MSS tried to make some sense of the letters by various means.

the mistaken omission of *Nicanor* would be very easy in this context, the two versions leave little firm ground for choice. We will return to this point; for the moment we can note three other, less problematic assumptions that should serve as a guide to criticism:

1) the lines appeared as two successive verses in Sevius' *satura*, and they must make grammatical sense as such--that is, a new clause must begin at the beginning of the first line (the preceding line was end-stopped; *Sevius Nicanor* is not the subject of some verb in the previous line), and *docebit* at the end of the second line must mark the end of a unit of sense--for that is how Suetonius quotes verse (he nowhere quotes verse by taking the line as the unit of quotation without regard for grammatical sense);

2) Suetonius was correct to take both lines as referring to the same *grammaticus*; and since his inference concerning the man's libertine status was clearly based on the first line, the inference concerning his *duplex cognomen* must have been based on the second;

3) *negabit* and *docebit* are a corresponding pair: i.e., whatever they may have meant in their original context (something we can no longer know), the two actions are being matched (as parallel) or contrasted (in antithesis) directly with one another.

As noted above, Robinson took the version of **X**, with repeated *Nicanor*, as the basis of emendation (the reason is not made plain in his only statment on the subject, diss., p. 89); and he was followed in this by della Corte and Brugnoli. All three adopt a form of Robinson's emendation *Pothus* (a slight correction of archetypal *posthus* or *posth'*), to provide the second cognomen that is wanted.⁴² The verses are printed by Robinson thus:

> Sevius Nicanor Marci libertus; negabit
> Sevius Nicanor Pothus idem; at Marcus docebit

by della Corte, in his 2nd edition (followed by Brugnoli), thus:

> Sevius Nicanor Marci libertus negabit:
> Sevius Nicanor Pothos idem ac Marcus docebit.

---

42 Robinson, ed., p. 11, cited half a dozen inscriptions for the Latin *Pothus* and several more for Greek Πόθος; H. Solin, *Die griechischen Personennamen in Rom: Ein Namenbuch* (Berlin and New York, 1982), 1:440 and 3:1367, records 43 more instances of *Pothus*, including one where it serves as a second cognomen (*CIL* 6.14705 C. Cestius Zosimus Pothus).

and by della Corte, in his 3rd edition, thus:

> Sevius Nicanor Marci libertus? negabit
> Sevius Nicanor. Pothos isdem ac Marcus docebit.[43]

None of these versions is satisfactory. Though Robinson did not explain his punctuation of the first line (which in effect simply reproduces the punctuation in O), it appears that he took the words *Sevius Nicanor Marci libertus* to be a fragmentary phrase (the completion of some preceding clause?), in the belief that Suetonius was quoting these lines merely to support his statement about Nicanor's status and nomenclature, and without regard to their context.[44] But as noted above, though Suetonius quotes verse dozens of times in similar contexts in the *DGR* and the *Caesares*, he never quotes in such a way as to produce a fragment of this sort: if *Sevius Nicanor Marci libertus* had been the subject of the verb in a preceding clause, he would have quoted all of that clause, even if it required beginning the quotation in the middle of a line.[45]

The versions printed by della Corte avoid this problem but are unacceptable on other grounds. In the case of the earlier version, neither della Corte (in his commentary) nor Brugnoli (in his edition) made plain how he understood the crucial words *idem ac Marcus*. In the text given, that phrase would most naturally mean that Sevius Nicanor Pothos is "the same person as Marcus"--viz., the Marcus just mentioned in the preceding verse, the *patronus* of the freedman; but in that case *Sevius Nicanor Marci libertus* plainly cannot be the same person as *Sevius*

---

[43] Della Corte translates this version as (3rd ed., p. 18): "è Sevio Nicanore il liberto di Marco? Servio Nicanore risponderà di no. Poto, che è la medesima persona di Marco, continuerà a insegnare." On the scenario presumed here, see below.

[44] Diss., pp. 89-90: "Inutile est quaerere quid Sevius negaturus fuerit aut quid Marcus docturus fuerit, neque haec ad rem pertinent; *nam Suetonius hos versiculos non nisi ad duas res demonstrandas profert*: Sevium libertum ac duplici cognomine fuisse." The italicized words are the closest Robinson comes to explaining his understanding of the first line; his general point about the purpose of the quotation is of course correct.

[45] Cf., e.g., *Jul.* 49. 1, with a quotation of Licinius Calvus (*FPL* frag. 17, p. 112 B.) consisting of the last 6 syllables of a hexameter plus a complete pentameter.

Nicanor Pothos, and Suetonius would therefore have blundered massively in reading the lines. The only alternative is to imagine that Sevius was using the words *idem ac Marcus* as though *idem ac = qui et*, to indicate that because he was *Marci libertus* his praenomen was also Marcus. So it no doubt was (cf. below), but this is nonetheless a very unattractive alternative: it entails giving *idem ac* a wholly unlikely meaning;[46] and it shrouds in even deeper obscurity the relation between *negabit* and *docebit*.

This improbable text was abandoned in della Corte's 3rd edition for a version that is impossible.[47] Della Corte based this version on the premise that Suetonius recognized a strict distinction between the terms *libertus* (as = *emancipatus*) and *libertinus* (as = *liberti filius*): that is, Sevius, when asked if he is a freedman (*Sevius Nicanor Marci libertus?*), will reply that he is not (*negabit / Sevius Nicanor*); from this Suetonius is supposed to have inferred that Sevius was a freedman's son, *libertinus* (thus "fecit . . . saturam . . ., in qua libertinum se . . . indicat"). It is scarcely credible that Suetonius (or anyone else) would draw such a conclusion from such a text, even if he did recognize the distinction assumed in della Corte's premise. In any case, that premise is demonstrably false, since Suetonius uses *libertinus*, throughout the *DGR* and the *Caesares*, to mean "freedman": compare, e.g., 10. 1 "<L.> Ateius Philologus, libertinus, Athenis est natus" (born in Athens, but brought as a slave to Rome, Ateius could not have been a *liberti filius*), *Aug.* 74 "neminem umquam libertinorum adhibitum ab eo cenae excepto Mena, sed asserto in ingenuitatem post proditam Sexti Pompei classem."[48] Here, too,

---

46 For *qui et* see the numerous examples in the index to *CIL* 6, pt. 7, fasc. 4; *idem ac* does not occur. The same difficulty (*int. al.*) brings to grief the discussion of E. H. Brewster, "On Suetonius *De grammaticis* 5," *CP* 10 (1915): 84-87.

47 For della Corte's interpretation, see the translation quoted above, n. 43, and his commentary ad loc., pp. 80-81.

48 In support of his premise, della Corte referred to *Claud.* 24. 1 "ignarus [sc. Claudius] temporibus Appi [sc. Caeci censoris] et deinceps aliquamdiu libertinos dictos non ipsos, qui manu emitterentur, sed ingenuos ex his procreatos": but as the passage shows, Suetonius not only knew of the earlier distinction but was also aware that it was obsolete in his own day (on the distinction see most recently E. W. Haley, "Suetonius *Claudius* 24.1 and the Sons of Freedmen," *Historia* 35 [1986]: 115-21). In his own writings Suetonius employs the words *libertus* and *libertinus* as they are

we meet the problem raised by *i(s)dem ac Marcus*: in this instance, della Corte did make clear that he took the phrase to indicate Sevius' praenomen (see above); but we have already noted the difficulties encountered by any text that retains *i(s)dem ac*.[49] Presumably, it was to avoid such difficulties that Robinson read *at Marcus*; a number of the early emendations noted in the apparatus above, incorporating some adversative word (*at, ast, sed*), were similarly motivated (after *idem* the temptation to write *ac* for *at* would of course be very strong).

If we wished, then, to persist along the lines laid down by X, we might retain Robinson's *Pothus*, as promising the neatest solution to the problem of the second cognomen, and attempt the following:

> Sevius Nicanor Marci libertus negabit
> (Sevius Nicanor Pothus idem), at Marcus docebit.
>
> Sevius Nicanor, the freedman of Marcus, will refuse[?]
> (Sevius Nicanor Pothus is the same man), but Marcus
>   will provide the information[?].

In this version, both *Marci* in the first line and *Marcus* in the second refer to a single person, viz., Sevius' *patronus*; the relation between *negabit* and *docebit* is antithetical, with the antithesis extending to the subjects of the two verbs (whereas the *libertus* will do one thing, his *patronus* will, in effect, do the opposite); and the second cognomen is revealed in an aside in the second line. The text would thus yield sense, in a way consistent with our initial assumptions.

But there is room to doubt that this is good enough--and room to doubt the wisdom of continuing to tinker with the testimony of X, faithful witness though it generally is. As noted above, X's repetition of *Nicanor* is as likely to be mistaken as Y's omission; and it may be that the latter here plays the unaccustomed role of

---

used in all extant Latin texts, the former to indicate the patronal relation (*libertus alicuius*), the latter to indicate social and legal status as a freedman.

[49] The text of della Corte's 3rd ed. also blunts the pointed correspondence of *negabit* and *docebit,* but that is a venial matter compared with the other problems in this version.

the more faithful witness. If so, there is one conjectural version that at least produces an intelligible meaning:

> Sevius Nicanor Marci libertus negabit,
> Sevius *Postumianus* idem *tunc* Marcus docebit.

This version incorporates Gronovius' *Postumianus* and Courtney's *tunc* (i.e., $\overline{tc}$) for *ac*;⁵⁰ *idem* thus = neut. sing. acc., not masc. sing. nom. The lines would then involve a play on Sevius' dual nomenclature:

> Sevius Nicanor, the freedman of Marcus, will say "no"[?],
> Marcus Sevius Postumianus will then give the same reply[?].

As *Marci libertus*, Sevius would also have had the praenomen Marcus (cf. above), hence *Marcus* in the second line; the cognomen *Postumianus* would most naturally be derived from a previous owner: with the full form of Sevius' name implied by the lines--M. Sevius M. l. Nicanor Postumianus--cf. *CIL* 6. 13979 T. Caesius Priscillae l. Hermes Postumianus. It must be noted that in this version the two lines do not by themselves make plain that Sevius Nicanor the *libertus* = M. Sevius Postumianus: to accept this text, one must further assume that the original context not only amplified the meaning of *negabit* and *docebit* but also showed that the lines must refer to one and the same man. This assumption is not difficult *per se*.

In the end, however, I cannot quite persuade myself that any of the versions canvassed above (or any of the numerous earlier proposals tacitly discarded) is clearly correct; and in view of the obscurities of the paradosis and the deficiencies of the context, it seems unlikely that any wholly compelling solution can be found.⁵¹ I intend to print the text as it is shown above, with obeli surrounding *posthus idem ac,* and to signal in my apparatus the last version considered, with the conjectures of Gronovius and Courtney.

---

⁵⁰ I wish to thank E. Courtney for showing this suggestion to me and for allowing me to refer to it in advance of its publication in his forthcoming commentary on the fragments of the Roman poets; note that Courtney's understanding of the lines differs somewhat from that suggested here.

⁵¹ The question is left open in the discussion of J. Christes, *Sklaven und Freigelassene als Grammatiker und Philologen im antiken Rom* (Wiesbaden, 1979), pp. 16f.

6.2 dimissa autem schola, Rutilium Rufum damnatum in Asiam secutus ibidem Zmyrnae **simul** consenuit composuitque variae eruditionis aliquot volumina, ex quibus novem unius corporis, **quae**--quia scriptores ac poetas sub clientela Musarum iudicaret-- non absurde et fecisse et <in>scripsisse se ait ex numero divarum et appellatione.

    simul **LQUE** : simulque ω   *post* corporis *lacunam statuit Robinson proposuitque* <cui est titulus Musarum>, *coll. Gell. NA* 1. 25. 17   quae *Bentley* : qui ω, *del.* **ed. Ven.**, *edd. plerique* inscripsisse *Bentley* : scripsisse ω

The passage concerns the career of Aurelius Opillus. Some have detected deeper corruption in the first part of the sentence (*dimissa . . . consenuit*): Krueger, displeased with *ibidem Zmyrnae*, proposed *Zmyrnae consenuit simulque ibidem composuit . . .*; Robinson thought that *simulque* pointed to a preceding lacuna, for which he suggested *vixit una familiarissime* (comparing 16. 1 "Q. Caecilius Epirota . . . ad Cornelium Gallum se contulit vixitque una familiarissime"; followed in part by della Corte, who printed *ibidem Zmyrnae <vixit> simulque consenuit* in his first two editions). But the presumed corruption in each case is difficult to explain, and such measures are anyway unnecessary. *simul*--an emendation of Pontano (**L**) also found in **UE** (and **Q**, contaminated from **L** or its exemplar as corrected by Pontano)--provides what is wanted (so most recently Brugnoli, followed by della Corte in his 3rd ed.): "Having followed Rutilius Rufus to Asia after his condemnation, he both grew old in his company at Zmyrna and composed . . ." (cf. Orosius 5. 17. 13 "qui [viz., Rutilius] Zmyrnam conmigrans litterarum studiis intentus consenuit"). The writings of Opillus that Suetonius goes on to mention belong, then, to the period after his withdrawal: cf. 8. 2 (on M. Pompilius Andronicus) "itaque . . . Cumas transiit ibique in otio vixit et multa composuit"; with *simul consenuit composuitque . . .* (where *simul* conveys little more than "both . . . and . . ."), compare (e.g.) 4. 2 "Valerium Catonem, poetam simul grammaticumque notissimum," *Jul.* 81. 4 "ob haec simul et ob infirmam valitudinem," *Aug.* 17. 3 "simul eius [sc. liburnicae] . . . fusis armamentis et gubernaculo diffracto." The archetype's *simulque*, if not a mechanical error (from, say, anticipation of *composuitque*), is probably no more than a misguided attempt to coordinate *simul* with the preceding adverbial phrase. With *ibidem Zmyrnae*, compare Suetonius' use of *ibidem* in the phrase *ibidem statim* at

Aug. 39, 87. 3, *Tib.* 44. 2, *Oth.* 12. 2, *Vit.* 13. 3, and cf. Cic. 2 *Verr.* 3. 6. 14 *ut ibidem in Sicilia . . . venderent,* Gell. *NA* 12. 8. 6 *ibidem in campo* (with *TLL* 7.1:156.53ff.).

On the remainder of the passage, a couple of secondary points can be noted first. Robinson thought that a relative clause had fallen out after *corporis,* "cum infra *fecisse . . . ex numero divarum ad novem unius corporis* pertinent, verba autem *scripsisse . . . ex . . . divarum appellatione* quo referantur non habeant. Lacuna sic fere explenda est, *cui est titulus Musarum.* Cf. Gell. I 25, 17: 'Aurelius autem Opillus . . . in primo librorum, quos Musarum inscripsit'" (ed., p. 12). But this is overly precise--the run of the sentence (especially with *Musarum* in the causal clause) leaves no doubt of the work's title--and Robinson has had no followers. Similarly, he has been followed only by Bione in rejecting (with Roth, earlier) Bentley's *inscripsisse,* in the belief that "*scribere* nonnumquam ab antiquis eodem significatu quo *inscribere* usurpatum esse" (diss., p. 111 n. 65): the belief has no firm foundation, being based only on another passage in the *DGR* where the text is problematic (21. 4, on which see below) and on a passage in Charisius (*GL* 1. 127. 17 = 162. 6-7 Barwick "'Didun': Ateius Philologus librum suum sic edidit <in>scriptum 'An amaverit Didun Aeneas'") where Barwick rightly printed Fabricius' *inscriptum* for the MSS' *scriptum.*[52] For the same error elsewhere in Suetonius (beyond 21. 4, below), see also *Ner.* 11. 2 "inducta Afrani togata, quae 'Incendium' <in>scribitur" (with Erasmus' correction).

Turning to the central question of the passage, we find the vulgate text: "composuitque . . . aliquot volumina, ex quibus novem unius corporis, [qui] quia scriptores ac poetas sub clientela Musarum iudicaret, non absurde et fecisse et <in>scripsisse se ait. . . ." So Reifferscheid, Rolfe, Brugnoli, Roth, and Bione (the latter two reading *scripsisse*), deleting the archetype's *qui* (as a product of dittography before *quia*) and regarding *novem* (sc. *volumina*) *unius corporis* as the object of the infinitives.[53] The result is

---

[52] Robinson, ibid., also referred to Gell. *NA* 18. 6. 3 "ei libro titulus est ingentis cuiusdam inlecebrae ad legendum; scriptus quippe est: 'de loquendi proprietate,'" where *titulus . . . scriptus* does not help his case; cf. rather *quos Musarum inscripsit* in the passage from *NA* 1. 25. 17 that Robinson cited in his ed., with *NA* praef. 6 "alii *Musarum* [sc. libros] inscripserunt . . ." (no doubt referring to the same work).

[53] Among modern editors only Robinson retains *qui,* as a connective relative beginning a new sentence after the (supposed) lacuna; della Corte

certainly intelligible; but Bentley's *quae*--which presumes an equally easy corruption--has more to recommend it, since it produces a structure typical of Suetonius' idiom: with "composuitque . . . **aliquot** volumina, **ex quibus** novem unius corporis, **quae** . . . non absurde et fecisse et <in>scripsisse se ait . . .," compare 10. 3 (in indirect discourse) "praecepisse autem **multis** et claris iuvenibus, **in quis** Appio et Pulchro Claudiis fratribus, **quorum** etiam comes in provincia fuit," or *Dom*. 5 "**plurima** et amplissima opera incendio absumpta restituit, **in quis** et Capitolium, **quod** rursus arserat." In all three cases the main clause presents a general category (some books, many pupils, a large number of public works) and is followed by a relative clause--lacking an explicit verb--that provides one or more specific examples; the relative clause is then followed by another subordinate clause that offers further detail. Note in particular the elliptical relative clause, which Suetonius also uses elsewhere when introducing examples from a general category: Robinson (ed., p. 12) well compares *Aug*. 29. 1 ("publica opera *plurima* extruxit, *e quibus* vel praecipua: forum . . ., templum . . ., aedem. . . .") and 36 ("auctor et *aliarum* rerum fuit, *in quis*: ne . . ., ne . . ., ut . . ., ut . . ., ut. . . ."); to these can be added, from the *DGR*, 3. 6 ". . . ac *nonnulli* de notissimis doctoribus peregre docuerunt, maxime in Gallia Togata, *inter quos* Octavius Teucer et Sescenius Iacchus et Oppius Chares--hic quidem ad ultimam aetatem . . ." (cf. also *Claud*. 14. 1 "consulatus super pristinum *quattuor* gessit, *ex quibus* duos primos . . ., sequentis . . .," *Vesp*. 22 "*nonnulla* eius facetissima extant, *in quibus* et haec: . . ." [two examples follow]). Slightly different in the forms of subordination used, but still comparable in its structure, is 7. 2 "scholam eius claros quoque viros frequentasse aiunt, in his M. Ciceronem, etiam cum praetura fungeretur": general statement > specific example (with *in his* rather than *in quibus*; cf. 18. 3 *in his Iullum Antonium*, in a similar context) > further detail.

7.3 scripsit [sc. Antonius Gnipho] **multa, quamvis annum aetatis quinquagesimum non excesserit--etsi Ateius Philologus duo tantum volumina de Latino sermone reliquisse eum tradit: nam**

---

deletes *qui* but punctuates with a semi-colon after *corporis*. I cannot see that either of these versions is desirable.

cetera scripta discipulorum eius esse, non ipsius, in quibus et suum alicubi reperiri nomen. [ut hoc]

> ut hoc *delevi* : ut hoc WNG²βQ, ut hic N¹Γ, *om.* OD, *post* hoc *lacunam notat* L² (*edd. nonnulli*), ut auctoris *Vahlen*, Ἀτήιος *della Corte*

The archetype almost certainly had *ut hoc*: that--despite the omission in O--was clearly the reading of X (here represented by W and by NG², contaminated from X), and it was very likely present in Y as well, attested here by β (= BVL, with Q contaminated from L or its exemplar, as often); *ut hic* appears only in the descendants of α (= N¹GI) and γ, whose agreement points to the origin of the reading in Γ, as either a conjecture or a simple blunder (on αγ = Γ see pp. 12-14). There is in any case little stemmatic justification for attributing the double reading *ut hoc / ut hic* to Y, and none at all for supposing that both readings go back to the archetype (*pace* Robinson, diss., p. 96, where *hoc* is attributed to G¹, not G²).

Bione printed *ut* †hoc†; Roth, Reifferscheid, and Rolfe followed the corrector of L (= Pontano) in marking a lacuna after *hoc*--not impossible, though the sense and structure seem complete with *nomen*. Robinson printed Vahlen's conjecture *ut auctoris*, which he found in the margin of Vahlen's copy of Reifferscheid: though Robinson judged that it "certe optimam sententiam praebet neque ita longe a fide codicum abhorret,"[54] it seems to me both superfluous and paleographically improbable; it would also be a remarkable coincidence if two successive chapters ended with the words *nomen ut auctoris* and *nomine auctoris* (thus the conclusion of chap. 8, which may in fact have prompted Vahlen's conjecture). Another of Vahlen's marginal suggestions--οὕτως ateius-- pointed the way for della Corte's Ἀτήιος (as if < ΑΤΗΙΟC), which was adopted by Brugnoli as ΑΤΗΟC.[55] Though greeted as

---

[54] Diss., p. 102, suggesting that the transmitted reading derives from VT-AVTHOIS "in antiquissimis libris."

[55] Vahlen's οὕτως *ateius* was reported in Robinson's ed. (p. 14); della Corte, basing his work on Robinson's, printed Ἀτήιον in his 1st ed. (p. 33, with app. crit.: "'Ἀτήιον vel Ἀτήιος *conieci*"), citing Vahlen's *ut auctoris* (from Robinson), with no mention of Vahlen's other suggestion; della Corte promoted Ἀτήιος to the text in his 2d ed. (so also in the 3rd ed.). Cf., e.g., della Corte's app. crit. at 5. 1 (3rd ed., p. 19, line 2), where he writes "Pothos isdem ac *conieci*" and neglects to mention Robinson's *Pothus*-- though he lists nine other emendations proposed ad loc.

"palmaire" (R. Verdière, rev. of Brugnoli's 1st ed., *Latomus* 19 [1960]: 801), this paleographically clever emendation is unsatisfying once one looks beyond the *ductus litterarum*. The reading Ἀτήιος presumes that Ateius Philologus, whose statement Suetonius is reporting in indirect discourse, wrote something like this: "duo tantum volumina de Latino sermone Gnipho reliquit: nam cetera scripta sunt discipulorum eius, non ipsius, in quibus *et meum alicubi reperitur nomen* Ἀτήιος"--yet it is far from clear why Ateius should have felt compelled to add his name (in Greek) to such a statement, as though to provide a fact that his reader would not already know.

If one wanted to emend according to the *ductus litterarum*, then *adhuc* could suggest itself; but that is hardly less otiose than the other emendations that have been proposed. I believe, in fact, that the archetype's *ut hoc* does not conceal the authentic text of Suetonius at all. Rather, the phrase is an interpolation that entered the text after it was jotted in the margin or between the lines by a reader inspired to suggest that, in the writings attributed to Gnipho, Ateius' name was occasionally found "like this" (*ut hoc*)-- i.e., as it happens to be found in this very passage of Suetonius. The version of Γ, with *ut hic* (= "as here"), then arose as an "improvement" on (if not as a simple corruption of) *ut hoc*. For one such interpolated jotting, compare the text of G at 10. 4-- "Philologi appellationem adsumpsisse videtur quia . . . multiplici variaque doctrina censebatur sic philologus"--where the last two words obviously began as a note keyed to Suetonius' explanation of the cognomen Philologus. For other interpolated glosses or notes, see on 25. 4 <*versare*>, and cf. on 25. 5 [*liber*], 25. 5 *appellatione Graeca*.

8.3 . . . adeo inops atque egens ut coactus sit praecipuum illud **opusculum** suum "Annalium" Enni elenchorum sedecim milibus nummum cuidam vendere.

Reifferscheid placed an obelus before *opusculum* (for reasons not made explicit) and noted in his apparatus the emendation *opus cui titulum* suggested to him by Otto Jahn; Hillscher (*Jahrb. f. class. Phil.* Suppl. 18 [1892]: 367 n. 1) said that he could find no parallel for the construction *opusculum . . . elenchorum*. But for the appositive or defining genitive ("a work consisting of / comprising . . ."), cf. Vell. Pat. 2. 9. 5 "opus belli civilis Sullanique . . . ab eo [sc. Sisenna] seniore editum est."

9.3 librum etiam cui est titulus Περὶ ἀλογίας edidit [sc. Orbilius] continentem querelas de iniuriis quas professores neglegentia aut ambitione parentum acciperent.

> Περὶ ἀλογίας *Turnebus* : perialogos ω (-leg- W, pialogos B), Περιαλγής *Toup*, Περὶ ἄλγεος *Robinson, alii alia*

The archetype's reading was *perialogos*, printed by Roth, Rolfe ("the word is evidently corrupt"), Bione (with an obelus), and della Corte (περιάλογος, translated as "L'illogicissimo"); such a word is nowhere found. Robinson, led by W's -*leg*- (i.e., *perialego sedidit*) to suppose that the -*e*- was authentic, conjectured Περὶ ἄλγεος;[56] but W's text is surely the result of a casual error,[57] and the open form of the genitive (-εος) is in any case not what one expects for a work that presumably was in prose.[58] Other suggestions are legion (cited here from Robinson and Brugnoli):

> *peri alogon* Beroaldus
> αἰτιαλόγος Statius
> Παιδαγωγός Auratus apud Turnebum
> Περὶ ἀλόγου vel Περὶ ἀλογίας Turnebus
> Περὶ ἀγωγῆς Voss apud Burman
> *Periautologus* Bentley
> Περὶ αὐτοῦ λόγος Baumgarten-Crusius
> Περιαλγής Toup
> Περισσολόγος Vahlen
> Περιαλουργός Hertz

---

56 Followed by Brugnoli (adopting the transliterated form *peri algeos*), app. crit. ad loc., p. 12: "quasi περὶ ἄλγεος id est 'De dolore' scil. plagarum qui sit in discipulis"--a very odd interpretation of the context (cf. della Corte, 3rd ed., p. 84).

57 Note, e.g., 11. 3 *medico* γ (for Y's *modico*; X's *modice* is correct) and 2.1 *acroasis*, where the texts of I (*acreoasis*) and NG (*acroasis*, with *e* written above the *o*) imply the reading *acreasis* (corrected with suprascript *o*) in α; cf. also X's *socius* for *secius* at 20. 2.

58 Prisc. *GL* 2:381.1 = *GRF* frag. 3 "Orbilius: 'quae vix ab hominibus consequi possunt'" (cited for the passive *consequi*) could well have stood in a work devoted to *querelae*: if so, the citation would confirm both the medium (prose) and the language (Latin, cf. below).

Most of these are best passed over in silence. Toup's Περιαλγής has found some favor;[59] but a title with περί seems a priori likely. In that case, the best choice is Turnebus' Περὶ ἀλογίας: the work in which Orbilius voiced his complaints was a moralizing polemic "On folly"--the folly, i.e., that characterized the pedagogical fashions of his day and the behavior of parents vis-à-vis their sons and their sons' teachers (cf. V. Ferraro, "La scuola di Orbilio," *RCCM* 9 [1967]: 234-38, comparing Tac. *Dial.* 25ff.). The Greek title need not indicate that the work was written in Greek: for contemporary prose works bearing a title with περί but written in Latin note M. Brutus' Περὶ καθήκοντος (Sen. *Epist.* 95. 45 "M. Brutus in eo libro quem Περὶ καθήκοντος inscripsit . . .," with Prisc. *GL* 2:199.8f. "M. Brutus de officiis: 'itaque patres familiae domini sumus'") and Varro's Περὶ χαρακτήρων (Charis. 246. 3f. B. "collativa sunt adverbia. Varro sic ait in III Περὶ χαρακτήρων, 'propius, proxime'").

9.4 fuit autem naturae acerbae, non modo in antisophistas, quos **omni occasione** laceravit, sed etiam in discipulos . . .

> omni occasione W²B : omni in occasione ΧαλQ : omni (-nes H) sermone γ, per omnem occasionem *Robinson*

There is little reason to retain the archetypal reading, here represented by Χαλ, though most editors do. Temporal *in occasione*, with the preposition, is attested exactly twice in earlier Latin (*TLL* 9.2:336.72ff.), at Livy 21. 14. 3 "non cunctandum in tali occasione ratus Hannibal . . ." and Sen. *Ben.* 2. 13. 2 ". . . ut in occasione potius quam in necessitate succurreret": in the latter case the use of *in* is motivated primarily by the absence of a modifier with *occasione* (cf. *in bello* / "in a time of war" vs. *secundo Punico bello* / "in the Second Punic War"), and perhaps secondarily by a desire for formal symmetry in the *sententia* (*in occasione . . . in necessitate*); in the former it is perhaps not excessively skeptical to point to the preceding *-duM* as a possible source of interpolation. Certainly Suetonius himself elsewhere uses only the bare ablative (*Claud.* 42. 1 "amorem praestantiamque linguae occasione omni professus," cf. *Jul.* 35. 2 "tunc occasione temporum bellantem,"

---

[59] Printed by Reifferscheid, cf. also Wessner, rev. of Robinson, diss., *PhW* 43 (1923): 539; Rolfe, ed., p. 408; Robinson, ed., p. 15; K.-E. Henriksson, *Griechische Büchertitel in der römischen Literatur* (Helsinki, 1956), p. 39.

Dom. 10. 3 "cuius criminis occasione philosophos . . . summovit"), which is the construction favored by other authors as well. The ease with which *in* could creep into the text after *omNI* (and with *in antisophistas* preceding, *in discipulos* following) scarcely needs saying; Reifferscheid was correct to prefer the reading of **B**, which appears also as the correction of a second hand in **W**.[60]

9.5 ac ne principum quidem virorum insectatione abstinuit [sc. Orbilius]: siquidem ignotus adhuc, cum iudicio frequenti testimonium diceret, interrogatus a Varrone <**Murena**>, diversae partis advocato, quidnam ageret et quo artificio uteretur, gibberosos se de sole in umbram transferre respondit, quod Murena gibber erat.

<Murena> *addidi* : *om.* ω

The criticism of this passage has been influenced by a parallel passage in Macrob. *Sat.* 2. 6. 4, which presents Orbilius in confrontation with C. Sulpicius Galba, the father of the emperor: "in eundem Galbam Orbilius grammaticus acerbius inrisit. prodierat Orbilius in reum testis. quem Galba ut confunderet, dissimulata professione eius interrogavit: 'quid artium facis?' respondit: 'in sole gibbos soleo fricare.'"[61] Motivated, apparently, by the discrepant identity of Orbilius' interlocutor in the two passages, earlier critics--Bentley among them--deleted the names *Varrone* and *Murena* from the Suetonian anecdote. They should not have done so. Whatever the historicity of Suetonius' story (which is not above question), the joke that Macrobius passes along is a pure

---

60 Robinson's argument for *per omnem occasionem* (diss., p. 146) is ingenious, and its motivation is understandable (Suetonius is fond of the phrase *per occasionem* [*-es*], using it five times in the *Caesares*); but it rests on a very unlikely double premise--viz., that γ's *omni sermone* goes back to a *duplex lectio* in the archetype (*sermone / omni in*) and that *sermone* is a corruption of *per omnem*. Nowhere can a reading unique to γ be referred with any probability to the archetype; in this case, *omni sermone* is probably what Wessner called "eine überflüssige Konjektur" (rev. of Robinson's ed., *PhW* 46 [1926]: 1226).

61 On the interpretation of this joke, see J. F. Killeen, "Suetonius De gramm. ix," *WS* 3 (1969): 233-34, and below at n. 63.

fabrication.[62] Though Orbilius, born in 113 or 112, lived *prope ad centesimum aetatis annum* (*amissa iam pridem memoria*, according to Suetonius, 9. 6), there is only the remotest chance that he could have appeared in the same courtroom as Galba's father, who was suffect consul in 5 B.C. (his son was born in 3 B.C.); the anecdote is a conflation, bringing together Orbilius--reported to have made a joke at a hunchback's expense--and a noted orator and hunchback (cf. Suet. *Galb.* 3. 3) about whose deformity other jokes were also handed down (cf. Macrob. *Sat.* 2. 4. 8, 2. 6. 3).

The passage from Macrobius also stands behind the emendation *Varrone* <*Gibba*> of della Corte, who followed Münzer ("Terentius (89)," *RE* 5 A [1934]: 704) in identifying the man in Suetonius' anecdote with M. Terentius Varro Gibba, an advocate mentioned by Asconius (55 Clark): the presence of the name Gibba would thus help to explain the confusion with Galba (della Corte, 3rd ed., p. 85). But to state della Corte's understanding of the passage with this emendation is to show why the emendation cannot be correct: Varro Gibba would be the advocate, but not the hunchback of the tale, despite his cognomen; the hunchback would be another man, a Murena, who must be understood to be Varro's client. It would be an unbearably awkward (and un-Suetonian) sort of story-telling to have the butt of the joke remain invisible until the punchline, where he must hastily be conjured up as an implied client; and in any case, as G. V. Sumner has noted, "Orbilius' point is that he intends to put his 'gibberose' interlocutor in the shade"--the butt of the joke must be the person Orbilius is addressing, the advocate.[63] Sumner plausibly suggests

---

[62] Note the clause *quem Galba ut confunderet* . . ., which is included because of the needs of the story: it explains--very lamely--why Galba would ask Orbilius his profession, and thus gives Orbilius the chance to deliver the punchline. The same narrative need is met in Suetonius' story by the phrase *ignotus adhuc*; its factual worth should probably not be taken for granted in attempting to "date" the episode.

[63] "Varrones Murenae," *HSCP* 82 (1978): 190. A secondary sense of Orbilius' retort may be: "I send hunchbacks back to school"; for *umbra* in this sense, see Juv. 7. 173 *rhetorica* . . . *umbra*, and cf. with our passage esp. Cic. *Leg.* 3. 6. 14 "doctrinam *ex umbraculis* eruditorum otioque non modo *in solem* atque in pulverem sed in ipsum discrimen aciemque produxit." The meaning of the joke is interpreted differently by Killeen, "Suetonius de gramm. ix"; however one takes the meaning, the joke is plainly made at the advocate's expense. Bione, also following Münzer, suggested the

that--*if* the story is authentic--the advocate would have been A. Terentius Varro Murena (born about 80 B.C. as the biological son of A. Terentius Varro, adopted by C. Licinius Murena sometime between 48 and 46), an orator, friend of Cicero, and curule aedile in 44.[64]

Be that as it may: since "Varro" and "Murena" must be one and the same man in Suetonius' version of the story, the fault in the transmitted text is plain. For Suetonius to introduce the advocate as "Varro" and then refer to him as "Murena" two lines later would be absolutely unparalleled; consider the following examples:

 2. 2 Laelius Archelaus Vettiusque Philocomus . . . Archelaum . . . Philocomum . . .
 10. 6 Asinium Pollionem . . . Asinium . . .
 16. 1-2 Cornelium Gallum . . . Gallo . . . Galli . . .
 18. 3-19. 1 Verrio Flacco . . . Verrius . . .
 Jul. 68. 4 Cassi Scaevae . . . Scaeva . . .
 Jul. 79. 1-80. 3 Epidius Marullus Caesetiusque Flavus . . . Caesetium et Marullum . . .
 Aug. 66. 1-2 Cornelium Gallum . . . Gallo . . .
 Cal. 58. 2 Cornelium Sabinum . . . Sabinum . . .
 Claud. 37. 2 Appium Silanum . . . Appium . . . Appius . . .
 Ner. 40. 1-41. 1 Iulio Vindice . . . Vindicis . . .
 Vit. 15. 2-3 Flavio Sabino . . . Sabinum . . .

In each case the man is introduced by reference to two of his names (cf. above, at 3. 3), and when he is mentioned again soon thereafter, only one of the names is used: that is Suetonius' regular practice (though not, of course, only Suetonius'). Suetonius never does what the archetype's text causes him to do here, viz., introduce a person by using only one of his names (nomen or cognomen), then refer to him in the same context by using another

---

deletion of *Murena* ("Note critiche," pp. 24f.), though he printed *Varrone . . . Murena* in his edition; see following.

[64] Sumner, ibid., pp. 189-90. The tale as Suetonius tells it, however, may bear only an attenuated relation to some real event: e.g., the anecdote *could* have originally featured Varro Gibba, as Sumner remarks, p. 190; in that case, a name more prominent among the *principes viri* had been installed by the time the story took the form known to Suetonius (cf. also next n.). On the instability of the details in such anecdotes (including the participants), see R. P. Saller, "Anecdotes as Historical Evidence for the Principate," *G&R* 27 (1980): 74ff. (with comment on this anecdote at p. 76).

of his names. It should be noted, too, that in the case of the name "Varro Murena," Suetonius elsewhere uses either the two names together or just "Murena," never "Varro" alone.[65] Rather than delete one or the other of the names, or both, as some have proposed in in the past, we need to add the name *Murena* when the advocate is first introduced. In minuscule script (esp. one with open *a*), *ar(r)on* and *uren* would look very much alike; *Murena* could easily be omitted.

10.1 <L.> Ateius Philologus, libertinus, Athenis est natus. (2) hunc Capito Ateius, notus iuris consultus, inter grammaticos rhetorem, inter rhetores grammaticum fuisse ait.

    L. *Roth (ex indice)* : *om.* ω

"Praeter indicem nostrum praenomen *L.* in indice [sc. auctorum] ad Plin. *N.H.* III invenitur" (Robinson, ed., p. 16); the man is otherwise referred to only as Ateius Philologus, without a praenomen. This is not the sort of evidence to buoy the spirits, particularly when one notices that the preceding entry in the *DGR*'s index--"L. Orbilius"--offers the same praenomen (hence a ready source of confusion) and that the evidence of the index in Pliny is worthless. Robinson refers to the latter listing as it has been printed since Detlefsen, "L. Ateio. <Ateio> Capitone," with the supplement proposed by Ritschl for the MSS' "L. Ateio Capitone";[66] but this supplement is certainly incorrect. Ritschl proposed it in the mistaken belief that the name "L. Ateius" recurs in the index to *HN* 32: that form of the name, however, does not occur anywhere in the *HN*; and when Ateius Philologus *is* listed in the index (to Book 4) that is the form his name takes--"Ateio Capitone. Ateio Philologo." Ritschl was right to think that a name had been omitted by haplography, but he chose the wrong solution: the correction needed is "L. <Aelio.> Ateio Capitone."

---

[65] *Aug.* 19. 1, *Tib.* 8 (*Varro Murena*), *Aug.* 56. 4, 66. 3 (*Murena*), all referring to the conspirator of 22 B.C. On "Varro Murena" as "the distinctive name of the family," see Sumner, ibid., pp. 192-93. The problem of sorting out individuals and relations within the family is a notorious prosopographical crux, mercifully irrelevant here: for refs. to earlier discussions see Sumner, ibid., p. 187 n. 1.

[66] F. Ritschl, *Parerga zu Plautus und Terenz I* (Leipzig, 1845), p. 374.

The man meant is L. Aelius Stilo: the listing appears in precisely that form in the *indices auctorum* to *HN* 14 and 15; and cf. 14. 93 "Scaevolam quoque et L. Aelium et Ateium Capitonem in eadem sententia fuisse video."

Even without the evidence of Pliny, however, there is some reason to think that the *DGR*'s index has it right.[67] First, it has long been supposed that Ateius was taken captive when Sulla plundered Athens in 86 B.C.: that is much the most likely explanation for his standing as a *libertinus, Athenis . . . natus*. Second, Ateius was clearly a slave and freedman of the family of Ateius Capito--and Capito's *avus* was a *centurio Sullanus* (Tac. *Ann.* 3. 75): family, rank, and chronology suggest that he was the man who captured Ateius and brought him to Rome. Finally, we know from the *Fasti Capitolini* that Capito's grandfather was a Lucius (*CIL* 1² p. 29 [a.u.c. 758] C. Ateius L. f. L. n. Capito): if he was the owner and then *patronus* of Ateius Philologus, the latter's praenomen would also have been Lucius, as the index gives it.

Note that this conclusion, if correct, also bears on Plutarch's report of Sulla's attack on Athens, *Sull.* 14. 3 (citing αὐτὸς ὁ Σύλλας ἐν τοῖς ὑπομνήμασι). There it is said that the first soldier to mount the city-wall was a man whose name the MSS give in the obviously corrupt form Μαρκον τηιον, corrected by Bryan to Μάρκον ᾿Ατήιον. This man is often identified as Ateius' captor; but if that is the case, the MSS' reading should perhaps be corrected instead to Λεύκιον ᾿Ατήιον--Capito's grandfather, the *centurio Sullanus*--a remedy that is both consistent with our other evidence and paleographically transparent, if the praenomen was at some point written in the abbreviated form ΛΑΤΗΙΟΝ, misread as ΜΤΗΙΟΝ (> ΜΑΡΚΟΝ ΤΗΙΟΝ). Alternatively, one might suppose that the praenomen was mistakenly reported by Sulla or mistakenly copied by Plutarch himself from Sulla (cf. "Ateius [5]," *RE* 2 [1896]: 1903 [Klebs]).

10.2 de eodem [sc. Ateio Philologo] Asinius Pollio, in libro quo Sallusti scripta reprehendit ut nimia priscorum verborum adfectatione oblita, ita tradit: "in eam rem adiutorium ei fecit maxime quidam Ateius, **praetextatis nobis** grammaticus Latinus, decla-

---

[67] Note that the initial for the praenomen was also omitted in the archetype at the beginning of chap. 9, on L. Orbilius Pupillus; it was inserted from the index by the second hand in **W**.

mantium deinde auditor atque praeceptor, ad summam Philologus ab semet nominatus."

> quidam ω : quidem B Q F, *Jahn*   pr(a)etextatis nobis X : praetextatus nobilis Y (Prae- *Casaubon*), *edd.*

To W. D. Lebek's support for X's *praetextatis nobis*--in place of "Ateius Praetextatus nobilis grammaticus Latinus," printed by nearly all modern editors--one is tempted to say, "At last!"[68] As Lebek notes, X's text has two clear advantages over the vulgate: it avoids the awkward juxtaposition of *quidam* (with contemptuous force, as the context demands) and *nobilis*;[69] and it provides a clearly marked sequence where one is wanted ("praetextatis nobis grammaticus . . ., declamantium deinde . . . praeceptor"),[70] placing Ateius' work as a *grammaticus* in a chronologically appropriate period, the boyhood of Pollio.[71] "Wie an mancher andere Stelle hat somit auch hier allein X das Richtige bewahrt."[72]

To Lebek's observations one need add only two points, concerning the cognomen Praetextatus, bestowed on Ateius by Casaubon's conjecture but attested for him (as Lebek remarks) nowhere else. First, Praetextatus is an utterly improbable cognomen for a late republican *libertinus*, in view of its intimate connection with the *toga praetexta*, one of the foremost tokens of

---

[68] "Eine pollionische Bemerkung Suet. Gramm. 10,1 (Rob.) und der Name des Ateius Philologus," *Hermes* 98 (1970): 127-28.

[69] This inconcinnity previously motivated Jahn's *quidem* (adopted by Reifferscheid), a correction also found in three Y-MSS.

[70] Cf., e.g., 6. 1 "Aurelius Opillus . . . philosophiam primo, deinde rhetoricam, novissime grammaticam docuit," 9. 1 "<L.> Orbilius Pupillus . . . primo apparituram magistratibus fecit, deinde in Macedonia corniculo, mox equo meruit." Lebek was probably mistaken to see another temporal marker in the phrase *ad summam* ("in short" / "in a nutshell"), taking it to signify a third stage in the sequence; but that does not affect the main point at issue here.

[71] Born in Athens, Ateius was probably taken captive there in 86 and brought to Rome, see above on 10. 1; Pollio was born in 76.

[72] Lebek, "Eine pollionische Bemerkung," p. 128, also demonstrating why della Corte's half measure--accepting X's *nobis* while retaining *Praetextatus*--will not do.

ingenuitas (cf. below, on 25. 5): since no freedman could ever have been a *puer praetextatus*, it is a fortiori unlikely that a freedman would be called Praetextatus--and it is therefore unsurprising that the name is in fact nowhere attested for any *libertinus*.[73] Second, double *cognomina* are something of a leitmotif in the *DGR*, for Suetonius draws special attention to them when he encounters them in three other *grammatici* (3. 2 "Aelius cognomine duplici fuit: nam et Praeconinus . . . vocabatur et Stilo . . .," 5. 1 "Sevius Nicanor . . . se . . . duplici cognomine esse per haec indicat . . .," 18. 1 "L. Crassicius . . ., cognomine Pasicles, mox Pansam se transnominavit"). Yet Suetonius simply gives Ateius' name as "<L.> Ateius Philologus" at the head of the chapter and then explains the significance of the cognomen Philologus in 10. 4; he has not a word to say about the appearance of the still more remarkable Praetextatus as a second cognomen. We should conclude that Suetonius, like our other sources, did not know that second cognomen.

In short, *Praetextatus* is objectionable enough in itself that we would be justified in suspecting corruption even it were the reading transmitted in all the MSS. Since it is not, since (on the contrary) it is attested only in that branch of the tradition which shows itself time and again to be even more deeply corrupt than the archetype, and since the alternative reading is clearly preferable on other grounds, there is not the least reason to persist in printing *Praetextatus nobilis*.

10.3 ipse [viz., Ateius Philologus] ad Laelium Hermam scripsit se in Graecis litteris magnum processum habere et in Latinis nonnullum, audisse Antonium Gniphonem eiusque †haeret† postea docuisse; praecepisse autem multis et claris iuvenibus, in quis

---

[73] Among the Praetextati collected by I. Kajanto, *The Latin Cognomina* (Helsinki, 1965), p. 300, none is a freedman and most are plainly of much higher status; it was because of this fact of nomenclature that Lebek's defense of *praetextatis nobis* was approved by H. Solin, *Beiträge zur Kenntnis der griechischen Personennamen in Rom, I* (Helsinki, 1971), p. 134 n. 2 (on p. 135). Della Corte imagined (3rd ed., p. 86) that Pollio called Ateius "Praetextatus" sarcastically, using the word as a synonymn for "puerile" or in an obscene sense; other explanations of "Praetextatus," similarly arbitrary or improbable, are attempted by Hillscher, *Jahrb. f. class. Phil.* Suppl. 18 (Leipzig, 1892), p. 365, Christes, *Sklaven*, pp. 44f., and Rawson, *Intellectual Life*, p. 74 n. 32.

Appio quoque et Pulchro Claudiis fratribus, quorum comes in
provincia fuerit.

> haere **WN¹V¹** (aere **G²**), Hermam **OWᵐY** (-niam **H**, mea **ΔF**),
> haeresin *Mercklin*, heredem *Vahlen (teste Robinson)*, heredem
> Hermam *Funaioli*, here<des; Hermam> *della Corte*

The problem here is of the sort for which only the obelus is adequate.[74] The distribution of the readings *haere* and *Hermam* among the MSS--with the division between **O** and **W**, the presence of *haere* as a variant in **V**, and the presence of *Hermam* as a variant in **W**--strongly suggests that the two readings were already present as variants in the archetype (cf. Robinson, diss., p. 74). If that is so, *Hermam* should probably be regarded as a conjecture, the name having been fetched from the beginning of the sentence as a palliative for the problem presented by *haere*; in that case, any further attempts at emendation should be based on *haere*, not *Hermam*. Beyond that, however, the path of probability does not lead: no secure solution has yet been proposed; and, strictly speaking, no secure solution *can* be proposed, since (*int. al.*) we do not even know whether the desiderated word(s) should be construed with *audisse* or with *docuisse* (see below).

Even if we set aside the latter difficulty for the sake of discussion, the solutions that have found favor with editors leave a great deal to be desired. Robinson printed ". . . audisse Antonium Gniphonem eiusque haeresin," adopting Mercklin's conjecture. There are, however, two difficulties with this solution. First, though Robinson took *haeresin* as = *dogma*, it should more properly denote what is usually called a *secta* in Latin (cf. Suetonius at 8. 1 *studio Epicureae sectae*, 18. 3 *Q. Sexti philosophi sectam*, 28. 1 *in re publica administranda . . . Isaurici sectam sequeretur*, and compare, e.g., Cic. *Parad.* 2 "Cato . . . in ea est haeresi [viz., Stoica] quae nullum sequitur florem orationis," with *TLL* 6:2502. 37ff.). As such, *haeresin* makes an odd object for *audisse*: just as no Latin-speaker would ever say *audire sectam*, so none ever says *audire haeresin* (a similar problem would remain if one were to read "audisse Antonium Gniphonem, eiusque haeresin postea

---

[74] Rolfe printed *eiusque †haere*, Roth *eiusque †Hermam†*, Reifferscheid *eiusque †Laelium Hermam†* (*Laelium* was a printer's error, as Reifferscheid noted in the addenda to his ed., p. 413 n.); Bione printed *eiusque <*> Hermam*, positing a lacuna.

docuisse").[75] More important, the conjecture does not provide the *idea* that is wanted here: *haeresis*, like *secta*, belongs above all to the world of the philosophical schools; it is never used in Latin of mere grammar, which did not know either the institutional continuity or the doctrinal sectarianism that characterized philosophy. Excuses could no doubt be made: one could say that *audire* finds its primary object in *Antonium Gniphonem*, to which *haeresin* is loosely appended; one could say that the Greek-born Ateius Philologus, whose words Suetonius is reporting, used the notion of *haeresis* loosely as well. That might just barely suffice if *haeresin* were the transmitted reading; but an emendation that requires multiple appeals to "loose usage" does not inspire confidence.

Similar considerations suggest that the other favored correction, *heredem* (or some variation on it), is still less satisfactory. Robinson reported (ed., p. 17) that Vahlen had written *eiusque heredem postea docuisse* in the margin of his copy of Reifferscheid, evidently intending *heredem* to be taken as the object of *docuisse* ("... and subsequently taught his [viz., Gnipho's] *heres*");[76] Funaioli proposed "... audisse Antonium Gniphonem eiusque heredem Hermam, postea docuisse," which was in turn modified by della Corte to produce "... audisse Antonium Gniphonem eiusque here<des; Hermam> postea docuisse." The meaning in each case is rather different, depending on the verb

---

[75] Mercklin himself anticipated this difficulty (*Philol.* 19 [1863]: 159, "Sollte *audire haeresin* anstössig sein ...") and so was prepared to abandon *haeresin* for the more extensive correction *et usque ad terminum vitae secutum* or *eiusque aere redemptum*.

[76] That, at any rate, is how Brugnoli understood the phrasing when he adopted the correction for his edition; see *Studi Suetoniani*, p. 102: "... affermare 'di avere' anche 'insegnato al successore' di Antonio Gnifone.... Chi fosse questo *heres* di Antonio Gnifone non possiamo sapere" (indeed: and Ateius' failure to name the supposed *heres* is one of the things that make this solution unlikely). Vahlen also jotted several other possibilities in his margin--*ad normam* or *artem* or *aere* (followed by a lacuna)--and suggested *theoremata* in his *De Verrio Flacco* (p. 7 n. = *Opusc. Acad.*, 1:48 n.). Other conjectures noted by Robinson (app. crit., p. 17, and Append. II, p. 60) include: *F(ilium) Hermam* Statius; *L(ibertum) Hermam* Gronovius; *more ignotus apud* Ihm ("Zur Ueberlieferung und Textkritik von Suetons Schrift *De grammaticis et rhetoribus*," *RhM* 61 [1906]: 551).

with which one chooses to construe the conjectured word(s), and none is unobjectionable.⁷⁷

But it should be stressed that the word *heres* itself raises the same fundamental problems for all three of these proposals. First, whatever meaning one attributes to the term *heres* here, it would be odd for the word to occur without further specification: we expect to be told the man's name, especially in a passage where Philologus was indulging in a fair amount of name-dropping (thus Gnipho preceding, the brothers Claudii following). Second, *heres* could not have its literal meaning, since it would be so used only in a context where Gnipho's will (vel sim.) was under discussion and where, consequently, emphasis on the strictly testamentary relationship would be relevant: there is no apparent reason to think that the present passage is such a context. We would therefore have to understand the term figuratively; but that is not a satisfactory alternative, either. In this context, *heredem* (or -*des*) would have to mean "successor(s)"--that is, it could only be serving as an equivalent to the Greek term διάδοχος; and those who favor this solution point to Cic. *Brut.* 332 "illa vetus Academia atque eius heres Aristus" for an example of that meaning (cf. also *TLL* 6:2655.1ff.).⁷⁸ So far from providing support, however, that passage actually suggests why a form of *heres* is not apt; for here again we find ourselves in the world of the philosophical schools--the world of scholarchs following one after another in a direct line of succession (διαδοχή), of sectarian distinctiveness and doctrinal continuity maintained by that succession, and of institutions, like the Academy and the Lyceum, that abided from one generation to the next while the "successors" came and went.⁷⁹ But scholarchs and διάδοχοι / *heredes*--and the

---

⁷⁷ On the texts of Funaioli and della Corte, see Brugnoli, *Studi Suetoniani*, pp. 101-2; on Vahlen's conjecture, cf. the preceding note. The choice of construction cannot help but be arbitrary (cf. above), especially since we know nothing useful about Laelius Herma's connection with Ateius.

⁷⁸ Della Corte believed that *heredes* could = "pupils" ("discepoli," 3rd ed., pp. 24, 86); but *heredes* could no more = *discipuli* than διάδοχοι could = οἱ παιδευόμενοι / οἱ φοιτῶντες / μαθηταί.

⁷⁹ See, e.g., J. P. Lynch, *Aristotle's School: A Study of a Greek Educational Institution* (Berkeley and Los Angeles, 1972). On the development of such institutions in the field of law, see R. Bauman, *Lawyers and Politics in the Early Roman Empire* (Munich, 1989), pp. 25ff. On Διαδοχαί ("Succes-

whole institutional culture that made them possible--are entirely foreign to the world of the *grammatici*: even at Alexandria, where we can trace five generations of teachers and pupils from the early third century to the middle of the second, "there were no διαδοχαί, as in the philosophical schools with their particular δόξαι."[80] No *grammaticus* is ever called the *heres* (or διάδοχος) of another, and with good reason: there were no "schools" of grammar in the sense relevant here--and least of all were there such "schools" in the late Republic, when formal grammar and its institutions at Rome were still in their infancy.

Given these considerations, then, together with the other uncertainties that attend this crux, I believe that the obelus is the only proper choice.

10.6 quos [sc. Sallustium et Asinium Pollionem] historiam componere adgressos, alterum breviario **rerum omnium Romanarum**, ex quibus quas vellet eligeret, instruxit [sc. Ateius Philologus] . . .

rerum omnium Romanarum ω (Romanorum **WIQ**)

The transmitted word-order is hardly what one expects. *res Romanae*--in the sense virtually = "Roman history"--is an idiomatic phrase whose elements cohere to convey a single idea (cf. *res publica* or *res gestae*), and one does not expect to see another adjective interposing itself between noun and modifier. Furthermore, one especially does not expect to see *omnium* thus interposing itself: among the more than three dozen places where Suetonius writes *omnium* in the *Caesares* and the *DGR*, it precedes the word (or phrase) that it modifies in all instances save four (*Aug.* 96. 1, *Cal.* 15. 4, *Vesp.* 21, *Tit.* 2); the expectation that *omnium* would precede the word it modifies no doubt explains, at least in part, the error *Romanorum* that is found in **WIQ** (printed by della Corte in his 2nd ed.). The unexpected order is doubtless correct, however: a precise parallel is provided by Livy 31. 1. 2, where the historian describes himself as "profiteri ausum perscripturum res omnes Romanas"; and for a variation on the

---

sions") as a genre in ancient "history of philosophy," see J. Mejer, *Diogenes Laertius and His Hellenistic Background* (Wiesbaden, 1978), pp. 62ff.

[80] R. Pfeiffer, *History of Classical Scholarship* (Oxford, 1968), p. 233.

phrase, cf. id. 33. 10. 10 "Polybium . . ., non incertum auctorem cum omnium Romanarum rerum tum praecipue in Graecia gestarum."

11.3 (= *FPL* frag. 2, p. 81 M. = p. 104 B.)

> Catonis modo, Galle, Tusculanum
> tota creditor urbe venditabat.
> mirati sumus unicum magistrum,
> summum grammaticum, optimum poetam
> omnes solvere posse quaestiones,
> unum **deficere** expedire nomen.
> en cor Zenodoti! en iecur Cratetis!

deficere *Toup* : difficile ω, difficilem *Bentley,* unum huic difficile *Heinsius* (*teste Burman*), at difficile *Burman*

According to Furius Bibaculus, quoted here, the grammarian P. Valerius Cato lost his Tusculan villa to bankruptcy; the punchline (6) turns on a pun, the two possible senses of the phrase *expedire nomen*, "to expound / give an account of the *nomen*" (sc. as a grammatical part of speech) and "to extricate (one's) name" (sc. from an entry in an account-book) = "to settle a debt." The balanced antithesis between line 5 and line 6 is obviously worked out with some care: *omnes . . . quaestiones*, framing line 5, is answered by *unum . . . nomen*, framing line 6;[81] *solvere*, holding second position in line 5, is answered by *expedire*, holding third position in line 6; and *posse*, holding third position in line 5, is answered by--what? Evidently some verbal idea, equivalent to *non posse*, to stand in second position and complete the chiastic balance of the predicates. Toup's *deficere* (accepted by Reifferscheid and Bione, and by Morel and Buechner in *FPL*) provides just the sense that is needed: Cato "failed to account for a single *nomen*" (for *deficere* used with a personal construction + inf. = "to fail / be unable" to do something, see OLD s.v. 9.c, *TLL* 5: 336.62ff.); and as R. Renehan points out to me, *deficere* may even participate appropriately in the pun, if it can suggest "fail" sc. because of insolvency (so later at Juv. 7. 129, *Dig.* 35. 2. 31 [Pompon.], 49. 14. 3. 8 [Callist.], cited at *TLL* 5:330.77ff.). By contrast,

---

[81] This aspect of the line's technique is effaced by della Corte's punctuation "unum difficile: expedire nomen" (the punctuation is accepted, with Toup's *deficere* for *difficile*, by Buechner in *FPL*).

the archetype's *difficile* (retained by Roth, Rolfe, Robinson, and Brugnoli) can be thought to respond adequately to *posse* only if it is assumed to be adverbial, modifying *expedire* with a force approaching that of *non*.

Both parts of this assumption are very problematic. First the matter of form: in Latin of the Republic, the regular form of the adverb (positive degree) is *difficulter*; apart from Cato *Agr. summ.* cap. 131 (*si difficile emittit vissica*), the form *difficile* is not attested before Velleius Paterculus.[82] Taken by itself, the morphological point would perhaps not be decisive: one could say that there is, after all, the evidence of Cato, that the positive degree *difficile* would seem to be implied by the comparative *difficilius* and the superlative *difficillime* (e.g., 6 times each in Cic., who does not use any form of the positive degree), and that *difficulter* would have been metrically intractable in Bibaculus' line. Nonetheless, a problem, and one that must be placed on the same side of the scale as the problem of sense, which is less easily dismissed.

As noted above, *difficile* can stand here only if--like *vix* or *haud*--it can have a sense approaching *non*: the point toward which Bibaculus has been building is that Cato did *not* "unum ... expedire nomen," not that he did so "with difficulty." Yet in all periods, *difficile* (or *difficulter*) most commonly retains its literal meaning (very often in litotes, *non difficile* = *facile*); and that is the *exclusive* meaning of the adverb in republican Latin. The earliest text in which I find the adverb used like *vix* is the same passage of Velleius in which the adverbial form *difficile* is securely attested for the first time since Cato: 2. 63. 3 "Plancus deinde dubia ... fide, diu quarum esset partium secum luctatus ac *sibi difficile consentiens*, et nunc adiutor D. Bruti ..., mox eiusdem proditor ..." (where *et nunc ..., mox ...,* in particular, indicate that Plancus did *not* succeed in *sibi ... consentiens*).[83]

On the most favorable assessment, then, *difficile* is a *lectio difficilior*; but the foregoing considerations of form and meaning suggest that it is simply *nimis difficile*. *deficere*, of course, is

---

[82] See *TLL* 5:1091.16ff.; for the passage in Paterculus, see below. The problem of the grammatical form was remarked by Bione, "Note critiche," p. 25.

[83] *TLL* is more conservative, classifying this passage among the literal uses of the term; if one followed the classifications in the article s.v. (5:1093.48ff.), *difficile* = *vix* would not be attested before Fronto.

entirely unproblematic--and that fact (combined with the conservatism of Suetonius' editors) probably explains its neglect: it seems almost too good, and suggests the danger that we have "uno dei casi in cui una congettura moderna migliora non l'opera di un amanuense, ma quella dell' autore."[84] But given the obvious care that Bibaculus took in crafting these lines, I think that danger is minimal.

13.1 L. Staberius Eros, †nametra† emptus de catasta et propter litterarum studium manumissus, docuit inter ceteros Brutum et Cassium.

> L. Staberius O (Staberius W, *spatio praeposit.*) : Staberius Y (Stra- α, L. Taberius ζ, V. Taberius H, Taberius KE)   (h)eros nametra X : (h)eros nametra *et* (h)ero suo Metre Y, Eros, natione Thrax *Funaioli*, Eros <libertinus>--nam erat *Robinson* (nam erat *iam Vahlen*), *alii alia*   emptus XG²βM : empturus αM²ζ

To take the praenomen first: Staberius' name happens to have been omitted from the index, which can therefore provide no assistance;[85] X and Y are divided in their testimony. Y had no praenomen (I take it that the *L. Taberius* of γ's descendant ζ is the result of clumsy "correction" by contamination: see below). X just as clearly had a praenomen: O reads *L.*; W wrote *Staberius* and left a large space before the name for a capital initial to be

---

[84] Bione, "Note critiche," p. 25

[85] The name was inserted in the index after P. Valerius Cato in O ("et. L. Staberius") and after Cornelius Epicadus in M ("Staberius heros l' hiero") and CΔ ("L. Taberius"); in each case it was obviously supplied from the text. In most other instances the teacher's praenomen appears in both the index and the archetypal text ad loc. (chaps. 7, 8, 16, 18, 20, 21, 22 [om. ζ], 23 [om. OWK, add. W^m], 27 [cf. the discussion ad loc.], 29, 30) or in neither index nor text (chaps. 5, 6, 12, 14, 15, 19). In two instances, the praenomen appears only in the index (chaps. 10, 28), whence editors regularly supply it in the text ad loc.; in two other instances, it appears only in the text (chaps. 24, 26; in the latter case, the scribes of BM inserted it in the index as well); and in three instances it appears in the index and in one or two MSS ad loc. (chaps. 9 [*L.* W²], 11 [*P.* OW², *Publius* B], 17 [*M.* W², *Marcus* B]). In these last instances editors typically assume that the praenomen was fetched from the index by individual scribes and inserted in the text; on W² in these cases, see n. 87.

added.⁸⁶ This was the usual practice of **W**'s scribe at the start of the biographical chapters and at a few other places elsewhere in the text (mostly chapter- or paragraph-breaks); the capital initials, however, were never provided.⁸⁷ The significance of this blank space was rightly seen by Robinson (diss., p. 83): had **W**'s scribe not found an initial for a praenomen in his exemplar, then--following his usual practice--he would have written *taberius* (cf. ζ), leaving a space for a capital *S*, just as he wrote *ornelius* at the start of the preceding chapter (leaving space for a capital *C*) and as he wrote *urtius* at the start of the next chapter (leaving space for a capital *C*). I see no reason to doubt either that an initial stood in **W**'s exemplar or that the initial was the *L.* we find in **W**'s brother, **O**.

Nor do I see any reason to reject the praenomen, as most editors do. I certainly cannot accept the view of Robinson (ibid.), the only editor to give a reason for his choice. On this view, the archetype had a double reading, *l. taberius* (as in ζ) and *staberius*, the result of confusion between minuscule *s* and *l*, and this double reading was combined by **X**'s scribe to produce *L. Staberius*. But the confusion posited seems to me improbable: if *staberius* was written without capital *S*, then the usual minuscule *st* ligature would make confusion with *l* unlikely; if it was written as *Staberius*, then confusion of *l* with capital *S* would be even more unlikely. Worse still, this view compels us to assume that ζ uniquely preserves an authentic memory of the archetype, a service that it performs nowhere else, and one that Robinson (following his own stemma) should not have expected it to perform.⁸⁸

---

⁸⁶ Brugnoli omits this detail from his app. crit., which thus fails to provide the information needed for a correct appraisal of the text. The apparatus of della Corte, who is the only editor in this century to accept *L.*, has no entry at all for this matter.

⁸⁷ In most cases a small initial was written in the vacant space, in a hand (as appears from my photographs) different from and presumably later than that of the scribe; cf. n. 85 and App. 2 (ad fin.), on 23. 1 *(Q.) Remmius*. The small initial was not written in our passage; cf. at 10. 5 *Hylen*, where **W**'s scribe wrote *ylen* and left space for a capital initial, though the *h* was not provided thereafter in any form.

⁸⁸ Robinson's stemma would necessarily imply the following sequence, if *l. taberius* is to be thought archetypal: Y copied both *l. taberius* and *staberius*; α and β both ignored the former reading and copied only the latter (mistakenly reproduced as *straberius* in α), while γ copied both; one

In this context, X's *L* is not likely to be either a mechanical error or a free conjecture;[89] it is more probable that Y's text is the result of simple omission.[90] Note that of the very few late republican Staberii whose praenomen we know, one was a Lucius.[91]

The problem in the text after the name *Staberius* is much less tractable. It is probably best to give the complete record of the MSS (based on Robinson, diss., p. 84, with Brugnoli's report of E; for the variants *emptus / empturus* in Xαβ, see the apparatus above: they do not enter into the central problem here):

X	α	β
heros nametra O	*eros nametra* N	*here suo Metre* B
eros nametra W	*hero suo metre*	*l' erosnametra*
	eros nametra G	*hero suo Metre* V
	nametra (om. *eros*) I	*hero suo metre* L
		(*herosnametra* L^m)
		hero suo morem D

γ

heros nametra MK (*hiero suo metre* M²ᵐKᵐ)
heros suo [spat. 10 litt.] *empturus nametra* H
[spat. 14 litt.] *hero emptus* U
hiero suo menea emptus heros nam&ra (*ramata* Δ) *empturus* CΔ
emptus post de catasta [cet. om.] F
hierausuomene emptus heros empturus Q
hyerasuomene emptus haeres empturus E

---

of γ's apographs, δ, in turn ignored the former reading and copied only the latter, while the other apograph, ζ, copied only the former and ignored the latter. Given the general character of ζ, its reading is far more likely due to contamination.

[89] Cf. Ihm, "Zur Ueberlieferung," p. 548 n. 4: ". . . *L.* freie Erfindung von O zu sein scheint"; but neither O nor any other MS indulges in such free invention at other places where a praenomen is lacking.

[90] For a slightly different explanation, leading to the same conclusion, cf. Wessner, rev. of Robinson, ed., *PhW* 46 (1926): 1228: the three variants *L. Staberius, L. Taberius,* and *Staberius* could all be derived from an archetype in which *L* appeared as a suprascript correction, with *Staberius* in the text.

[91] L. Staberius, a Pompeian officer in command at Apollonia in 48 B.C. (*MRR* 2:284): probably too young to be the man who purchased Staberius *de catasta*, though he could be that man's son.

X plainly had *eros* (or *heros*) *nametra*; as α, β, and MK (= δ) show, Y too had *(h)eros nametra*, and a second reading as well, *hero suo metre* (the aporia or gibberish evident in HUCFΔQE results from the combination of the two readings in their common ancestor, ζ). We can therefore unequivocally claim at least *(h)eros nametra* for the archetype; it is possible that *hero suo metre* also appeared in the archetype, as a second reading (so Robinson, ibid.), though it could just as well have originated in Y.[92]

Whichever is the case, attempts at emendation must proceed from the reading *(h)eros nametra*, as Robinson correctly emphasized (diss., pp. 84-85): "nam huic grammatico nomen esse *Staberio Eroti* Ios. Scaliger *ad Manil.* p. 4, Plinium N. H. XXXV 199 proferens, primus ostendit." That is, *(h)ero suo Metre* represents an attempt to extort at least partial sense from the transmitted letters by a scribe or reader who did not recognize *Eros* as a cognomen: *(h)erosna . . .* became *(h)ero suo*, a reference to Staberius' "master," to be fitted together with *emptus de catasta*. If this is the case, then modern emendations based on *(h)ero suo Metre* can be discarded (Roth's *Eros suomet aere emptus*, Beck's *Eros a sua matre emptus*, neither one giving desirable sense in any case).[93]

Of the remaining emendations proposed by earlier scholars, two seem *prima facie* unlikely. Following from the analysis summarized above, Robinson proposed *Eros <libertinus>--nam erat emptus . . .*: that is, omitted *libertinus* followed by a parenthesis with Vahlen's *nam erat* (for *nametra*), "quae coniectura neque unam quidem litteram addit neque tollit"; but the latter consideration, I think, impressed Robinson too much (here as occasionally elsewhere), and I would be reluctant to posit the omission that *nam erat* entails. Brugnoli's *Eros nomine, Thrax emptus* (with *Thrax* taken over from Funaioli, see below) proceeds from a

---

[92] Brugnoli, app. crit. ad loc., p. 18, writes: "in codice Hersfeldensi lectionem fuisse eros | | ometra . . . suspicatus sum quam ex familia Y (eros | | ometre . . .) cum X (eros | | ametra . . .) collata plane deducere possumus" (cf. *Studi Suetoniani*, p. 117). I do not see how one can deduce those readings for X and Y from the evidence noted above, or how one can arrive at such a reading for the archetype.

[93] I mention here also Doergens' *Heros cognomine. Et redemptus* and Voss' *Eros Syrophoenix emptus*, which do not have any chance of being right.

mistaken reading of the MS evidence (see above, n. 92); and in any case, *nomine* here both is superfluous and involves a form of phrasing (teacher's name followed by abl. *nomine* at the start of a chapter) that Suetonius employs nowhere in the *DGR*.[94] The only earlier conjecture worth serious consideration is Funaioli's *natione Thrax* (> *name t(h)ra(x)*: on *name*, see below), proposed at *GRF* 1:106: this at least provides information of the sort one expects (on the man's origin) in the form one expects it to take (cf. 8. 1 "M. Pompilius Andronicus, natione Syrus," 20. 1 C. Julius Hyginus, Augusti libertus, natione Hispanus," with, e.g., 16. 1 "Q. Caecilius Epirota, Tusculi natus").

There are, however, two points requiring further consideration. The first is paleographical, and concerns *natione*: if that word was corrupted to *name*, the corruption would most probably be explained as a misreading of an abbreviation--say, $\overline{nao}e$ or $\overline{nac}$;[95] compare the two errors found in cod. **B**, *Rome* for *ratione* (i.e., $\overline{ro}e$) at 10. 6 and (conversely) *ratione* for *Romae* at 14. 2. Now such an abbreviation could have appeared neither in the Hersfeldensis nor in any other MS of the ninth century or before-- though that is not exactly the point. As I have argued in Chapter 1, the stemmata of the *DGR* and Tac. *Dial.* are in all relevant respects identical; and there is clear evidence that a Renaissance archetype stood between the Hersfeldensis and the Renaissance hyparchetypes of the *Dial.* (i.e., the equivalents, for that work, of **X** and **Y**).[96] It would therefore be far from surprising if the *DGR*, too, descended from the Hersfeldensis by way of a Renaissance archetype antecedent to **X** and **Y**. (As remarked in Chap. 1, it

---

[94] Brugnoli (app. crit. ad loc., p. 18, sim. *Studi Suetoniani*, pp. 120-21) sought support from 4. 6 *repeto quendam Principem nomine*, where Suetonius refers *obiter* to a teacher (*quendam* = *quendam* sc. *grammaticum*, as in the preceding sentence *quorundam* = *quorundam* sc. *grammaticorum*): but *quendam* there makes all the difference ("a certain one, Princeps by name"); and *nomine* was especially desirable in that context, to make plain that the preceding word was being used as a proper name (*Princeps*), not as a common noun (*princeps*).

[95] For the latter (= *nacione* = *natione*), see Capelli, *Dizionario di abbreviature*[6], p. 231; the former would = *na-* + the compendium $\overline{oe}$ (= *-tione* : see Capelli, p. xxiii, L. Schiaparelli, *Avviamento allo studio delle abbreviature latine nel medioevo* [Florence, 1926], p. 88).

[96] See Chap. 1 at nn. 14 and 57.

would be surprising if the *DGR* were not so descended, in view of its close relation to the *Dial.*: it is for this reason that I have avoided using "Hersfeldensis" and "archetype" as interchangeable terms in these discussions.) The point, rather, is this. If we take *name* to represent the misreading of such an abbreviation, it is necessary to accept one of two alternatives: either that abbreviation stood in the Renaissance archetype (representing *natione* in the Hersfeldensis), whence it was independently miscopied as *name* by the scribes of *both* **X** *and* **Y** (since, as we saw, the reading *name* appeared in both of the these MSS); or the corrupt *name* already stood in the Renaissance MS antecedent to **X** and **Y**, where it was the result of the miscopying of an abbreviation in a *previous* Renaissance MS. In other words: either the same mistake would have been made twice, independently, by the scribes of **X** and **Y**; or there would have been (at least) two Renaissance MSS between the Hersfeldensis and **XY**. Either of these alternatives would be possible; and in view of comparable sequences of error found in Tac. *Dial.* (cf. Chap. 1 at n. 14), the second alternative might even be thought likely--if the paleographical point could be viewed in isolation.

But this brings us to the second point, which is raised by Pliny *HN* 35. 199 (cf. above): "Publilium <Anti>ochium, mimicae scaenae conditorem, et astrologiae consobrinum eius Manilium Antiochium, item grammaticae Staberium Erotem eadem nave advectos videre proavi." If the cousins Publilius and Manilius, both Syrians of Antioch, reached Rome on the same ship as Staberius, it might at first glance seem natural to assume that Staberius was a native of Syria too:[97] this assumption, which would obviously rule out *Thrax*, eventually caused Funaioli himself to hesitate (cf. "Staberius (4)," *RE* 3 A [1929]: 1924). The assumption, however, is *per se* quite insubstantial: even if we were to place full faith in Pliny's story, it should be noted that he does not say the ship *came* from Antioch, merely that the three men-- two of them cousins from Antioch, the third of unspecified origin-- were on it;[98] the ship could have come from some other port in the

---

[97] Thus della Corte conjectured *natus in Syria* (rev. of Bione, *RFIC* 70 [1942]: 138): "si può leggere NA<TUS> IN <S>YR<I>A, dove paleograficamente è avvenuto il mutamento di IN in M e di Y in T" (plus the loss of 5 other letters).

[98] As Christes suggests, *Sklaven*, p. 53 n. 364, if the passage implies anything at all about Staberius' origin, it is that he was *not* from Antioch.

East, propelled by Sulla's adventures or by the more ordinary currents of the slave trade.[99] Yet the passage does suggest another cause for hesitation. Pliny, who is discussing the chalk used to whiten the feet of foreign slaves presented for sale *in catasta* (*HN* 35. 199-201), and Suetonius, who records that Staberius was *emptus de catasta*, both ultimately reflect the same tradition about Staberius' background. (Suetonius is not likely to be drawing on Pliny himself, for the latter does not mention Staberius' manumission.) Since Pliny does not record Staberius' origin, it probably means that his origin--unlike that of the Antiochene cousins--was not in the version of the tradition Pliny knew; and since Suetonius was drawing on the same tradition (though not necessarily the same version of it), he too may not have known Staberius' origin. In that case, of course, any attempt to restore that origin here would be misguided, however likely one judged the corruption of *natione* to *name*.

Though the foregoing considerations do not prove that Funaioli's conjecture is mistaken, I am unable to convince myself that it is correct. I am also not quite able to embrace the much simpler solution proposed to me by C. E. Murgia, viz., *Eros, a Metra emptus* . . ., according to which *Metra* would be the cognomen of Staberius' master.[100] Nor can I myself propose anything prefer-

---

[99] It has been customary since Hillscher (*Jahrb. f. class. Phil.* Suppl. 18 [Leipzig, 1892], p. 366) to associate the arrival of this ship at Rome with the return of Sulla from Athens in 83. Note, however, that if Staberius came to Rome as late as that, then (acc. to Suetonius' story) he must have been manumitted *very* quickly indeed, to have been teaching *Sullanis temporibus*; cf. S. Treggiari, *Roman Freedmen during the Late Republic* (Oxford, 1969), pp. 115f. In fact, the story may well be "a myth," in whole or in part, as Teuffel thought ("ein Mythos," 1^4:254, changed to "ein Märchen" by L. Schwabe in the 5th ed. of 1890, 1^5:269): that Staberius is identified as the *conditor* of grammar, to match the other two *conditores artium*, is an obvious fairytale element; other aspects of the anecdote--its dating to the time of Pliny's *proavi*, the chronology of Publilius, the identity of Manilius--can give comfort neither to those who would believe it nor to those who would date it to the mid-80s B.C. These questions of credibility and chronology are not central to the textual problem here; I discuss them fully in my commentary.

[100] The name Μητρᾶς is very sparsely attested, not least at Rome: Solin, *Griech. Personennamen* 1:371, lists but five examples, none before the 1st cent. A.D. Comparing the phrases *venalium trans maria advectorum* and *nave advectos* in Plin. *HN* 35. 199, R. Renehan suggests that something

able.¹⁰¹ I therefore intend to place *nametra* in the text, surrounded by obeli.

14.1 Curtius Nicia <ad>haesit Cn. Pompeio et C. Memmio.

adhaesit *Heinsius (teste Burman)* : haesit ω

Heinsius' *adhaesit* was accepted by Reifferscheid; it was also proposed independently (it appears) by Osann, though his reasoning --"haud novi aliud exemplum, quo *haerere* alicui idem sit ac ex partibus alicuius stare" (p. 65)--was rightly rejected by Robinson (ed., p. 22: "Quo . . . iure iudicavit Suetonium dicere voluisse Niciam Pompei et Memmi partibus adhaesisse, potius quam ipsis Pompeio et Memmio haesisse?"), who printed the archetype's *haesit*, citing Plin. *Epist*. 7. 27. 2 (*obtinenti Africam comes haeserat*), Quint. *Inst*. 1. 2. 10 (*minores . . . haerere singulis . . . non indignantur*), and Verg. *Aen*. 10. 779-80 (*missus ab Argis / haeserat Evandro*).

Robinson has been followed by all subsequent editors. Nonetheless, I believe that Heinsius and (if for the wrong reason) Osann were correct: when Suetonius elsewhere wishes to express the idea appropriate here, he does not use the simplex *haerere*, which for him has only the sense "to be stuck" (sc. in a difficulty, vel sim.) or "to remain / persist" (used with *circa* + acc. or *in* + abl.: *Aug*. 71. 1, *Ner*. 56, *Galb*. 4. 4, *Dom*. 12. 1); instead, he employs the compound *adhaerere*.¹⁰² The opportunity for loss of *ad-* by haplography after *Nicia* is obvious.

---

along the lines of *Eros, nave tra<nsvectus atque> emptus de catasta et . . . manumissus* might be considered (for the sequence A *atque* / *ac* B et C, cf. 24. 2 *emendare ac distinguere et adnotare*, 26. 2 *inflatum ac levem et sordidum*, 30. 2 *circumcise ac sordide et tantum non trivialibus verbis*); but he adds, rightly, that "certainty is up on some crater of the moon."

101 I once suspected that *nametra* was the result of physical damage in an ancestor of the archetype--a hole in the parchment through which letters from a preceding or following page were seen and mistakenly copied (for an example of the phenomenon in the 9th-cent. Vergil MS Bern. 165 [b], see my *Tradition of the Text*, p. 222 n. 8); but there is no such sequence of letters at any reasonable distance before or ahead.

102 *Galb*. 14. 2 "regebatur trium arbitrio, quos una et intra Palatium habitantis nec umquam non adhaerentis paedagogos vulgo vocabant," *Oth*. 6. 3 "ad principia devenit, obvio quoque . . . adhaerente"; that neither

14.3 cur **ego** illi molestus esse <velim, cum mihi ille iucundus esse> non possit?

> ego B (*Iens., ed. Rom. Cic.*) : ergo ω (*codd. Cic.*)   velim . . .
> esse *suppl. Aldus e Cic.* : *om.* ω   non possit XN¹M : non possim W² : possim V¹H, possem βθ, possum α (non possum G²)US, non possit possum I

This sentence, part of a quotation from Cic. *Att*. 12. 26. 2, involves the most notable lacuna that is securely attributed to the archetype of *DGR*, the omission of *velim . . . esse* produced by *saut du même au même*.¹⁰³ The suppletion is unproblematic. A nice methodological question is raised, however, by a smaller matter in the sentence, the conjecture *ego* that is found in the twin editiones principes of the *ad Att., ad Q. fr., et ad M. Brutum* (the editio Romana and the edition of N. Jenson, both 1470); though not previously reported, *ego* also occurs in cod. B of *DGR*, in place of the archetype's *ergo*. The conjecture, accepted by Shackleton Bailey, is certainly attractive and probably correct: *ergo* is otiose, while *ego illi . . . mihi ille* suits the point and emphasis of the antithesis. But if *ego* is correct, does an editor of the *DGR* nonetheless print *ergo*--and thereby assume that that is what Suetonius himself wrote, because the corruption had already occurred by the time he quoted from the letter? Or does the editor print *ego*--and thereby assume that the corruption found in the MSS of Cicero (*cuR ego > cuR eRgo*) occurred independently in the tradition of *DGR*? I can see no decisive reason for choosing one assumption over the other; but given the general state of the *DGR* 's tradition, I prefer the latter.

15.2 ac tanto amore erga patroni memoriam extitit ut Sallustium historicum, quod eum (frag. II. 16, p. 65 M.) "oris probi animo inverecundo" scripsisset, acerbissima satura laceraverit, lastaurum et lurconem et nebulonem popinonemque appellans, et vita

---

of these places invites or requires explicit use of the dative I take to be irrelevant.

[103] The process we see still underway in the MSS--the attempt by various paths to make some sense of *non possit* after the lacuna--demonstrates that the omission occurred quite recently in the text's history, very likely in the archetype itself.

scriptisque monstrosum, praeterea priscorum **Catonis[que]** verborum ineruditissimum furem.

<small>Catonis "vet(eri) impr(esso)" (teste Statio), Bentley : Catonisque ω</small>

The subject of the sentence is Lenaeus, freedman of Pompey and staunch defender of his memory. Explaining his acceptance of the archetype's *priscorum Catonisque verborum,* Robinson wrote (ed., p. 23): "*Priscorum* substantive capio, quod etiam in c. 10, 1, fieri possit." It is not clear whether Robinson took *priscorum* as a substantive dependent on *verborum,* parallel with *Catonis* ("thief of the words *of the ancients* and of Cato"), or (as in some older editions) as a substantive dependent on *furem,* parallel with *verborum* ("thief *of the ancients* and of the words of Cato"); his reference to 10. 1 (= 10. 2 in my text) suggests the former.[104] It hardly matters, however: though Robinson's view (tacitly assumed by subsequent editors) is possible, at least in principle--for *prisci* can of course be used substantively--that use is in fact much less common than it is in the case of *maiores, antiqui,* and *veteres*;[105] and it is most unlikely to be present here.

First, Robinson was certainly mistaken to seek support in 10. 2, where a similar criticism of Sallust (by Asinius Pollio) is at issue: "Sallusti scripta reprehendit ut nimia priscorum verborum adfectatione oblita." That *priscorum* here is a substantive dependent on *verborum* (i.e., *priscorum verba*) is not only improbable in itself but is shown to be false when Suetonius returns to the subject later in the same chapter and refers to Pollio's criticism with the phrase *antiqua . . . verba* ("quo magis miror Asinium credidisse antiqua eum verba et figuras solitum esse colligere Sallustio").

---

[104] That one could retain *Catonisque* while yet regarding *priscorum* as an adjective here--". . . of ancient [words] and of Cato's words"--seems to me inconceivable, *pace* W. D. Lebek, *Verba Prisca: Die Anfänge des Archaisierens in der lateinischen Beredsamkeit und Geschichtsschreibung* (Göttingen, 1970), p. 328 n. 83.

[105] Since Suetonius is quoting or paraphrasing Lenaeus here, his own usage does not carry the weight it ordinarily would; but it is worth noting that he uses *priscus* infrequently (four times only), and only as an adjective (*Aug.* 43. 2 *prisci decorisque moris, Ner.* 38. 2 *domus priscorum ducum, Tit.* 5. 3 *de more . . . rituque priscae religionis;* on *DGR* 10. 2, see following), in contrast to his use of *antiqui* four times as a substantive, and *maiores* fifteen times.

Furthermore, it is not clear where one *could* find support for Robinson's view, since it must be doubted that any Roman would write *priscorum verba* instead of *prisca verba*--for that is the phrase regularly used when "archaic" or "old-fashioned" language is at issue.[106] I have found no instance of *priscorum verba* (vel sim.) used in such a context; it surely rests with those who would accept the transmitted text to show that a Latin author would write in such an odd way.

We should read *priscorum Catonis verborum* ("Cato's archaic diction"), with the correction attributed to an "old printed edition" by Statius and conjectured independently by Bentley. Sallust's debt to Cato, specifically, is still evident, despite the fragmentary state of Cato's historical and oratorical works; that debt struck the ancients, too, as one of the most salient features of Sallust's style, and was singled out for praise or blame: compare especially the anonymous couplet quoted by Quintilian (*Inst.* 8. 3. 29), "et verba antiqui multum furate Catonis, / Crispe, Iugurthinae conditor historiae."[107] It is unlikely that this distich is Lenaeus' own, as has sometimes been thought: Suetonius apparently had Lenaeus' text at hand, and he calls it a *satura*, a term he elsewhere uses to refer to poetry in dactylic hexameters.[108] Clearly, though, the lines make the same criticism.

As for the genesis of the error, we need only consider that in the course of the eight words immediately preceding our phrase, the scribe twice had occasion to write *-que* linking paired nouns ("nebulonem popinonem*que* appellans, et vita scriptis*que* monstrosum, praeterea . . ."). He was therefore prepared to see in *priscorum*

---

[106] See, e.g., Cic. *Dom.* 123, *Balb.* 36, *Brut.* 83, *Or.* 202, Sen. *Epist.* 108. 35, Tac. *Ann.* 4. 19, Fronto *ad M. Ant.* 4. 7 (p. 145. 2 v. d. Hout), and the *liber de verbis priscis* of L. Cincius (*GRF* 1:372-74); on the subject, see Lebek, *Verba Prisca*, esp. pp. 23ff.

[107] See also Suet. *Aug.* 86. 3, and cf. (in a favorable judgment) Fronto *ad M. Caes.* 4. 3. 2 (p. 56. 25f. v. d. H.), with Lebek, ibid., pp. 316ff.

[108] See 2. 2 *Lucili saturas*, and 5. 1 *fecit . . . saturam* (on Sevius Nicanor, followed by quotation of the two hexameters discussed above). Lucilius, it is true, composed in other meters, including elegiacs (in Books 22-25); but like Horace (or because of Horace), Suetonius would surely have thought of him primarily as a writer of hexameter *satura*.

Catonis yet another pair, and he accordingly produced the expected *-que*.[109]

15.3 traditur autem puer adhuc **catenis subreptis** refugisse in patriam perceptisque liberalibus disciplinis pretium suum domino rettulisse, verum ob ingenium atque doctrinam gratis manumissus.

 catenis ω (cath- **BDMQT**, Kathenas **K**) : Athenis *Heinsius* (*teste Graevio*) subreptis] surreptis **XL²** : surreptus **Y** (-rectus α)

The story concerning Lenaeus that Suetonius passes along (*traditur*) in this sentence is difficult to credit on any reading. (How many slaves, having made good their escape, later returned docilely, and despite the likelihood of dreadful punishment, to offer their master the price of their freedom?) But a strange tale is made still stranger by the two forms of the text commonly printed.

 Earlier editors (Baumgarten-Crusius, Roth, Reifferscheid, Rolfe) regularly preferred a version with Heinsius' conjecture *Athenis*, a version that (by implication, at least) compounds Lenaeus' adventures: he did not simply slip his chains and return to his homeland; rather (in Rolfe's translation) "he was stolen from Athens [*Athenis subreptus*], made his escape [sc. from his kidnappers] and returned to his native land"--kidnapping, escape from his kidnappers, and only then flight *in patriam*. But beyond the objection that Lenaeus has no known connection with Athens (so Robinson, ed., p. 24), there is the fact that this version requires three distinct verbal ideas to be expressed by only two verb-forms: the phrase *refugisse in patriam* cannot mean what it seems to mean--that Lenaeus simply fled from slavery back to his homeland--but must work double-time (as in Rolfe's version), to indicate both his escape from the alleged kidnappers (who prudently remain invisible) and his return home.[110] To accept this

---

[109] It is possible to imagine other forms of corruption here: e.g., Lebek, *Verba Prisca*, p. 328 n. 83, suggested a lacuna, "praeterea <pravissimum imitatorem> priscorum Catonisque verborum ineruditissimum furem." But in the context the solution given here seems preferable.

[110] Cf. Robinson, ed., p. 24: "Nonne . . . hoc obscurat, si verba *subreptus* et *refugisse* non ad unam atque eandem rem, scilicet ad fugam Lenaei, pertinere intelligimus, sed ad duas diversas res, capturam eius et fugam?"

version, then, we would have to suppose that Suetonius discreetly left much of the thrilling detail to his reader's imagination.

Though I cannot believe this version is correct, it at least gives *subreptus* its proper value, something that cannot be said for the version, with *catenis subreptus*, that has been printed since Robinson. The latter did not make clear what he took the phrase to mean:[111] presumably, that Lenaeus "escaped"--that is, "removed himself / stole away from his chains" (cf. della Corte's translation, "sfuggito alla prigionia").[112] That, however, is a meaning the phrase cannot have. *subripere* has the sense "remove oneself stealthfully / steal away" only with the reflexive pronoun (see OLD s.v. 2.c, citing examples only from Plautus). *subreptus* must mean "removed stealthfully / stolen" sc. by the agency of another: *puer . . . subreptus* should in fact suggest "kidnapped" (thus the classification of this passage in OLD s.v. 1.c, and cf. above on Heinsius' conjecture); note especially that a *servus subreptus* was not a "runaway slave" (= *fugitivus*) but a slave that had been "stolen" (cf. the distinction at *Dig.* 15. 1. 48 *neque in fugitivo neque in subrepto*, with *servus subreptus* vel sim. in the following sections of *Dig.* 47. 2 *de furtis*: 14. 7; 46. 1, 5; 48. 5; 52. 28; 81 pr., 2; 83. 2). But if we understand *catenis subreptus* in the correct sense, we see that it goes rather oddly with *refugisse*: for while the former phrase connotes the agency of another ("while still a boy he was stolen / kidnapped" sc. by someone else), the latter verb connotes an action performed on his own initiative ("he ran away"). We are then faced with an inconcinnity similar to that produced by *Athenis subreptus*.

We should therefore read *catenis subreptis*, with X:[113] the two infinitive constructions dependent on *traditur* are then completely

---

[111] He did note (ibid.) "locutionem *catenis subripere* nusquam repperi"--with good reason, since the correct Latin phrase would be *catenas subripere* or *se (e) catenis subripere*; see following.

[112] Similarly, Christes, *Sklaven*, p. 57 n. 395, attributes to the participle a "middle" sense, referring to Cic. 2 *Verr.* 4. 10; but no form of *subripere* occurs in that passage, and the participle is used exclusively in the passive sense both by Suetonius himself elsewhere (*Tib.* 60. 1 *militem . . . ob subreptum . . . pavonem capite puniit*) and by all prose authors before him.

[113] The ablative also appears as a (later) correction by Pontano in L; on L² = Pontano, see Chap. 1, n. 36.

parallel, with an ablative absolute--*catenis subreptis . . . perceptisque liberalibus disciplinis*--introducing each and denoting the prelude ("his chains having been stealthfully removed . . . his lessons in the liberal arts having been learned") to each of the main actions, *refugisse . . . rettulisse*. Since it was one of Robinson's great contributions to have recognized the value of **X**, it is curious that he seems to have ignored its reading here (cf. above on 10. 2 *praetextatis nobis*); perhaps he believed that it was merely a casual error, *-tus* > *-tis* after *catenis*. But the error in **Y** is no more difficult, given the preceding *puer* and Suetonius' great fondness for placing a nominative participial phrase at the head of a clause; and we should remember that the confusion at word-end between -if and the ligature ư (= *-us*) could run both ways.[114]

16.3 primus [sc. Caecilius Epirota] dicitur Latine ex tempore disputasse, primusque Vergilium et alios poetas novos praelegere coepisse; quod etiam Domiti Marsi **versiculus indicat**: "**Epirota**, tenellorum nutricula vatum."

> versiculus indicat **XVL¹Γ** : versiculis indicat **BLQ** : versiculis indicatur *Robinson* (*item Brugnoli: quorum alter post* indicatur, *alter post* vatum *lacunam statuit*)   Epirota **ζ** : et Epirota **ω** (*Robinson*)

The archetype read *versiculus indicat et Epirota*, corrected by **ζ**, with the deletion of *et*, to the reading printed above; **BL** (and **Q**, contaminated from **L** or its exemplar) had the nonsensical reading *versiculis indicat*. Combining the latter ("dubito an hoc sorti attribui possit") with the archetype's *et*, Robinson came to the following conclusion (diss., p. 129):

---

[114] In the second ablative absolute the MSS are divided between *perceptis* (**ONV**) and *praeceptis* (**WB Γ**). The latter was preferred by Oudendorp (more recently by T. Wiedemann, rev. of Christes, *Sklaven*, CR 32 [1982]: 75), on the ground that we should expect some expression to show how Lenaeus came by the *pretium* (cf. Wiedemann: "Lenaeus *teaches* grammar as a runaway, and is thus in a position to buy himself free"). But since (acc. to the terms of the story) Lenaeus is *puer adhuc*, we equally expect some expression that tells of his education, the *sine qua non* of his later career (cf. 21. 1 "altiora studia percepit ac Maecenati pro grammatico muneri datus est"); and *praeceptis* would in any case not fully meet the need perceived by Oudendorp, since it would leave unclear whether the "lessons in the liberal arts were taught" *to* Lenaeus or *by* Lenaeus.

> Mihi quidem clarius luce apparet Suetonium non unum sed duos versiculos protulisse, quorum prior de Epitora [sic] Vergili interprete ageret, alter eiusdem in aliis poetis novis interpretandis studia memoraret. Prior autem versus delapsus est, vocula *te* [sic] quae olim duos versiculos iungebat tamquam pars alterius versus in textu permansit. Locum sic restituo:
> *quod etiam Domiti Marsi versiculis indicat<ur>:*
> < * * * >
> Et:
> *Epirota, tenellorum nutricula vatum.*

Brugnoli was persuaded by Wessner that *et* was merely the result of dittography before *Ep-*;[115] but he accepted Robinson's major premise, that a verse had fallen out in which Domitius Marsus mentioned Epirota's concern specifically with Vergil. He therefore retained *versiculis indicatur* and posited a lacuna after *vatum*.[116]

Robinson's premise, however, was mistaken. It is true, of course, that Suetonius often does cite verse as the source or basis of a statement; so, for example, 9. 6 "vixit [sc. Orbilius] prope ad centesimum aetatis annum, amissa iam pridem memoria, ut versiculus Bibaculi docet: 'Orbilius ubinam est, litterarum obivio?'"[117] But comparison of such a case with the present passage--"quod *etiam* Domiti Marsi versiculus indicat . . ."-- shows how the latter should be understood: ". . . a fact which a verse of Domitius Marsus *also* indicates. . . ." *etiam* makes all the difference: Suetonius is citing Marsus' line as something *in addition to*--corroborative of and subsidiary to--his preceding statement, not as the source or basis of that statement.[118] Suetonius happened to know--from what source, he does not specify--that Epirota was the first teacher to lecture on Vergil and the other

---

[115] Wessner, rev. of Robinson, ed., *PhW* 46 (1926): 1227. For confusion of *p* and *t*, cf. **X**'s *capulo* (for *Catulo*) at 3. 5; for the dittography, cf. the archetype's *nerenuntiatum* (for *renun-*) at 25. 2.

[116] See his app. crit. ad loc., pp. 20-21, with *Studi Suetoniani*, pp. 133-34.

[117] Whether Suetonius correctly *interpreted* Bibaculus' verse here--or that of Domitius Marsus at 16. 3--is a different question, which does not concern the *method* of citation that is our present concern. I discuss the problems of interpretation in my commentary ad locc.

[118] Cf. 4. 3 "sunt qui . . . existiment. . . . quorum opinionem Orbilius *etiam* exemplis confirmat. . . ."

poetae novi, just as he happened to know that Epirota *primus . . . Latine ex tempore disputasse*--a statement for which, again, no source is specified, even on Robinson's reconstruction; he also happened to know Marsus' verse, which (correctly or not) he took to indicate Epirota's concern with the *vates*, as Vergil and other *poetae novi* styled themselves. The connection was close enough for Suetonius, who therefore simply cited the latter as a supplement to the former. There is no reason to posit the loss of a verse in which Marsus specifically mentioned Epirota's *praelectio* of Vergil.

A similar failure to attend to the nuance of a similar conjunction--*quoque*, this time--has caused unnecessary difficulty in another passage:

23.7 sed maxime flagrabat [sc. Palaemon] libidinibus, **in mulieres** usque ad infamiam oris; dicto quoque non infaceto notatum ferunt cuiusdam qui eum in turba osculum sibi ingerentem quamquam refugiens devitare non posset: "vis tu," inquit, "magister, quotiens festinantem aliquem vides, abligurire?"

in mulieres *del. Reiff.*, in mares *Jernstedt*

Suetonius previously alluded to Palaemon's reputation for wide-ranging sexual vices (evidently including pederasty: 23. 2 ". . . principem locum inter grammaticos tenuit, quamquam infamis omnibus vitiis palamque et Tiberio et mox Claudio praedicantibus nemini minus institutionem puerorum vel iuvenum committendam"); he here caps the *vita* by treating the subject explicitly. The first clause notes that Palaemon's lusts, in the case of women, extended *usque ad infamiam oris*: the point of specifying *mulieres*, together with the latter phrase, is to make plain that he served as a *cunnilingus*, a sexual practice that was commonly considered degrading (see, e.g., *Priap.* 78, Martial 4. 43, 11. 47, 61, 12. 85, Juv. 9. 3-4, Auson. *Epigr.* 82, 86, 87; della Corte should not have attempted *infamiam <am>oris*). The anecdote that follows, on the other hand, concerns a witticism produced at Palaemon's expense by a *man*: the joke turns on a pun involving a colloquial and obscene sense of *festinare* ("to hurry" [sc. toward climax]), and appears in context to allude to Palaemon's predilection for *fellatio*.[119]

---

[119] On *festinare* see A. E. Housman, "Praefanda," *Hermes* 66 (1931): 412 = *Classical Papers*, 3:1183-84, with J. N. Adams, *The Latin Sexual Vocabulary*

Modern attention has focused on the different sexes of the partners in the two parts of the passage, distinguishing between what we would call heterosexual and homosexual acts, and so finding a discrepancy on the basis of that distinction: hence both Reifferscheid's desire to delete *in mulieres* and Jernstedt's conjecture, *in mares*.[120] But these attempts, and the distinction on which they are based, miss the point of the passage, which does not depend on the sex of the partner but focuses instead on the behavior of Palaemon himself--behavior that would have been regarded as shameful *irrespective of the partner's sex*: both the *cunnilingus* and the *fellator* were thought to be equally degraded; the implied point here is that Palaemon was *doubly* degraded, since he was thought to enjoy both roles (for such double duty as a sign of dissolute character see Lucian *Rhet. praecept.* 23 and esp. Auson. *Epigr.* 78; cf. also Martial 3. 88, 12. 59). Hence the force of *quoque*, which is the same as that of *etiam* in 16. 3, above: Suetonius notes that Palaemon was chiefly notorious for his lusts, *in mulieres usque ad infamiam oris,* and then goes on to add: "dicto *quoque* non infaceto notatum ferunt. . . ."--"They *also* say that he was stigmatized. . . ." The second statement, with the anecdote, is not meant to justify the first statement or to establish the basis for it (as the emendations of Reifferscheid and Jernstedt assume); the anecdote simply provides another detail that belongs under the rubric *libidines Palaemonis* and that Suetonius here adds as a supplement to the first, just as at 16. 3 he adds the verse of Domitius Marsus (marked as a supplement by *etiam*) to elaborate the detail just reported (cf. *Tib.* 44-45 "maiore adhuc ac turpiore infamia flagravit, . . . quasi pueros . . . institueret ut natanti sibi inter femina versarentur ac luderent lingua. . . . feminarum *quoque* . . . capitibus quanto opere solitus sit inludere, evidentissime

---

(Baltimore, 1982), p. 144, and esp. W. D. Lebek, "Festinare (Suet. gramm. 23, 6; CIL IV, 4758; Hor. Epist. 1, 1, 85)," *ZPE* 45 (1982): 53-57; cf. also Brugnoli, *Studi Suetoniani*, pp. 123-24, and id., *Studi sulle "Differentiae verborum"* (Rome, 1955), p. 98 (n.). Attempts to emend *festinantem* have been too lamentable to mention; see Brugnoli's app. crit. ad loc., p. 26.

[120] The latter accepted by (*int. al.*) Mazzarino at *GRF* 2:71 (test. 8), Christes, *Sklaven*, p. 100 n. 76, tentatively approved by Brugnoli ("fort. recte") in his apparatus ad loc. Ernout's proposal, *in mulieres hominesque*, was similarly motivated (rev. of Robinson's ed., *REL* 4 [1926]: 270), though as Brugnoli points out, *homines* would not serve the intended purpose.

apparuit Malloniae cuiusdam exitu . . .": again, two categories of sexual *infamia* are at issue, the first here concerned with males of various ages, the second with females, the two joined with *quoque*). In this case Robinson got the nuance exactly right (ed., p. 33): "Haud recte haec verba delere voluit Reifferscheid, cum ea quae postmodo narrantur solum ad verba *usque ad infamiam oris* spectent." The phrase *usque ad infamiam oris* is the peg on which Suetonius hangs the related (if not quite identical) detail, with *quoque* as the connective.

If further proof is wanted, consider 4.1, where we see Suetonius using *quoque* in exactly the same way:

> appellatio grammaticorum Graeca consuetudine invaluit, sed initio litterati vocabantur; Cornelius *quoque* Nepos . . . litteratos vulgo quidem appellari ait eos qui aliquid diligenter et acute scienterque possint aut dicere aut scribere, ceterum proprie sic appellandos poetarum interpretes, qui a Graecis grammatici nominentur.

The two parts of the passage concern the same general topic--the relation between the terms *grammaticus* and *litteratus*--just as the two parts of 23. 7 concern the same general topic (Palemon's *libidines*, esp. his alleged predilection for oral sex). At the same time, however, the two parts of the passage are concerned with different aspects of the relation (or with the relation approached from different angles), just as (again) the two parts of 23. 7 concern different kinds of oral sex: in the first pair of clauses, Suetonius makes a point that is essentially diachronic, regarding the historical development of the terminology (i.e., *initio . . . vocabantur > appellatio . . . Graeca . . . invaluit*), whereas the citation from Nepos approaches the matter synchronically, to make a prescriptive distinction between "vulgar" and "correct" usage, what is commonly said vs. what ought to be said (*vulgo . . . appellari* vs. *proprie . . . appellandos*). The citation from Nepos plainly does not provide the basis for Suetonius' first statement but supplements it; the relation between the two parts of the passage is the same as that in 23. 7, and the relation is articulated in the same way: "X is the case; someone also says Y." The soundness of the text at 4. 1 has of course never been questioned, even though the "discrepancy" between its two parts is at least as great as that at 23. 7.

In all three passages examined above--16. 3 (with *etiam*), 23. 7 and 4. 1 (with *quoque*)--one might fault Suetonius for applying slack criteria of relevance in citing the supplementary matter, or for failing to make quite clear what connection he thought existed between the details being marshalled (though before finding fault, latter day *homines scholastici* should ask how often they themselves have written "cf. also . . ." where the relevance was not clear or the connection not precise). But fault Suetonius or not, in none of these cases should we suspect the text.

21.4 atque, ut ipse [viz., C. Melissus] tradit, sexagesimum aetatis annum agens libellos "Ineptiarum," qui nunc "Iocorum" **inscribuntur**, componere instituit absolvitque centum et quinquaginta. . . .

inscribuntur **GLU** : scribuntur ω

As Suetonius knew from internal evidence ("ut ipse tradit," presumably in a preface), the books that in his own day bore the title *Ioci* ("qui nunc *Iocorum* inscribuntur") were called by their author *Ineptiae*: such is the meaning of the sentence with the correction *inscribuntur* found in **GL**(= Pontano)**U**, in place of the archetype's *scribuntur*; for Suetonius' use of internal evidence in a similar case, cf. 6. 3, on Aurelius Opillus ("huius cognomen in plerisque indicibus et titulis per unam <L> litteram scriptum animadverto, verum ipse id per duas effert in parastichide libelli qui inscribitur *Pinax*"). As in the latter case, so here Suetonius' observation shows that he had firsthand knowledge of the books he mentions: for the implications regarding Melissus, see the discussion of 3. 5 *Gaius Melissus*, above.

Inscribuntur is accepted by all editors save Robinson and Brugnoli. The former retained *scribuntur* because he believed, mistakenly, that it could have the meaning *inscribuntur*.[121] Brugnoli preferred *scribuntur* in the belief that "hoc loco Suetonium non alteram intitulationem Melissiani libelli nobis proferre velle sed suae aetatis auctorum" (app. crit. ad loc., p. 23, cf. *Studi Suetoniani*, pp. 121-22): that is, the *Ineptiae* written by Melissus were the same *type* of composition as the books written in his own day

---

[121] Cf. above on 6. 2 *inscripsisse*, with Robinson, diss., p. 111 n. 65. In his note on the present passage (ed., p. 29) Robinson refers to his diss. but adds: "Hoc loco fortasse non valet [sc. *scribuntur*] idem quod *inscribuntur*, sed pro *vocantur* positum est."

under the title *Ioci*.[122] If that is what Suetonius meant to say, however, he chose an extraordinarily compressed and obscure way of saying it (I can find him writing thus nowhere else, nor does Brugnoli offer any parallels): other considerations aside, there is the fact that Brugnoli's text--"libellos *Ineptiarum* qui nunc *Iocorum* scribuntur componere instituit," with specific antecedent followed by *qui* + indicative--is hardly normal Latin for the kind of *generic* relative clause Brugnoli has in mind ("books . . . *of the sort that / such as* now are written . . ."), for which one expects either *quales* + indicative or *qui* + subjunctive ("wo . . . der Adjektivsatz . . . eine nähere Bestimmung eines Gegenstandes nach seinem Wesen angeben soll," Kühner-Stegmann 2.2:291 [sec. 194.1]).

22.1 M. Pomponius **Porcellus**, sermonis Latini exactor molestissimus . . .

Porcellus *scripsi* : Marcellus ω (*an recte, lapsu Suet.?*)

Thus Suetonius introduces his entry for this "extraordinarily bothersome overseer of the Latin language": the man's name appears only at the head of the chapter, whence it was included in the index at the start of the work. The cognomen presents a problem; the relevant data are as follows.

(1) Suetonius' entry consists of two anecdotes and an epigram (the epigram, attributed to Asinius Gallus, does not tell us anything that bears upon the present discussion). The first anecdote is set in a courtroom, where the grammarian, appearing as an advocate, exasperates the noted orator Cassius Severus by harping on a solecism that the latter has supposedly committed ("in advocatione quadam . . . soloecismum ab adversario factum usque adeo arguere perseveravit quoad Cassius Severus . . . dilationem petit . . ."). In the second anecdote, the grammarian reproves an error in Tiberius' diction, remarking that the emperor "can give citizenship to men, but not to words" (on the text of this anecdote, see the following discussion). The two anecdotes combine to place the grammarian's *floruit* in the latter part of Augustus' reign (before the exile of Cassius Severus in A.D. 8 or

---

[122] Cf. *Studi Suetoniani*, p. 122, ". . . opere del genere di quella di Melisso. . . ." Brugnoli is followed by E. Bower, "*Ineptiae* and *Ioci*," *Latomus* 33 (1974): 528, who also believed that Melissus' 150 *libelli* consisted of light verse; see rather above, on 3. 5 *Gaius Melissus*.

12) and the early part of Tiberius' (before the death in A.D. 22 of Ateius Capito, another participant in the second story; cf. also below). This dating is in turn consistent with the epigram attributed to Asinius Gallus (41 B.C.-A.D. 33).

(2) The second of Suetonius' stories is also told by Cassius Dio (57. 17. 1-3), who sets it in A.D. 17: the criticism of Tiberius is presented in precisely the same terms; but both witnesses to Dio's text--cod. M and the epitome of Xiphilinus--call the critic Πόρκελλός τις, without nomen and with the relatively uncommon cognomen Porcellus.[123] Xylander's emendation, Μάρκελλός τις, was adopted by Boissevain, to bring Dio's text into conformity with Suetonius'.[124]

(3) At *Suasoriae* 2. 12-13 the elder Seneca recalls, and rightly deplores, the vexatious pedantry of a grammarian named Porcellus, who used to claim that the Augustan poet Cornelius Severus had committed a solecism when he wrote "stratique [sc. milites] per herbam / 'hic meus est' dixere 'dies'" (*FPL* frag. 11, p. 150 B.), because the 1st pers. sing. possessive *meus* responds incorrectly to the plurality of *milites* who are speaking ("illud Porcellus grammaticus arguebat in hoc versu quasi soloecismum quod, cum plures induxisset, diceret 'hic meus est dies,' non 'hic noster est,' et in sententia optima id accusabat quod erat optimum," with further acerbic comment on the *grammaticorum calumnia*). The date of Severus and the reminiscence of Seneca combine to show that Porcellus was active at the same time as the grammarian sketched by Suetonius; he is not otherwise attested, unless he is the "Procellus" cited in the *Verborum differentiae* of pseudo-Palaemon.[125]

---

[123] Kajanto, *Latin Cognomina*, p. 328, counted seven instances in *CIL*, plus one Porcella; Marcellus, by contrast, is among the most common cognomina, with 460 instances in *CIL*, plus another 324 Marcellae (ibid., p. 173).

[124] Boissevain notes, ad loc., "Πο⟨μπ⟩ώνιος Μά⟨ρ⟩κελλός τις ne scribamus vetat τις quod sequitur": i.e., when Dio uses τις with nomen and cognomen, it either precedes them both--thus τινος 'Ατείου Καπίτωνος in the same passage--or stands between the nomen and cognomen, e.g., 59. 8. 3 'Ατάνιός τε τις Σεκοῦνδος, 60. 23. 3 Οὐαλερίου τινὸς Λίγυος.

[125] P. 310. 28-31 in Roth's ed. of Suetonius = Brugnoli, *Studi sulle "Differentiae,"* p. 103: "Tribunal an tribunale et animal an animale: Porcellus [*Roth* : Procellus *cod. Montepess. H. 30. b*] ait: 'quae l littera finiuntur in declinatione, geminant eandem litteram, tamquam mel

Faced with these data, Antonio Mazzarino drew two conclusions: only one grammarian is concerned in all three texts; and Seneca, like Dio, should be emended to conform to Suetonius--hence his proposal *Po<mponius Ma>rcellus* (*GRF* 2:24).[126] Now the latter conclusion is surely unacceptable, since it not only requires us to believe that precisely the same error, replacing the common name Marcellus with the uncommon Porcellus, chanced to arise independently in both Seneca and Dio,[127] but it also assumes that the *auctoritas* of Suetonius' MSS should be given absolute priority in this matter--an assumption that most readers of these pages will find very doubtful. Mazzarino's first conclusion, on the other hand, is just as surely correct. If Seneca's Porcellus is not to be regarded as the same man as Suetonius' grammarian, it must follow that the latter had a contemporary whose one recorded activity--an extremely pedantic form of solecism-hunting--just happens to match precisely the behavior reported in Suetonius' first anecdote, *and* whose uncommon name just happens to match precisely the name transmitted in the passage of Dio that corresponds to Suetonius' second anecdote. Furthermore, if the grammarian of Seneca is distinct from the grammarian of Suetonius, we must also assume either that the confrontation with Tiberius actually involved the former but was mistakenly attributed to the latter by Suetonius, or that the latter was somehow confused with the former by Dio--for that Dio himself *wrote* Πόρκελλός τις should now be very difficult to doubt.

The only probable conclusion here is also the simplest: there is only one grammarian, and the error concerning his name occurs in Suetonius alone, where *Porcellus* has been replaced by the vastly more common cognomen *Marcellus*, after the praenomen

---

mellis et fel fellis, facit ita tribunal tribunallis et animal animallis.' sed erravit. . . ." Roth's emendation (ed., p. xcvii) was accepted by Brugnoli but rejected by Funaioli, *GRF* 1:508.

[126] Approved in principle by H. Dahlmann, who preferred the correction *Marcellus*: *Cornelius Severus*, Abh. d. Akad. d. Wissen. und d. Lit. (Mainz), Geistes- und sozialwiss. Kl., Jahrg. 1975, nr. 6 (Mainz, 1975), pp. 60-61.

[127] An objection already made by Brugnoli, *Studi sulle "Differentiae,"* p. 103 n. 4, though his remarks on the state of Dio's text are, unfortunately, confused.

Marcus. (Note that for the genesis of the error it would not much matter whether the praenomen here was spelled out or abbreviated, for someone reading or copying *M.* would tend to say or think "Marcus," just as we do.) I therefore intend to print *Porcellus*, on the assumption that the error occurred in the course of transmission. I would not be at all surprised, however, if the slip in this case was Suetonius' own: it may be relevant that the first "Pomponius Marcellus" of whom we are securely informed was Suetonius' contemporary, Q. Pomponius Marcellus (*PIR* P.552), who became suffect consul in April 121, when Suetonius was nearing the end of his time in Hadrian's service.

22.2 hic idem [sc. Pomponius] cum ex oratione Tiberi verbum reprehendisset, adfirmante Ateio Capitone et esse illud Latinum et si non esset futurum certe iam inde, "mentitur," inquit, "Capito: tu enim, Caesar, civitatem dare potes hominibus, **verbis** non potes."

> Tiberi verbum *Madvig* : Tiberius verbum X, Tiberium Y
> verbis *Faernus (teste Statio)* : verba ω, verbo H

The incident obviously enjoyed a certain renown: Cassius Dio recounts it in detail, quoting the grammarian in a form nearly identical to that found here (57. 17. 3, see below); and Pomponius' trope--the conceit of "giving citizenship" to words--reappears in Seneca and Gellius (Sen. *Ep.* 120. 4 "hoc verbum cum Latini grammatici civitate donaverint . . .," sim. *NQ* 5. 16. 4; Gell. *NA* 19. 13. 3 "verbum hoc a te civitate donatum aut in Latinam coloniam deductum"). As virtually all editors agree, the archetype's *verba* must be corrupt:[128] the choice lies between two conjectures, H's *verbo* (adopted by editors since Osann) and Faernus' *verbis* (the vulgate before Osann).

Either one could be right: if *verbo*, the error should be understood to be primarily paleographical (merely *-o* > *-a*); if *verbis*, the corruption must be understood to be primarily psychological / interpretive (dat. pl. *verbis* > acc. pl. *verba* because of the apparent parallel with *civitatem*). The former is somewhat easier,

---

[128] The only recent exception is della Corte, who prints *verba* and takes the phrase to mean "imporre . . . un vocabulo"; but this ignores both the other evidence for Porcellus' *sententia* and the meaning of the idiom *verba dare* (= "deceive," "cheat," "fool").

no doubt--but only somewhat. The latter is made preferable both by the evidence of Dio ("σύ, Καῖσαρ, ἀνθρώποις μὲν πολιτείαν Ῥωμαίων δύνασι δοῦναι, ῥήμασι δὲ οὔ") and--more important-- by the demands of the context. Ateius Capito, whom Pomponius is contradicting, offered a defense of the particular word Tiberius had used (thus *illud*, which must look back specifically to *Tiberi verbum*, as Madvig saw): it was a good Latin word, Capito said, and if wasn't before, it certainly would be from then on. But in his rebuttal Pomponius went a step further, and produced a generalizing *sententia* concerning the emperor's authority--authority not over this word or that, but over words in general, as over men in general. Just as the generalization has *hominibus*, so too it seems to want *verbis*. These considerations would not, perhaps, weigh heavily enough to justify emending *verbo* if that were the transmitted reading; but since we know (as Osann did not) that both readings are conjectural, these considerations are enough to tip the scale.

23.4 nomen suum in "Bucolicis" non temere positum sed **praesagiente** Vergilio fore quandoque omnium poetarum ac poematum Palaemonem iudicem.

praesagiente UΔ (-gente C) : -gante ω

The 1st-conjugation form of the verb is not otherwise attested before Apuleius (*Met*. 9. 38 *praesagaverant*, *Apol*. 43 *praesagare*); Suetonius himself elsewhere uses the classical, 4th-conjugation form (*Aug*. 96. 1 *praesagiente*). If we wished to retain the archetype's *praesagante*, we would probably need to assume that the form was used by Remmius Palaemon, whose boast Suetonius is reporting here in indirect discourse: so Robinson (diss., p. 165 n. 293), followed by subsequent editors. This is conceivably correct. Yet there is no particular reason to think that Palaemon used what apparently occurs in Apuleius as one of his colloquial forms (there is no evidence to suggest it was one of his archaic revivals): note especially that the participial forms *praesagans* and *praesagatus* (sim. *praesagator*) occur subsequently in Jerome and Cassiodorus, and then in later medieval texts (citations in Forcellini, 3:826; Du Cange, 4:467; Arnaldi, 2:562). To a medieval copyist, then, the participle *praesagante* may well have been the expected form, *praesagiente* the *vox inusitatior*, vulnerable to alteration. Though the question *utrum in alterum abiturum erat* does not admit of a sure answer here, I find the latter alternative more likely and so intend to print *praesagiente*.

23.4 gloriabatur etiam latrones quondam sibi propter nominis celebritatem **pepercisse**.

> pepercisse **OLUS** (percisse **W**) : parcisse **Y** : parsisse **V¹DHΔ**, *edd. nonnulli*

The boaster, again, is Remmius Palaemon. Reifferscheid and Roth read *parsisse*; Robinson chose *pepercisse* and gave the correct explanation for the variants in the MSS (diss., p. 82). There the matter could rest, were it not for the fact that in reviving *parsisse*, Brugnoli misunderstood Robinson's argument (app. crit. ad loc., p. 25, sim. *Studi Suetoniani*, p. 122): "Ihm et Robinson . . . codicum lectionem <pe>per-cisse fuisse iudicaverunt ex eo quod perfectum 'parsi' nusquam adhibuisset Suetonius: at verba sunt Palaemonis!" In other words, *parsisse* is to be defended in the same way that Robinson defended *praesagante* just above, as the form used by Palaemon, whose boast Suetonius is reporting. But this is to conduct the argument on the wrong ground. True, Robinson (citing Ihm) did note that Suetonius nowhere uses the form *parsi* for the perfect of *parco*; but (despite Brugnoli's "ex eo quod . . .") that was not the primary reason for his choice of *pepercisse*.[129] Rather, Robinson rightly observed that the MS variants point unmistakably to the presence of p̲cisse in the archetype (i.e., *pepercisse*, with the first syllable lost through haplography, the second represented by the compendium p̲): this was copied as *percisse* (or, conceivably, p̲cisse) in **X**, whence we find *percisse* in **W** and the correction *pepercisse* in **O**; but p̲cisse was copied as *parcisse* in **Y**, whose scribe took the compendium as = *par*, a value that it had in the 15th century, though not in the 9th.[130] The error *parcisse* then gave rise to the "correction" (or *Schlimmbesserung*: Wessner, rev.

---

[129] At *Studi Suetoniani*, p. 122, Brugnoli compounds his error by attempting to stigmatize *pepercisse* as "la lezione dei codici *deteriores*," though it occurs in **O**.

[130] Robinson, again correctly, compared 18. 2 *pergula*, where the correct reading occurs only as a conjecture in **Δ** and **ed. Ven.**: the archetype evidently had p̲cula (written thus in **OMH**), which gave rise to *parcula* in α V θ. Cf. also, e.g., 9. 1 *apparituram*, written as ap̲pituram in **V**, ap̲pituram in **B**.

of Robinson's diss., *PhW* 43 [1923]: 540) *parsisse*, perhaps in Y itself: the form appears as a suprascript variant in V and in the text of three more of Y's descendants; other members of the family introduced *pepercisse* (L[= Pontano]US). *parsisse* thus has no standing as an inherited reading. Of course, one might claim that *parsisse* had been ousted by *pepercisse* earlier in the text's history; but that would plainly be gratuitous.

23.6 cuius [sc. rei familiaris] diligentissimus erat, cum . . . agros adeo coleret ut vitem manu eius institutam satis constet **CCCLXV <dies quotannis> uvas** edidisse.

CCCLXV ω : CCCLX *Ursinus*   dies *suppl. Murgia, post quem* quotannis *addidi*   uvas *Ursinus* : vasa ω

Pliny, too, testifies to Palaemon's great success in viticulture (*HN* 14. 49-52), and he even specifies the vineyard's yield, in terms of *cullei* per *iugerum*, in the period after Palaemon sold the property to Seneca (ibid. 52, 7 *cullei / iug.*; cf. Col. 3. 3. 3, evidently referring to the same property as Seneca's possession and reporting a yield of 8 *cullei / iug.*, with n. 133 below). But it is plain that Suetonius' version of the story cannot be derived from Pliny's account: the vine-yield reported here corresponds to nothing in the latter, whatever reading one adopts (see below); moreover, Suetonius' version has as its premise Palaemon's earnest, hands-on involvement ("agros adeo coleret ut vitem manu eius institutam . . .," cf. *diligentissimus* preceding), whereas Pliny repeatedly stresses that the success was due to Palaemon's agent, the freedman Acilius Sthenelus (ibid. 49 *Stheneli opera*, 50 *cura Stheneli*), while Palaemon's role was that of a trifling dilettante (ibid. 50 "haec adgressus excolere non virtute animi sed vanitate primo, quae nota mire in illo fuit, . . . agricolam imitatur"). Suetonius, therefore, must have relied on an alternative version of Palaemon's success: how did that version report the productivity of the vine that Palaemon planted with his own hand?

The archetype's reading, *CCCLXV vasa*, will not do. It is no sort of description to say that a vine produced "365 vessels" (of must, i.e.), without specifying the unit of measure (cf. Robinson, ed., pp. 32-33). Nor can we simply to assume that the generic *vasa* is a gloss that has replaced some more specific term, for the liquid measures commonly used to express productivity in viticulture-- the *culleus, amphora,* and *urna*--all produce absurd results when substituted for *vasa* here: the remarks of Pliny (*HN* 14. 52) and Columella (3. 3. 3) suggest that a noteworthy yield would be 7-10 *cullei* per *iugerum* (= 140-200 *amphorae* = 280-400 *urnae* = ca. 3,620-5,170 liters),[131] and Varro reports that yields of as many as 15 *cullei* per *iugerum* (= 300 *amphorae* = 600 *urnae* = ca. 7,750 liters) were known (*R.R.* 1. 2. 7);[132] but such figures represent the combined production of *hundreds* of vines, not the yield of a single *vitis*.[133] Even if one chooses a smaller unit of measure--the *congius* (= 1/4 *urna*), the *sextarius* (= 1/6 *congius*), or the *hemina* (= 1/2 *sextarius*)--one does not emerge with plausible results (365 *congii* = 45.6 *amphorae*, 365 *sextarii* = 7.6 *amphorae*, 365 *heminae* = 3.8 *amphorae*); and in any case, these smaller units do not appear to have been used to measure vine-yield.

The solution commonly chosen is Ursinus' CCCLX *uvas* (i.e., CCCLX VVAS EDIDISSE > CCCLX VVAS AEDIDISSE > CCCLXV VASA EDIDISSE); and Columella does at one point report the yield of a single vine in terms of *uvae* (3. 3. 3, see below). But this emendation produces a sense ("360 bunches of grapes") that is only apparently acceptable. Robinson printed the correction with great reservation, noting "numeros . . . *ccclx* corruptissimos esse valde suspicor" (ed., p. 33); Bione and Brugnoli put CCCLX *uvas* in their texts but placed an obelus before the number, evidently to indicate that though they thought *uvas* correct, "numerus ille CCCLX corruptissimus videatur, longe certe minor quam qui non ridicule a Suetonio memoria dignus

---

[131] For the conversion to liters, cf. R. P. Duncan-Jones, *Economy of the Roman Empire: Quantitative Studies*² (Cambridge, 1982), p. 372.

[132] Columella 3. 3. 11 indicates that a minimally acceptable yield would be 3 *cullei* (= 60 *amphorae*) per *iugerum*: if the yield falls below that, *exstirpanda vineta censemus*.

[133] Thus Christes' remarked (*Sklaven*, p. 101 n. 84) that the transmitted text is intelligible only if *vitis* is taken as = *vinea*, *vas* as = *amphora*; but the latter detail is not quite correct. In fact, a conventionally realistic text can be obtained only if one accepts Ursinus' CCCLX (for CCCLXV), inserts *iugeratim* (vel sim.), *and* rejects both *vitem* in favor of *vineam* and *vasa* in favor of *urnas*--"*vineam* manu eius institutam . . . CCCLX urnas <*iugeratim*> edidisse" (360 *urnae* / *iug.* = 180 *amphorae* / *iug.* = 9 *cullei* / *iug.*); but even a rewriting on this scale produces a text that agrees with neither of the other reports of the same property's yield, Col. 3. 3. 3 (8 *cullei* / *iug.*) and Plin. *HN* 14. 52 (7 *cullei* / *iug.*).

existimari possit" (Brugnoli, app. crit. ad loc., p. 26). It is difficult not to agree with the last point, given that Columella--when he does report outstanding production in terms of *uvae*--is speaking of a vine that produced *over 2,000* bunches of grapes (3. 3. 3 "aliqua vitis . . . excederet uvarum numerum duorum milium"). Granted, many factors could affect the yield of a vine--e.g., its age and the length to which it was allowed to grow, the type of pruning it received--so that it is difficult to say, in general, what would constitute remarkable productivity.[134] Granted, too, that Columella characterizes the yield he reports as virtually miraculous (*prodigialiter . . . accidisse*). Nonetheless, a number that is more than six times smaller simply seems too small.

I do believe that Ursinus' *uvas*, for *vasa*, points in the right direction. It does not necessarily follow, however, that the number is corrupt; rather, the fault may lie with the way in which we have tried to understand it. As C. E. Murgia has pointed out to me, it is remarkable that the transmitted number, *CCCLXV*, should be the same as the number of the days in the year according to the Julian calendar. Perhaps, then, the marvelous feature of this vine was not the absolute *quantity* of its production (measured in bunches of grapes, vel sim.) but the *duration* of its production: "the vine produced grapes for 365 days out of the year, that is, every day."

So Murgia, who adds that this would of course be "sheer fable"--but a fable not unsuited to the context. Suetonius' entire

---

[134] Palaemon's vineyard presumably took the form most common in Italy, the *arbustum*, a plantation of trees to which vines were married. According to Columella's prescriptions for this method (5. 6; cf. Pliny *HN* 17. 199-214), the tree should be left bare of branches to a height of 7 or 8 feet (depending on the quality of the soil), at which point the first "stage" should begin (ibid. 15-16), formed by 3 branches allowed to grow in even intervals around the circumference of the trunk, with the arms of the vines trained out onto the branches; a second stage should begin no less than 3 feet higher, with a similar arrangement of branches, and so on (Pliny, ibid. 201, suggests 20 feet as the maximum height for the tree). Obviously, the yield of a given vine would largely depend on the number of stages, a matter (Columella suggests, ibid. 24) that involved a trade-off between quality and quantity: whereas most growers crowded the lower stages, *uberiorem fructum et magis facilem cultum sequentes*, Columella recommends that those *qui bonitati vini student* should extend the vine in stages all the way to the top of the tree. Palaemon seems to have been among those *uberiorem fructum . . . sequentes*.

account of Palaemon is to a large extent a compound of the vivid gossip that surrounded this controversial figure (cf. *ut ferunt* and *ferunt* framing the chapter) and the wild self-congratulation to which Palaemon's arrogance supposedly led ("arrogantia fuit tanta ut . . . secum et natas et morituras litteras iactaret . . .," with the other boasts recorded in the two passages discussed immediately above): the present report may simply have originated as a gossipy (or boastful) exaggeration of the viticultural success that Pliny reports more prosaically. Note, in particular, that the *locus classicus* for fruit trees and vines that flower and bear constantly throughout the year is *Od.* 7. 112-32, the description of Alcinous' miraculous garden: the claim that Suetonius here retails as sober fact (*ut . . . constet*) may well have begun as an appropriately literary witticism about (or by) the highly successful *grammaticus*-viticulturist, who thus was assimilated to (or assimilated himself to) the fabulous Phaeacian king. In fact, as Pliny informs us, not only did gossip attend Palaemon's success, but that gossip specifically concerned Palaemon's status as a scholar: though Pliny himself gives the credit to Palaemon's agent, Sthenelus, he reports that the neighborhood folk, finding their own sluggishness put to shame, defended themselves by attributing Palaemon's success to his "higher learning" (ibid. 51 "litteris eius altioribus contra id pigra vicinitate sibi patrocinante"). It is to the echoes of such talk that we should probably attribute the origin of Suetonius' version.

However the story may have got its start, understanding the passage in this way cuts the knot: read CCCLXV <dies quotannis> uvas. Murgia suggested *dies* (i.e., CCCLXV D. VVAS EDIDISSE > CCCLX VASA EDIDISSE); I would prefer to add *quotannis*, which seems desirable in point of sense ("for 365 days every year": Suetonius uses *quotannis* 15 times in the *Caesares*, e.g., *Claud*. 1. 3 "circa quem [sc. tumulum] deinceps stato die quotannis miles decurreret"; in this case the same leap of the scribe's eye from *V* to *V* would have been abetted by the clustering of ascending and descending strokes in *quotANNIS* before *VVAS*). That the archetype was plagued with omissions emerges most obviously in those places where Suetonius' quotations from Cicero can be compared with the extant works (cf. n. 4 above); but see also the discussions of 9. 5 *Varrone* <*Murena*> above, 24. 2 *legerat* <*enim*> and 28. 1 <*Servili*> *Isaurici* . . . *consularis Isaurici* below.

24.1 M. Valerius Probus, Berytius, diu centuriatum petit, donec taedio ad studia se contulit. (2) legerat <enim> in provincia quosdam veteres libellos apud grammatistam, durante adhuc ibi antiquorum memoria necdum omnino abolita sicut Romae.

<enim> *addidi* : *om.* ω

enim may appear to be an "unnecessary" conjecture; I wish to suggest the opposite. In both the biographical entries and the other chapters in the *DGR*, Suetonius regularly links his sentences, one to the next, by introducing each sentence with a conjunction, an inferential or adversative particle, a connective relative or demonstrative pronoun, an adverb marking a stage in a sequence, or some other continuative word. He omits such a link *only* when (but by no means always when) he is passing on to a new and clearly separate subject: so, e.g., at the end of this chapter, after reviewing the course of Probus' career and the nature of his teaching, Suetonius concludes with a few brief remarks on a different matter, his written scholarship--simply, "nimis pauca et exigua . . ."; similarly, at the end of the chapter on Orbilius (9. 6), he concludes by noting a few miscellaneous facts about the man--that he lived a long time, that there was a statue of him at Beneventum, that he left a son--each in a sentence unconnected with the preceding ("vixit prope ad centesimum aetatis annum. . . . statua eius Beneventi ostenditur. . . . reliquit filium Orbilium. . . .").[135]

In the sentences before us, however, Suetonius is not moving from one distinct topic to another, nor is he noting discrete, miscellaneous facts. He is dealing with a single subject, the course of Probus' career, from frustrated military aspirations to literary studies; more specifically, he is continuing and elaborating in the second sentence the key idea--Probus' *studia*--introduced in the first, by describing (*via* the pluperf. *legerat*) the experience that provided the crucial background to these *studia* (for the nuance of pluperf. *legerat* here, cf. the remarks at pp. 48f. above, on 3. 6 *nam*

---

[135] Cf. 17. 3, for a similar inventory at the end of the entry on Verrius Flaccus: "decessit aetatis exactae sub Tiberio. statuam habet Praeneste. . . ." The other sentences begun without some linking word, all of the same sort, occur at: 4. 3 and 6, 5. 2, 7. 2 (*bis*) and 3, 10. 4, 11. 2 and 3, 13. 2, 20. 2, 22. 3, 23. 4 and 5, 25. 5 and 6; of course, each biographical entry begins with the subject's name, with no linking word.

... *penetraverat*). Unless we wish to decide, then, that Suetonius here chose, for no apparent reason, not to write like Suetonius, it is necessary to conclude that some connecting word has fallen out at the start of the second sentence: I suggest *enim*, which could easily have been lost through haplography before *in*.

24.2 hos cum diligentius **repetere** atque alios deinceps cognoscere cuperet, quamvis omnes contemni magisque opprobrio legentibus quam gloriae et fructui esse animadverteret, nihilo minus in proposito mansit multaque exemplaria contracta emendare ac distinguere et adnotare curavit, soli huic nec ulli praeterea grammaticae parti deditus.

repetere ω (recepere O) : repeteret Δ, **ed. Rom.,** *edd. plerique*

The subject is Valerius Probus' resumption of his studies, which he devoted to early and unfashionable authors (cf. above). *repeteret*, the reading of Δ and the editio Romana, has proved very popular with editors since Osann first promoted it to the text (p. 82: "*repeteret . . . quod ut vel sine codice reponatur sententia flagitat*"); though only Brugnoli prints the archetypal reading, *repetere*, it is more likely correct.

The sentence consists of four clauses--2 subordinate, 2 independent--which stand in a chiastic relation. *nihilo minus in proposito mansit* is motivated primarily by the preceding *quamvis*-clause (Probus' perseverance vs. the low esteem in which these texts were held), while *multaque exemplaria contracta . . .* responds to the introductory circumstantial clause:[136] it was when (or, because) Probus desired to resume and deepen (*diligentius repetere*) his study of these texts, and then extend his study to others, that he gathered together many copies, corrected and punctuated them, and provided them with critical *notae*.[137] Indeed, the phrasing "in *proposito* mansit" in the first independent

---

[136] Bione and della Corte punctuate with a semi-colon after *mansit*, which misses the structure of the sentence.

[137] The phrase *multa . . . exemplaria contracta* is of course controversial: I take it to mean that because Probus wished to study many authors, he acquired many books--not that he acquired many copies of each author, in the manner of a modern editor engaged in *recensio*. I discuss this matter in my commentary: in either case, the textual point at issue here is not altered.

clause itself looks to *cuperet* as the primary verbal idea of the *cum*-clause: all the steps Probus took were determined by his "purpose," i.e., his "desire." The reading *repeteret*, if not simply a mechanical error, is probably the faulty correction of a reader too impatient to allow *repetere* to receive its construction from *cuperet*.[138]

25.4 sed ratio docendi nec una omnibus nec singulis eadem semper fuit, quando vario modo quisque discipulos exercuerunt. nam et dicta praeclare per omnes figuras <**versare**> et apologos aliter atque aliter exponere et narrationes cum breviter ac presse tum latius et uberius explicare consuerant . . .

    versare *Haupt* (percurrere *iam Madvig*) : per casus ω

The passage concerns three school-exercises intended to develop flexibility and variety of expression; they are listed in ascending order of complexity, according to the material of each, from individual sentences through brief fables (*apologi*) to more extensive mythological *narrationes*. The first and simplest exercise is the *chria*, in which a student was presented with a notable saying (*dictum praeclare*)--for example, "Marcus Porcius Cato dixit litterarum radices amaras esse, fructus iocundiores" (Diom. GL 1:310. 3-4)--and was supposed to rework it by stressing a different case-relationship in each successive version: first the nominative (just quoted), then the genitive ("Marci Porcii Catonis dictum fertur . . ."), then the dative ("Marco Porcio Catoni placuit dicere . . ."), and so on, through the singular and plural (more elaborate examples are also known). So Robinson (ed., p. 39), who appears to have been the first editor since F. A. Wolf to understand the basic structure and meaning of this sentence; previous editors regularly punctuated as though *apologos* were the object (with *casus*) of *per* (see below).[139] The exercise of the

---

[138] Δ's text in fact reads ". . . necdum omnino abolita. sicut Romae hos diligentius repeteret . . .," punctuating after *abolita* (with the rest of γ save C) and omitting *cum* after *hos*.

[139] On the *chria*, see Quint. *Inst*. 1. 9. 4-5, Theon *Progymn*. 5 (pp. 96. 19-106. 3 Stengel), Hermog. *Progymn*. 3 (pp. 5. 25-7. 10 St.) = Prisc. *Praeex*. 2. 8-10 (*RLM* pp. 552-53), with J. Cousin, *Etudes sur Quintilien*, vol. 1 (Paris, 1935), pp. 80-81, S. F. Bonner, *Education in Ancient Rome* (Berkeley, 1977),

chria is thus parallel to those involving the *apologus* and the *narratio*.

Madvig and Haupt saw what was wanted here, but no editor has been willing to provide it, presumably on the ground that emendation is "unnecessary"--that is, one can identify some sort of construable Latin sentence without it. But what sort?

Consider the text presented by the archetype:

nam
    et dicta praeclare per omnes figuras per casus
    et apologos aliter atque aliter   **exponere**
    et narrationes cum breviter ac presse
                              tum latius et uberius   **explicare**
consuerant. . . .

We have a sentence with the verb *consuerant* preceded by three parallel *membra*; the *membra* are articulated by *et . . . et . . . et . . .*; each *et* is followed by a noun in the accusative and an adverbial expression; the second and third *membra* both end with an infinitive. With what sort of word should the first *membrum* end? The answer is, obviously, an infinitive--because that is the only sort of word that should stand at that place in that sentence. This conviction can only be strengthened when we note that Suetonius goes on to list four more exercises after *consuerant*, all similarly described in parallel *membra*, each similarly concluded with an infinitive dependent on *consuerant* ("interdum Graecorum scripta *convertere* ac viros illustres *laudare vel vituperare*, quaedam . . . *ostendere*, saepe fabulis fidem *firmare aut demere*"). If we then see that in the first *membrum* there is no infinitive--only two a-syndetic and essentially synonymous prepositional phrases, one of which is superfluous--then the equally obvious conclusion is that one of the prepositional phrases is a gloss on the other and has ousted the infinitive that Suetonius wrote.

Emendation here is not "unnecessary," because without emendation the structure and meaning of the passage are seriously distorted: to assume that Suetonius meant "{*et dicta praeclare* per omnes figuras per casus *et apologos* aliter atque aliter *exponere*} et {narrationes . . . explicare}"--so, evidently, the editors, the only way the passage can be construed without emendation--is to

---

pp. 256-58, H. Lausberg, *Handbuch der literarischen Rhetorik*[3] (Stuttgart, 1990), pp. 536-40.

emphasize pointlessly the conjunction of *dicta* and *apologos* with the act of *exponere* and to obscure the fact that Suetonius is referring to three distinct exercises, each involving a different kind of literary operation. The assumption thus blunts the point of the passage only slightly less than did former editors who took *apologos* to be the object of *per*. We therefore want an infinitive to govern *dicta*, parallel with *exponere* and *explicare*. We do not want both *per omnes figuras* and *per casus*--the asyndetic juxtaposition is sufficient to arouse suspicion by itself--because in this context, concerned with the *chria*, the phrases mean the same thing: to cause a *dictum* to pass through all the cases is to display it in its various grammatical constructions, or "postures" (= *figurae* / σχήματα).

The cure, however, is more difficult than the diagnosis. In conjecturing *percurrere* for *per casus*, Madvig evidently assumed that the former was corrupted directly to the latter. This is possible, though *percurrere* is not really the most suitable verb here; and as suggested above, it seems more likely that one of the prepositional phrases originated as a gloss on the other (that assumption is implied by Haupt's *versare*). If that so, then the probable culprit is *per casus*, since *casus* is the term that a reader would ordinarily associate with the *chria* and so the term that would suggest itself as a gloss on *per omnes figuras*. For the phenomenon, compare 4. 5, where X had the correct *meditationum*, while Y had *institutionum*, an obvious gloss, or (conversely) 30. 1, where Y had the correct reading *eas partes*, while X conflated that reading with the gloss *eius moris* (producing *eius partis mores* in O, *eius patris mores* in W);[140] cf. also ".i. interrogationes," a gloss on *acroasis* that slipped into the text of U at 2. 1, and the discussion of 7. 3 *ut hoc*, above.

As for the infinitive: if the word chosen by Suetonius was replaced by *per casus*, we could expect to recover it only by a great stroke of luck. Haupt's *versare* provides acceptable sense;[141] one

---

[140] On 30. 1 see App. 2, at n. 16.

[141] Haupt compared Quint. *Inst.* 5. 14. 32 "non mille figuris variet ac verset [sc. orator]?" and 11. 3. 176 "intra se quisque vel hoc [sc. exemplum] vel aliud quod volet per omnes adfectus verset"; though neither of these passages has to do with the *chria*, a similar direction may be pointed by Theon *Progymn.* 5 (p. 101. 9-10) τὰ γὰρ ἐν τῇ χρείᾳ πρόσωπα εἰς τοὺς τρεῖς ἀριθμοὺς ἐναλλάττομεν.

could as well suggest *ducere* (cf. Quint. *Inst.* 1. 9. 5 "in his omnibus ... declinatio per eosdem ducitur casus," on the *chria*) or *variare* (cf. Diom. *GL* 1:310. 2 "chriarum exercitatio in casus sic variatur") or even *declinare* (cf. Theon *Progymn.* 5 [p. 101. 21-23] φανερὸν δὲ ἐκ τούτων, πῶς καὶ τοὺς ἄλλους τρόπους κλινοῦμεν). But in a situation such as this, there is no point in multiplying mere guesses: *versare* can be printed as a stopgap, *exempli causa*.

25.5 venalicius cum Brundusi gregem venalium e navi educeret, formoso et pretioso puero, quod portitores verebatur, bullam et praetextam togam imposuit; facile fallaciam celavit. Romam venitur, res cognita est, petitur puer quod domini voluntate fuerit [liber] in libertate.

> venalicius · *Robinson* : -lici ω   educeret **X** : -ent **Y**
> verebatur **XN**[1] : -bantur **Y**   imposuit ... celavit **XN** : -erunt (*vel* -ere) ... -arunt **Y**   venitur **Y** : venit **XN**   res cognita est **XNG**[2]**D** (rec- **W**) : recogniti sunt **Y** (resc- **VL**)   liber *delevi* (*iam dubitant. Winterbottom*) : liber in libertate ω, liber in libertatem **B**, *Vinetus* (*edd.*)

Suetonius has told us about *controversiae* that have been *collectae editaeque*, "ex quibus" (he says) "non alienum fuerit unam et alteram exempli causa ad verbum referre"; this is the second example that he quotes. The passage incurred numerous corruptions, most notably in the subject and verbs of the first sentence, where the singular *venalicius* (cf. gen. sing. *domini*) became *venalici*, with the verbs then altered to the plural in **Y** (see Robinson, diss., pp. 90-91). The problem that concerns us now stands at the end of the second sentence, where the archetype's *liber in libertate* cannot be correct.

The point of the sentence is that discovery of the slave-dealer's deception resulted in a *causa liberalis* (viz., *vindicatio in libertatem*), a civil action in which the *puer* was claimed as free by someone (here unspecified, because irrelevant) who acted as *adsertor libertatis*.[142] All modern editors print "petitur puer, quod domini voluntate fuerit liber, in libertatem," adopting the emendation *libertatem* offered by one MS (**B**) and Vinetus. The pre-

---

[142] *Causa liberalis*: W. W. Buckland, *The Roman Law of Slavery* (Cambridge, 1908), pp. 652ff., A. Watson, *The Roman Law of Persons in the Later Roman Republic* (Oxford, 1967), pp. 218ff.

sumed corruption is obviously easy (merely the loss of a stroke above the final *-e*), and the resulting text is appropriate, insofar as *petere* in such a context--like *adserere, proclamare*, and *vindicare*--is regularly accompanied by the phrase *in libertatem* (*Dig.* 40. 12. 29 *in libertatem petitus*, sim. 3. 3. 39. 5, 38. 2. 16 pr., 43. 16. 1. 21). If the correction offers any obvious cause for doubt, it lies with the striking hyperbaton that is produced, the separation of *petitur* from *in libertatem* by the intervening causal clause (cf. the remark of Winterbottom, quoted below): rather awkward in itself, the hyperbaton is also noticeably at odds with the simple style of the quotation; and because the causal clause makes plain the meaning of *petitur puer*, the phrase *in libertatem* is left looking rather limp and superfluous by the time we finally reach it.

Ceteris paribus, we might wink at the hyperbaton and join the editors in accepting the correction. As it happens, however, there is independent evidence that gives backbone to doubt. First, pseudo-Quintilian *Decl.* 340, which in essence presents the very example that Suetonius here adduces: "QUI VOLUNTATE DOMINI IN LIBERTATE FUERIT, LIBER SIT. Mango novitium puerum per publicanos transiecit praetextatum. dicitur ille liber." Once again, the slave-dealer dresses the *puer* as an *ingenuus* (thus *praetextatum*: see above on 10. 2) and smuggles him past the tax-collectors; and the stipulation according to which his freedom is proclaimed--"qui voluntate domini in libertate fuerit"--is cast in the same words that we find in Suetonius' MSS--minus *liber*.[143] The use of the phrase *in libertate* is not inconsequential in the context, since the *declamatio* that follows takes that phrase as the key to its argument (concerning the distinction between *in libertate esse* and *liber esse*). More important, the use of the phrase is not fortuitous: precisely the same stipulation--"qui voluntate domini in libertate fuerit"--is the basis of a second *declamatio* that soon follows (342 "ancilla in archipiratae nuptias missa"), where again the phrase *in libertate* is the key to the arguments presented (the same distinction is involved); and precisely the same phrasing-- *voluntate domini in libertate* (sc. *esse* vel sim.)--occurs in the

---

[143] Note that a further detail links the two texts: in Suetonius's version the *puer* is *formosus et pretiosus*; in the second declamation on the theme in ps.-Quint. (p. 345 Ritter), the *puer* possesses *species*, "beauty," and (therefore) *videtur mangoni . . . pretiosus* (the slave-dealer accordingly *timuit ne magno aestimaretur*).

jurists.[144] Clearly we are dealing with a phrase from law that the *scholastici* took over and incorporated in their exercises, the *controversiae iudiciales* that Suetonius mentions in the following sentence (on that sentence, see the next discussion); and all these occurrences of the phrase show that the reading *liber* would be wrong as a matter of law: in such circumstances the *puer* would be vindicated as free, not *quod domini voluntate fuerit liber*, but *quod domini voluntate fuerit in libertate*. Since that is the case, since Suetonius makes a point of saying that he is quoting the example *ad verbum*, and since *in libertate* is what Suetonius' MSS give us, that must be what he wrote.

The correct solution, therefore, is to print "petitur puer quod domini voluntate fuerit [liber] in libertate." This conclusion was already tentatively reached by Michael Winterbottom in his commentary on [Quint.] *Decl.* 340:[145] noting the passage in the *DGR* he remarked that "the order [sc. with *in libertatem*] is very strange, and it may be that we should delete *liber* and read *libertate* with most of the manuscripts: if, that is, *petitur* by itself could mean 'claim for liberty.'" On the latter point there need be no doubt, since the context makes the meaning of *petitur puer* clear and complete in itself. With this absolute (or elliptical) use of *petitur*, compare 21. 2 "quamquam *adserente matre*, permansit tamen in statu servitutis praesentemque condicionem verae origini anteposuit": here again, the context concerns a *causa liberalis* (the mother is claiming the freedom of her son, the grammarian C. Melissus); and a form of *adserere* is used absolutely, instead of the more common *adserere in libertatem*.

---

[144] *Dig.* 40. 12. 24. 3 (Paulus) and 40. 12. 28 (Pomponius) (bis), cited by Buckland, *Roman Law*, p. 661; also in *frag. Dosith.* 5 (= *FIRA*² 2:617 "qui domini voluntate in libertate erant"), cited by Watson, *Law of Persons*, p. 197, and S. Treggiari, *Roman Freedmen*, p. 30 n. 1. On the phrase *in libertate fuisse*, see also *Dig.* 40. 12. 10 (Ulpian), and cf. ibid. 12 (id.). On the legal background to *Decl.* 340 and 342, see B. Sirks, "Juridical Rationality in Rhetorics," *Atti del III Seminario Romanistico Gardesano (22-25 ottobre 1985)* (Milan, 1988), pp. 333-59, esp. the suggestion (p. 347) that the principle "qui voluntate domini in libertate fuerit, liber sit" is derived from the *lex Iunia* (17 B.C.?) concerning informal manumission. My thanks to K. R. Bradley for bringing Sirks' paper to my attention and providing me with a copy of it, and for his other helpful responses to this discussion.

[145] *The Minor Declamations Ascribed to Quintilian* (Berlin and New York, 1984), p. 535.

With this solution the corruption to be assumed is obviously not quite as easy as a misplaced stroke of abbreviation, but that does not mean it is difficult. The word *liber* most likely began as an interlinear gloss inserted by a reader unfamiliar with the legal expression *esse in libertate*; other explanations are also possible.

25.5   olim autem eas **appellatione Graeca ὑποθέσεις** vocabant, mox controversias quidem, sed aut fictas aut iudiciales.

>appellatione Graeca *Schott* : appellationes Graeci **Οαζ**, a- Graece **WβM**, appellationes *crucibus incl. Robinson (lacun. postposit.), del. Brugnoli*, compellationes, Graeci *della Corte, alii alia*   ὑποθέσεις *Wolf* : syn(sin-)taxis **WαVDL¹M**, -tasis **OB**, -t(h)esis **LKHE**, -thasis **QUC**, συνθέσεις **S**, θέσεις *Gronov.*, συστάσεις *Bonner*

The sentence concerns the labels given to the exercises that came to be known as *controversiae; eas* refers to "them," i.e., the exercises, of which Suetonius has just quoted two examples (see the preceding discussion). The only deep difficulty here concerns the Greek label that is to be supplied; we can take the earlier part of the sentence first.

The archetype had *appellationes Graeci* or *Graece* (probably with a double reading for the latter word). Brugnoli's text nicely illustrates why *Graeci* cannot be correct: "olim autem eas [appellatione] Graeci συντάσεις vocabant, mox controversias quidem. . . ." This could only mean that the Greeks once called these exercises συντάσεις, but presently called them *controversiae*-- though the Greeks, of course, never called them *controversiae* at all. Robinson ("olim autem eas †appellationes† <* * *>, Graeci συντάσεις vocabant; mox controversias quidem . . .") and della Corte ("olim autem eas conpellationes, Graeci συντάσεις, vocabant: mox controversias quidem . . .") retained *Graeci*, too, avoiding Brugnoli's error, but at the cost of introducing (*int. al.*) some very improbable punctuation.[146] All this makes unnecessarily heavy weather of a straightforward sentence: Suetonius'

---

[146] To fill the supposed lacuna, Robinson tentatively suggested "olim autem eas <meditationes rhetores Latini conten>tiones, Graeci συντάσεις vocabant . . ."; della Corte emended *appellationes* to *conpellationes*, though the latter term is no more attested in the required sense than is the former. W. Stegemann, rev. of Bione, *PhW* 61 (1941): 344 n. 2, proposed "olim autem eas <praepar>ationes, Graece syntaxis, vocabant."

point is not that the Romans once called these things X, the Greeks Y, whereas subsequently the Romans called them Z; it is simply that the Romans once used a Greek term to label them, but presently adopted a Latin term.

We must therefore decide whether we want to read *Graece* (which entails deleting *appellationes*) or Schott's *appellatione Graeca* (adopted by Reifferscheid and Rolfe).[147] The former solution, according to which the archetype's *appellationes* must be regarded as an interpolated gloss, is possible:[148] we have already seen two instances where such a gloss had clearly infected either X or Y, and two other instances where (I believe) a gloss had already infected the archetype itself (see on 7. 3 and 25. 4 above); and the marginal note *Appellatio ude* [i.e., ûde] ᾱ̄τ that appears in cod. K here (see Robinson, diss., p. 151) suggests the sort of environment in which the interpolation could have arisen. But it is surely easier, in this case, to suppose that *appellatione* passed to *appellationes* after *eas*, with *Graeca* then altered to *Graeci* or *Graece* to produce a construable clause: with the phrase *appellatione Graeca* here, compare 4. 1, where Suetonius makes a similar observation on the history of a technical term ("*appellatio grammaticorum Graeca consuetudine invaluit, sed initio litterati vocabantur*": in this case use of the Latin term preceded adoption of the Greek); for the form of the clause as a whole, compare *Aug.* 82. 2 "insidens ligneo solo, quod ipse *Hispanico verbo* duretam *vocabat*," 97. 2 "aesar ... *Etrusca lingua* deus *vocaretur*."

We next need to decide what the Greek label was. Here we find certainty on every side, all of it conflicting. Robinson is sure that only συντάσεις can be correct, Bonner is equally sure about συστάσεις; Stegemann and Cousin have no hesitation where συν-

---

[147] Roth printed *eas appellationes Graece synthesis vocabant*, though what sense he attached to *appellationes* is not clear; S. F. Bonner, "Rhetorica," *CR* 61 (1947): 85-86, attempted to defend *appellationes* because it "has complete manuscript authority." Bione printed the same text as Roth, with an obelus before *appellationes*; but that is needlessly despairing, and is based on the mistaken belief that *eas* "manca di referimento" and so needs a noun to follow it: the referent of *eas* is unmistakable in the context.

[148] Cf. Brugnoli, app. crit. ad loc., p. 30: "*appellationes codd. ... quod corruptum ex glossula* appellatione *iudico, inde expungendum*." If this is correct, the archetype's *appellationes* should appear in brackets, not its hypothetical source, [*appellatione*].

τάξεις (or *syntaxis*) is concerned, while Fairweather is certain that only ὑποθέσεις will do.[149]

Fairweather is correct. As Robinson stressed (ed., pp. 41-42, cf. Fairweather, *Seneca*, pp. 115ff.), Suetonius' discussion of the development of the *controversiae* has a close parallel in Sen. *Contr.* 1 praef. 12. In describing the stage that corresponds to Suetonius' sentence here ("olim autem eas appellatione Graeca . . . vocabant, mox controversias quidem . . ."), Seneca says "declamabat autem Cicero non quales nunc controversias dicimus. . . . controversias nos dicimus, Cicero causas vocabat"; and the Greek term--the *only* Greek term--that corresponds to what Cicero called a *causa* is ὑπόθεσις (see Cic. *Top.* 79 "definitum [sc. genus quaestionis] est quod ὑπόθεσιν Graeci [sc. appellant], nos causam," Quint. *Inst.* 3. 5. 7 "hae ὑποθέσεις a Graecis dicuntur, causae a nostris," and cf. *TLL* 6:3161.27ff., with Fairweather, ibid., pp. 125-26, Lausberg, *Handbuch*[3], pp. 63-64): that is, a matter for debate defined by specific circumstances (times, places, persons), like the two examples Suetonius has just quoted ("aestivo tempore adulescentes urbani cum Ostiam venissent . . .," "venalicius cum Brundusi gregem venalium e navi educeret . . ."). None of the other Greek terms promoted as candidates here-- σύντασις or σύνταξις or σύστασις--occurs in anything remotely like the required sense; the first two, in fact, are nowhere used as rhetorical terms at all, while the third (a metaphor drawn from the palaestra) means only the "setting-up of the case" (*constitutio causae*), a sense that has no place in this context.

Now it is plain that these latter readings have been favored only because of the power of the *ductus litterarum*: thus Robinson (ed., p. 43) says "ὑποθέσεις . . ., non est infitiandum, sententiae optime congruat. . . . Sed *hypothesis* e lectione *syntasis* vel *syntaxis* numquam efficias"; similarly Bonner, while acknowledging that ὑποθέσεις gives the correct sense, asks ("Rhetorica," p. 85) "but how could ὑποθέσεις possibly have become any of our manu-

---

[149] See Robinson, ed., pp. 41-43; Bonner, "Rhetorica," pp. 84-86; W. Stegemann, "Die ältere griechische Bezeichnung für rhetorische Kontroversen," *PhW* 57 (1937): 509-12 (discussing the reading *syntaxis* adopted by W. Hofrichter, *Studien zur Entwicklungsgeschichte der Deklamatio* [Breslau, 1935], p. 2; Stegemann amplified his remarks in his rev. of Bione, *PhW* 61 [1941]: 344 n. 2); J. Cousin, rev. of Bione, *REL* 18 (1940): 207; J. Fairweather, *Seneca the Elder* (Cambridge, 1981), pp. 350-51 (n. 36).

script readings, which all begin with συν?" I will not claim that I can answer that question--beyond noting that all our manuscripts are descended from a single MS, the archetype that we know to have been deeply corrupt; accordingly, "we need not be so sure that the word Suetonius wrote began with [συν-] as we would ... be if a wide range of medieval manuscripts were extant, all attesting such a reading."[150] I assume that the archetype read *syntaxis*:[151] I do not know how ὑποθέσεις (or *hypothesis*) passed to *syntaxis*, but I am satisfied that neither *syntaxis* nor anything like it can be correct.

27.1 M'. Otacilius Pitholaus servisse dicitur atque etiam ostiarius vetere more in catena fuisse, donec ob ingenium ac studium litterarum manumissus accusanti patrono subscripsit. (2) deinde rhetoricam professus Cn. Pompeium Magnum docuit patrisque eius res gestas nec minus ipsius compluribus libris exposuit, primus omnium libertinorum, ut Cornelius Nepos opinatur, scribere historiam orsus, nonnisi ab honestissimo quoque scribi solitam ad id tempus.

> M'. Otacilius Pitholaus *Lewis* (Otacilius L[=*Pontano*]E, Pitholaus *Gyraldus*) : L. Oltacilius Pilutus **Χαβ** (Olta- **XV**, Octa- **αD**, Otta- **B**), L. Voltacilius Pilutus **γ** (Vola- **U**, Volcatius **CΔQT**), Voltacilius Pitholaus (*del.* L.) *Robinson*, L. Voltacilius Plotus *Reiff.*, L. Voltacilius Plutus *della Corte*

The archetype almost certainly had *L. Oltacilius Pilutus* (so **XV**, with minor variations in other members of **αβ**; the reading *Otacilius* found in L [and E] is a conjecture by Pontano, see below); **γ**'s *L. Voltacilius Pilutus* represents the influence of the index, which has the same reading. Independent testimony is provided by Jerome, who appears to have read *Vultacilius Plotus* when he

---

[150] Fairweather, *Seneca*, p. 350. She continues: "the Greek word seems to have been transmitted in Latin characters; uncomprehending western scribes could have distorted it considerably in the transmission of the text before the Renaissance."

[151] The *syntasis* of **OB** could be the trace of a double reading in the archetype, though it is more likely to be a coincidental error in the two MSS. The reading *synthesis* or *-thasis* that occurs in **LKζ** is surely just a further distortion (or, in the case of *synthesis*, a misguided conjecture).

excerpted this chapter of Suetonius for his extension of Eusebius' *Chronicle*.[152]

Criticism of this passage has also been influenced by a passage in Macrobius (*Sat.* 2. 2. 13)--"'M.,' inquit, 'Otacilius Pitholaus, cum Caninius Rebilus [cos. suff. 45] uno tantum die consul fuisset, dixit, *ante flamines, nunc consules diales fiunt*'"--where the archetype had *Votacilius* (*Octacilius* T [s. XV]), while editors regularly print *Otacilius*, a conjecture of Pontano and Casaubon.[153] Further, the man who made this joke at the expense of one of Caesar's consuls is probably to be identified with the Pitholaus mentioned by Suetonius (*Jul.* 75. 5) as the author of *carmina maledicentissima* directed against Caesar himself. (It has been customary, since Bentley, to identify him also with the *Rhodio . . . Pitholeoni* mentioned at Hor. *Serm.* 1. 10. 22, where it must be assumed that the form *Pitholeon* is used, *metri causa*, for *Pitholaus*; but this, I think, is to cast the net too wide.) It was long ago suggested that this anti-Caesarian wit and literary man is the same person as the teacher of Pompey sketched in our passage, who recorded the *res gestae* of Pompey and his father: hence Gyraldus' conjecture *Pitholaus* for *Pilutus* (with the assumption that *Voltacilius* is the *gentilicium* in both Suet. and Macrob.). The process of identification was carried to its conclusion by R. G. Lewis: the man in our passage and the Pitholaus of Macrobius and Suet. *Jul.* 75. 5 (and, acc. to Lewis, the Pitholeon of Horace) are indeed all the same person, whose name was M'. Otacilius Pitholaus. He would thus be a freedman of the Otacilii, who "[i]n the first century B.C. . . . were adherents of the Pompeii. One of

---

[152] *Vultacilius* is the reading of the 5th-century Bodleian MS (O) and most other MSS; *vulc-* also occurs, along with the trivial errors *Vultacius* (B) and *Acilius* (XC). Jerome gives no praenomen: *pace* Robinson (ed., p. 44), no significance should be attributed to this omission, since Jerome elsewhere omits the praenomen from his excerpts (e.g., 30. 1 C. *Albucius Silus Novariensis* Suet. vs. *Albucius Silo* [sic] *Novariensis* Hieron.) The marginal notes *Voltacilius Plotius* and *Volcaedius Plotus* that appear in two MSS of the *Ad Herenn.* (1. 18, at the words *noster doctor*) probably are derived from Jerome and have no independent value: so Robinson, ed., p. 45, following Marx.

[153] Pontano thus made the same conjecture in both Suet. and Macrob., see above. The text of Macrob. is otherwise disturbed here, with the MSS showing *maius servilius* (NDP) or *gaius servilius* (cett.) in place of *Caninius Rebilus*.

them, perhaps [the] young son of a contemporary legate of the same name, served under Cn. Strabo in the Social War. He is probably the man who held Lissus for Pompey in 48 B.C. . . . The *praenomen* of these two Otacilii active in the Social War is *Manius*."[154] The connections and sympathies of our rhetor would fall into place; and as Robinson noted (ed., p. 45), Pitholaus would be an appropriate cognomen for a rhetor.

The modern vulgate reading is *L. Voltacilius Plotus*--essentially, the praenomen and nomen found in the index (whence γ) combined with the cognomen found in Jerome. *Pilutus*, the cognomen in the MSS, though printed by Roth and Brugnoli, cannot stand: it is a *vox nihili*, unattested as a cognomen (or in any other way) and with no apparent meaning. The only reasonable choice lies between *Plotus* (Reifferscheid et al.) and *Pitholaus* (Robinson);[155] and that choice will depend on one's view of the identification of the man described by Suetonius with the man quoted in Macrobius.

Here the question of the praenomen and nomen arises. Most editors have been content to print the *L.* transmitted in the index and the text ad loc. (which would then count against identification with Macrobius' man). The only dissenter has been Robinson, who regarded the archetype's *L. Oltacilius* as a corruption of *Voltacilius* arising from confusion of capital V and capital L (i.e., *Voltacilius > Loltacilius > L. Oltacilius*).[156] He accordingly printed

---

[154] "Pompeius' Freedman Biographer: Suetonius, *De Gramm. et Rhet.* 27 (3)," *CR* 16 (1966): 272.

[155] Della Corte printed *Plutus*, the reading of X in the index; but this is probably nothing more than a corruption of the transmitted *Pilutus*.

[156] See his ed., ad loc., p. 44, with diss., p. 94 n. 195: in the latter place he compares, for the confusion of V and L, 13. 1 (see above), where H has *V. Taberius*, against the *L. Taberius* of its close kin. A different explanation for the same corruption was given by Wessner in his rev. of Robinson's ed., *PhW* 46 (1926): 1228: *Voltacilius* was the transmitted reading, above which *L.* (the praenomen found in the index) was written as a suprascript supplement; but instead of being regarded as an addition (to *Voltacilius*), it was treated as a correction (for V). The two analyses entail different assumptions about the form of the name in the index: on Robinson's view, the index's *L.* would apparently be derived from the corruption in the text, while on Wessner's view the index's reading would apparently be the source of the corruption in the text.

Voltacilius and (more tentatively) *Pitholaus*, accepting the identification with the man in Macrobius' anecdote. But no editor seems to have attended to the fact that the name *Voltacilius* (or *Vulta-*) is only slightly less problematic than the cognomen *Pilutus*. As Lewis stressed, the *gentilicium* is far from secure: in fact, if the editors of Macrobius are correct in reading *Otacilius*, it occurs only in Suetonius--or, to be precise, only in the index and in Jerome's version of Suetonius, for the text of the archetype ad loc. was *Oltacilius*, a form midway between *Voltacilius* and *Otacilius*. The latter name, by contrast, *is* well attested; and as noted above, it makes excellent sense in the context besides.

Hence the attraction of Lewis' proposal. That proposal, as Lewis presented it, was open to some substantive objections;[157] but almost all these objections fall away if one does not insist on the identification with Horace's Pitholeon, an identification that I find forced and unnecessary in any case. Without that identification, there remain only objections *ex silentio*: in his sketch of the rhetor, Suetonius does not identify the man's *patronus*, which "suggests that he was not of high position"; and Suetonius does not mention here the *carmina* that he mentions in the *vita* of Caesar. These objections carry no weight. By giving us the name of the rhetor, a freedman, Suetonius *does*, in effect, identify his *patronus*, since their praenomen and nomen would in the ordinary way of things have been the same (cf., conversely, 15. 1 *Lenaeus, Magni Pompei libertus*, where Suetonius gives only the teacher's cognomen, since it is obvious that the rest of his name would have been Cn. Pompeius). As for the *carmina*, Suetonius is markedly inconsistent in the coordination of such details, not only between different works (e.g., *DGR* 16. 1 vs. *Aug.* 66. 2: a detail on the fall of Gallus provided in the former, omitted in the latter), but also between different parts of the same work (within the *De vir. ill.* note, e.g., *DGR* 23 vs. *DGR* frag. 5, Palaemon's feud with the rhetor Antonius Liberalis mentioned in the life of the latter, but not of the former; *DGR* 9. 4 vs. *Vit. Hor.*, Hor. mentioned as a student of Orbilius in the former, Orbilius ignored as a teacher of Hor. in the latter); and if the *Caesares* postdates the *DGR* (as Treggiari and most scholars believe), then Suetonius may simply

---

[157] See S. Treggiari, "Pompeius' Freedman Biographer Again," *CR* 19 (1969): 264-66, and cf. her *Roman Freedmen*, p. 118 n. 8.

not have learned of the *carmina* until he was collecting material for Caesar's biography.

The deformation of the reading M'. *Otacilius Pitholaus* would have to be quite old, since it was already found in the text known to Jerome; but corruptions were as likely to occur in the second or fourth century as in the ninth and fifteenth. The corruption would certainly not be difficult, either in capital or in cursive script (the only two likely alternatives, given the presumed date of the error). Lewis remarked (p. 272) that *M'*. --or its compendium, *M* plus virgule (M)--would easily pass to *LV*, through confusion of the ascending and descending strokes. As for the cognomen, the corruption of *PITHOLAVS*, or *PITOLAVS*, to *PITOLVS* would be equally easy; and once that change had occurred, the attempt to produce a Latin-looking name would be nearly irresistible--hence *PLOTVS*, a reading aided (if not actually abetted) by the name *L. PLOTIVS Gallus* in the chapter immediately preceding. This is the form of the name that Jerome found in his text of Suetonius. In the strand of the tradition represented by our archetype, *PLOTVS* had been further corrupted to *Pilutus*; and in the text at the start of the chapter, *L. Voltacilius* had fairly recently been copied as *L. Oltacilius*, an error that coincidentally brought the name one letter closer to the correct reading.[158]

On the one side, then, *M'. Otacilius Pitholaus*, an emendation that relieves the text of one of Mumpsimus' relatives, provides in its place a name perfectly suited to the context and open to no substantive objection, and presumes an early but fairly easy corruption. On the other side, *L. Voltacilius Plotus*, a very questionable *gentilicium* coupled with a praenomen and cognomen that look uncomfortably like importations from the preceding chapter. Certainty is not attainable, but on balance the former alternative seems preferable.

28.1 <M.> Epidius, calumnia notatus, ludum dicendi aperuit docuitque inter ceteros M. Antonium et Augustum: quibus

---

[158] In other words, capital *V* was not replaced by capital *L* out of confusion of the two forms (as Robinson supposed, see n. 156), it was omitted because of that confusion. I say that this error had occurred fairly recently--perhaps in the archetype itself--because it had not had time to be "corrected" by comparison with the index, as we see happening in γ; cf. p. 88 n. 103, on the omission of *velim . . . esse* at 14. 3.

quondam **Ti.** Cannutius--obicientibus sibi quod in re publica administranda potissimum <Servili> Isaurici sectam sequeretur--malle respondit **consularis** Isaurici esse discipulum quam Epidi calumniatoris.

M. *suppl. Roth (ex indice)* : *om.* ω   Ti. *Ernesti* : C. ω, *del.* Oudendorp   Servili Isaurici . . . consularis Isaurici *conieci* (consularis *ante* esse *iam transposuit* Acidalius) : consularis Isaurici . . . Isaurici ω

Two more questions involving nomenclature. On the first, Robinson writes, preparatory to retaining the praenomen C. (ed., p. 46): "Vix dubium videtur quin noster Cannutius idem fuerit ac Ti. Cannutius tribunus plebis a. 710/44 . . . [cf. *MRR* 2:323-24]. Quapropter Ernestius *Ti.* restituendum, Oudendorpius *C.* delendum existimavit. Vide tamen ne ipsius Suetoni sit error." But choosing which is more likely to be in error here--Suetonius or the archetype--involves no choice at all; the only real choice lies between Oudendorp's deletion of *C.*--as a product of dittography before *Cannutius*--and Ernesti's emendation *Ti.* The error in either case is easy, and either option is possible (Brugnoli follows Oudendorp, della Corte follows Ernesti); but Suetonius' habits make the latter much more likely. As noted above (see at 3. 3), Suetonius does sometimes refer to a man by only one of his names; but such persons tend to be--especially in the *DGR*--well-known figures from literature and politics. Cannutius was not a literary man, nor was he a famous historical figure--a Brutus or a Cassius or an Augustus. Had Suetonius not known or not cared to give his praenomen, he would not have written just the *gentilicium,* but would have said *Cannutius quidam* (cf. 4. 6 *quendam Principem nomine,* 11. 1 *Burseni cuiusdam*).

The second question, concerning Cannutius' *dictum,* is less straightforward. "malo consularis Isaurici esse discipulus quam Epidi calumniatoris": that (or something very much like it) must be what Cannutius said, for the retort lacks bite, and is hardly memorable, without the presence of *consularis* in antithesis to *calumniatoris.* The question is, how did Suetonius report the *mot?* The correct answer suggests itself if we put the question in this form: did Suetonius first set up his report by placing the phrase *calumnia notatus* where he did, to prepare the reader for *calumniatoris,* but then almost immediately deface the report by misplacing *consularis?* So the archetype's text implies, but I think that is unlikely: the clumsiness we confront here is not characteristic of Suetonius but suggests the intervention of one or more ham-handed scribes.

V. Acidalius already proposed the transposition of *consularis* to precede *esse*;[159] I would prefer to read *Servili Isaurici . . . consularis Isaurici*. For the form of the name, compare *Tib.* 5 *Servili Isaurici* (= the man at issue here, cos. 48 and 41), and *Jul.* 3 *Servilio Isaurico* (= the latter's father, cos. 79). For the sequence nomen + cognomen > cognomen only, compare, in a similar context, 22. 2 *Ateio Capitone . . . Capito* and *Jul.* 78. 2 *Pontium Aquilam . . . Aquila*: in both places the two names are given in the passage leading up to a quotation, while the single name stands in the quotation itself; cf. also the remarks at 9. 5 *Varrone <Murena> . . . Murena*, above. I take it that a scribe wrote ". . . potissimum consularis Isaurici esse discipulum . . .," omitting "Servili Isaurici . . . respondit" through a *saut du même au même*; amends were then made by inserting "Isaurici sectam sequeretur malle respondit" between *consularis* and *Isaurici*. Other explanations of the error are possible.

28.2 hic Epidius ortum se a C. Epidio Nucerino praedicabat, quem ferunt olim praecipitatum in fontem fluminis Sarni paulo post cum cornibus **aureis** extitisse ac statim non comparuisse, in numeroque deorum habitum.

 aureis **ON**, aurib' **W** : *om.* **Y**, taureis *Jahn*, arietis *dubitant. Robinson*, <pro> auribus *della Corte*

That **X** had *aureis* is guaranteed by the agreement of **ON** (the latter here, as elsewhere, contaminated from **X** independently of **OW**); **W**'s *aurib'* (i.e., *auribus*) must be a peculiar error, after *corn*IBUS.[160] We should therefore suppose that *aureis* stood in the archetype, and attribute its absence in **Y** to simple omission; it is hardly likely to have been introduced as a mechanical error or arbitrary interpolation in **X**.

---

[159] *Valentis Acidalii Notae in Taciti Opera* (Hanau, 1607), p. 298 (ad *Dial.* 21). The conjecture is correctly reported by Robinson; adjust Brugnoli's app. crit. ad loc.

[160] Della Corte based his conjecture *cornibus <pro> auribus* on **W**'s error (rev. of Bione, *RFIC* 20 [1942]: 139, where the MS is mistakenly identified as **V**); the suggestion is not likely to be correct in any case.

I see no reason to accept Y's text (with Roth); and absent a demonstration that in these miraculous circumstances the man-become-god could *not* have had "golden horns," I see no reason to emend *aureis* to *taureis* (with Jahn, followed by Reifferscheid and Rolfe; the epithet occurs only in poetry) or to obelize *aureis* (with Robinson). The epithets χρύσεος (-σοῦς) / *aureus* were very generally applied to the possessions or attributes of divinities: see LSJ s.v. I.1, III.1.a, *TLL* 2:1489.9ff. passim; cf. also χρυσόκερως, used of Pan (Cratin. frag. 359. 1, 4:296 K.-A.) and Dionysus (*Anth. Gr.* 9. 524. 23 [anon.]), similarly *aureo cornu* at Hor. *c*. 2. 19. 29; and esp. Verg. *G*. 4. 371f. "*gemina auratus* taurino *cornua* vultu / Eridanus," Martial 10. 7. 6 *cornibus aureis*, of the Rhine.[161] Robinson tentatively suggested *arietis*, noting that "quosdam nummos e Nuceria Alfaterna provenientes litteris Oscis inscriptos caput iuvenale cum cornu arietino ostendere";[162] but as he also noted (ibid.), "nihil ... repertum est quod illud caput iuvenale in nummis ... depictum certa ratione cum deo Epidio coniungeret." Still, Robinson's suggestion does not deserve to be forgotten (I will mention it in my app. crit.), since the image on the coin *could* represent the personified Sarnus, to whom Epidius was thought to have been assimilated.[163]

29.1 Sextus Clodius ... male oculatus et dicax par oculorum in amicitia M. Antoni triumviri **extrisse se** aiebat.

>   extrisse se *Statius* (extinctum esse *Robinson, alii alia*) : extricte se ΧαβMᵐCQ (-tae se TE), extitisse se Y, extitisse Δ

---

[161] The latter cited by Bione, "Note critiche," p. 33.

[162] Ed., p. 46, citing (*int. al.*) A. Sambon, *Les Monnaies antiques de l'Italie* (Paris, 1903), pp. 378-79, and B. V. Head, *Historia Nummorum*² (Oxford, 1911), p. 11; see also *British Museum Catalogue of Greek Coins*, vol. 1 (London, 1873), p. 121, and for a photograph, J. Svoronos and B. V. Head, *The Illustrations of the "Historia Nummorum"* (Chicago, 1968), pl. II,9.

[163] This identification is assumed, e.g., at *Roscher-Lexicon* 4 (1910): 387 and *RE* 2 A (1921): 26-27. Note that a wallpainting in the *Casa del labirinto* at Pompeii represents the Sarnus as an *old* man, with a white beard and no horns: see W. Helbig, *Wandgemälde der vom Vesuv verschütteten Städte Campaniens* (Leipzig, 1868), p. 21 (no. 65), G. K. Boyce, *Corpus of the Lararia of Pompeii*, MAAR vol. 17 (Rome, 1937), p. 50 (no. 185) with pl. 21.1.

The Sicilian rhetor Sextus Clodius, who had weak eyes and a ready tongue, used to say that he had ruined his eyesight in the friendship (i.e., in the service and companionship) of Mark Antony: that is clearly the sense of the passage (cf. the slightly different metaphor at Sen. *Contr.* 1 praef. 17 *oculorum aciem contuderat*, of the rhetor Latro). The archetype must have had *extricte se*, the reading of X and of two of the sub-families of Y (αβ; it also occurs in the text or as a marginal variant in several γ-MSS); *extitisse se* is evidently the garbled result of an attempted correction in γ.[164] Of the emendations that have been proposed, only Statius' *extrisse se* and Robinson's *extinctum esse* merit consideration;[165] of these two, *extrisse se* is surely preferable, since it provides better sense--merely impaired ("worn out") vision, not actual blindness (as *par oculorum . . . extinctum* would imply)--and is slightly easier in the error it assumes (simply minuscule ſſ mistaken for the ligature &).[166]

30.2 sed ex eo clarus [sc. C. Albucius Silus] **propria auditoria instituit, solitus proposita controversia sedens incipere et calore demum provectus consurgere ac perorare. declamabat aut genere** vario, modo spendide atque **ornate**, tum--ne usque quaque scholasticus existimaretur--circumcise ac sordide et tantum non trivialibus verbis.

> declamabat autem genere *Steph.* : declamare aut gemere ω
> ornate *conieci* (adeo ornate *iam* Heinsius, *teste* Burman) :
> adoranter ω, adornate λ (*edd.*), eleganter S, ardenter Δ

All modern editors print Stephanus' *autem genere* for the archetype's *aut gemere*; none prints his equally excellent *declamabat*

---

[164] I.e, *extitisse* written above *extricte se*, then copied as *extitisse se*: so MK(=δ) HU(=η), with *extitisse* (om. *se*) in Δ; see Robinson, diss., p. 145. *Pace* Robinson, however, I see no reason to think *extitisse* already stood as a variant in the archetype; it is the sort of lame conjecture typical of γ. Cf. Wessner, rev. of Robinson, ed., *PhW* 46 (1926): 1228-29.

[165] The others are: *stetisse sibi* Muretus (reading *pari oculorum amicitiam . . . stetisse sibi*), *extersisse se* Doergens, *perdidisse se* Guietus.

[166] Brugnoli essentially followed Statius but printed *extrivisse se*, "cum ad rem paleographicam magis consentanea lectio esse mihi videatur" (app. crit. ad loc., p. 32, sim. *Studi Suetoniani*, p. 127); he does not elaborate, and I confess that I do not see his point.

for the archetype's *declamare*, presumably because it is not obviously "necessary" (cf. above, on 24. 1-2). The subject here is the rhetor Albucius Silus, who made his reputation from the discomfiture of the orator Plancus just described (*sed ex eo clarus . . .*). Suetonius first notes Silus' establishment of his *auditoria* and describes the manner of his performance there (*solitus . . . sedens incipere et . . . consurgere ac perorare*). He then takes up Silus' variable *verbal* style--a related but nonetheless separate and broader matter, calling for a new sentence: note especially that in the parallel account of Albucius at Sen. *Contr.* 7 praef., the corresponding characterizations of performance and verbal style occur not merely in different sentences but in separate paragraphs (cf. praef. 1 "incipiebat enim sedens, et si quando illum produxerat calor exsurgere audebat," with ibid. 3-4 "inaequalitatem in illo mirari licebat. splendidissimus erat; idem res dicebat omnium sordidissimas . . . nihil putabat esse quod dici in declamatione non posset. erat autem illa causa: timebat ne scholasticus videretur"). It should come as no surprise that Suetonius uses *autem* exclusively as a sentence-modifier, introducing it only at the start of a new independent clause, often where the verb of the new clause (as here) is placed first: 7. 2 *docuit autem . . .*, 9. 4 *fuit autem . . .*, 10. 3 *praecepisse autem . . .* (in indirect discourse), 15. 3 *traditur autem . . .*, 24. 4 *reliquit autem. . . .*[167] Once *autem genere* was corrupted to *aut gemere*, *declamabat* was doomed to be "corrected" to *declamare*.

The archetype offered another corruption a few words further on in the sentence, *splendide atque adoranter*. The MSS show several attempts to make sense of the last word by conjecture, with *eleganter* in **S**, *ardenter* in **Δ**, and *adornate* in **λ** (= the common ancestor of **DVL**; *adornate* also occurs in **Q**, by contamination from **L** or its exemplar); all modern editors agree in printing the last. Now even if *adornate* were the transmitted text

---

[167] The other instances of *autem* as sentence-modifier in the *DGR* are 6. 2, 12. 2, 25. 3, 25. 5, 30. 6. Suetonius' use of *autem* in the *Caesares* (just over 100 times) is identical, including a marked tendency for the verb to precede; there are a very few exceptions (e.g., *Jul.* 46 "habitavit primo in Subura modicis aedibus, post autem pontificatum maximum in Sacra via domo publica," sim. *Aug.* 81. 2, *Claud.* 14, 38. 3), with the only striking departure occurring at *Tib.* 60 ". . . gratulanti autem inter poenam, quod non et locustam . . . obtulisset," where *gratulanti* resumes *piscatori* from four lines earlier.

it would still be problematic; but since we know that it is a conjecture, it must be judged as such, and as such must be found wanting. Not only does this adverbial form appear nowhere else in Latin (as Robinson noted ad loc., ed., p. 48), but *adornare* itself is scarcely attested as a term of stylistic practice or criticism (the only relevant example noted in the *Thesaurus* is Fronto *ad M. Ant.* 4. 7 [p. 145. 2 v. d. H.] *prisco verbo adornares*); in this respect it is clearly distinct from the simplex *ornare* (for *ornate* as a stylistic term, cf. *TLL* 9.2:1034.16ff.). If a critic today offered a conjecture with these credentials--an unattested form of a word used in an all but unattested application--it would properly receive a chilly reception; there is no reason to embrace the same conjecture because it happens to have been made 500 years ago. With Heinsius, I believe that Suetonius wrote *ornate*, though I cannot agree with his *adeo*.[168] I assume that *ad-* was generated from the preceding *ATque*.

---

[168] Suetonius uses *adeo* as a simple emphatic particle--"in fact" / "quite" / "fully" (without following *ut*)--relatively seldom, and then only postpositively: *Jul.* 14. 2 *obtinuisset adeo*, *Claud.* 25. 5 *et haec et cetera totumque adeo . . . principatum*, 37 *nulla adeo suspicio*, *Ner.* 35. 4 *nullum adeo necessitudinis genus*, *Galb.* 14. 1 *maiore adeo favore et auctoritate*.

APPENDIX 1

ROBINSON AND DELLA CORTE

Della Corte's third edition includes a long discussion of the history of the text (pp. viii-xxxvii) that did not appear in the earlier editions.[1] The discussion departs from Robinson's analysis of the stemma in four places; one of these has already been remarked (cf. Chap. 1, n. 26), another is unimportant.[2] The other departures, if correct, would be quite important indeed.

1) Della Corte states that the five main MS-families identified by Robinson--X, α, β, δ (= MK), ζ--all descend *independently and directly* from the Hersfeldensis (pp. xiiif.): "Del *codex Hersfeldensis* . . . si fecero varii apografi, dei quali, allo stato attuale degli studi sia su Tacito minore sia sul minore Svetonio, si possono riconoscere almeno cinque famiglie: χ, α, β, δ, ζ." That is, δ and ζ do not descend from γ, and αβγ do not descend from Y, for γ and Y do not exist (concerning ζ and γ see also (2) below): on this view, we have a tradition composed not of two branches but of five ("almeno"). This view, however, is merely asserted, with no argument or documentation; it is incredible, and can be recognized as such by anyone who has read Robinson's diss. at all attentively. That della Corte did not read Robinson attentively is, however, suggested by the footnote appended to the sentence quoted above: "Il Robinson . . . distingueva due sole famiglie X e Y, ma onestamente riconosceva [diss., p. 61]: 'tanta est confusio familiae Y testimoniorum, ut librorum dispositionem in ipso Y

---

[1] Contrast 2nd ed., p. 20, accepting Robinson's view of the tradition and noting that the ed. was based "in gran parte sul lavoro del Robinson."

[2] Della Corte claims, p. xx, that **ed. Inc.** reproduces the text of H, though the basis of the claim is not made clear; Robinson argued, diss., pp. 159ff., that **ed. Inc.** and H had a common source.

praestare vix audeas.'" This is (at best) a gross misunderstanding of Robinson: by the phrase "librorum dispositionem" Robinson simply meant the order of the *libri*--Tac. *Dial.* and *Germ.* and Suet. *DGR*--that Y itself contained; the phrase "confusio familiae Y testimoniorum" merely refers to the fact that the various MSS of the Y-family preserve these *libri* in quite different combinations and orders. The statement does not "honestly recognize" that the testimony of the MSS is too confused to allow us to reconstruct the *existence* of Y--something Robinson (correctly) never doubted--it merely (and, again, correctly) acknowledges that the testimony of the MSS does not allow us to reconstruct the order in which the *Dial., Germ.,* and *DGR* stood in Y.

As for the question how della Corte arrived at his singular view of the tradition: it appears that he simply chose to make the *DGR* fit the schema proposed for the *Germania* by J. Perret, according to whose *Recherches* each of five MS-families (X, α, β, φ, s) descended from the archetype independently of the others; though della Corte does not actually cite Perret at the relevant spot, the direction is pointed by the reference to the "stato attuale degli studi . . . su Tacito minore" in the sentence quoted above, and by references to Perret on other matters in the near vicinity (p. xii n. 4, p. xiv. n. 2). Perret's schema, however, is scarcely more supportable for the *Germ.* than della Corte's is for *DGR*, and it has been universally rejected. Furthermore, it would challenge a Procrustes simply to impose that schema on the *DGR* even if it were valid; for while the three families Xαβ are essentially the same for both works, the remaining two families--δζ in the *DGR* and Perret's φs in the *Germ.*--are composed of entirely different MSS and have nothing at all to do with one another.

2) On p. xix della Corte notes the subscription to C--"hic antiquissimum finit exemplar: quod non integrum videtur: Fabius scripsit Romae"--and concludes: "è probabile che Fabio non sia l'amaneuense di C, ma di ζ, e l'*antiquissimum exemplar* sia senz'altro l'archetipo in scrittura carolina." This may or may not imply that C should be thought a direct copy of ζ (important if true, since C would then be--on della Corte's view--only one copy removed from the archetype, and stemmatically on a par with O and W; but this, again, is incredible, in view of the actual character of C's text). More to the point is related evidence that della Corte

failed to note.³ First, there is a virtually identical subscription in H: "hic antiquissimum exemplar finit & non integrum videtur"; this tends to confirm della Corte's conjecture that the subscription was already in ζ, the common ancestor of C and H. But there is also a similar subscription in M, a MS of the δ-family (regarded as independent by della Corte, but derived with ζ from γ by Robinson): "non videtur integrum hoc exemplar." The very similar wording ("non videtur integrum hoc exemplar" vs. "exemplar . . . non integrum videtur") strongly suggests that the two versions of the subscription are derived from a common source--namely, γ, the common ancestor of Mζ that della Corte failed to acknowledge ("hic antiquissimum . . . finit" may have stood already in γ--omitted by δ but copied by ζ--or it may represent a further elaboration by the scribe of ζ: we cannot tell).

---

3 The failure seems due to the fact that Robinson omitted this information--but not the subscription to C--from his descriptions of the MSS, on which della Corte appears (tacitly) to have depended: cf. Robinson, diss., pp. 29ff., with della Corte, pp. xivff.

APPENDIX 2

O AND W

Not quite twenty years ago D. Bo challenged the *communis opinio* that **O** and **W** are *gemelli* descended independently from a common hyparchetype (**X**), for which **O**--though certainly not flawless--is overall a better witness than **W**, whose scribe, Ugo Haemste, gives repeated signs of ignorance, negligence, and haste.[1] Bo began from three distinctive features of **W** that he took to prove its immediate descent from the Hersfeldensis itself:[2] **W** is the only MS to carry the *Germ.*, *Dial.*, and *DGR* in that order,

---

[1] See D. Bo, ed., *Cornelii Taciti "Dialogus de oratoribus"* (Turin, 1974), pp. lxxii-lxxx, and id., "Avvaloramento del codice Vindobonense 2960 in relazione al *Dialogus de oratoribus* di Tacito," *AAT* 110 (1976): 89ff.: the argument in both places is the same in its essentials (for the one noteworthy difference, see n. 5 below); in what follows I refer mainly to the more recent, slightly fuller version. On **O** and **W** in the *Dial.*, see Winterbottom, "Transmission," pp. 114f., and the earlier discussions cited there, n. 3, esp. F. Scheuer, "De Tacitei de Oratoribus Dialogi Codicum Nexu et Fide," *Breslauer philologische Abhandlungen* 6. 1 (Breslau, 1891); on **O** and **W** in the *DGR* see Robinson, diss., pp. 38ff. Throughout this discussion the *Dial.* is cited according to the chapter- and section-numbers in Winterbottom's OCT; the sigla used are those customary for the *DGR* (i.e., **O** for the *DGR* = Winterbottom's **E** for *Dial.*, **W** = **V**, **L** = **b**, **γ** = **φ**, **ζ** = **ψ**, **I** = **C**, **V** = **B**, **H** = **Harleianus 2639**, **M** = **Q**).

[2] These features do not constitute proof *per se*, and it is otherwise clear that neither **W** nor any other extant MS can be a direct copy of the Hersfeldensis (see Murgia, "The Length of the Lacuna," pp. 223f., 234f., with the discussion at Chap. 1, pp. 8-11, esp. nn. 16, 17); but these points may be set aside so that Bo's argument can be taken on its own terms. The same three features of **W** were already remarked by Robinson, "Germania," pp. 10ff., 153, though they of course did not lead him to the same conclusion.

the same order in which they occurred in the Hersfeldensis; it alone attributes the *Dial.* to Tacitus in its *subscriptio* but not in its *inscriptio*, a pattern that may have been present in the Hersfeldensis too;³ and it marks the lacuna at *Dial.* 35-36 both by leaving a space blank (as do the other MSS: in W's case, a folium minus two lines) and by using the unique formula "hic est defectus unius folii cum dimidio."⁴ At the same time, Bo realized that O posed an obstacle to this view: the distinctive errors shared by OW against the other MSS guarantee either that they are *gemelli* or that one is descended from the other; but their standing as *gemelli* would effectively rule out the view that W is also a direct copy of the Hersfeldensis. (*Int. al.*, the shared errors of OW would then presumptively be the legacy of the Hersfeldensis itself, and *all* the corresponding correct readings shared by the other MSS-- including those that supply text omitted in OW--would have to be the result of conjecture in their common hyparchetype(s), something that is scarcely conceivable.) Bo was therefore compelled to argue that O was descended from W (to account for their shared errors), with contamination from another MS (to account for the places where O departs from W to agree with the other MSS); the source of contamination Bo identified as a descendant of Pontano's MS, L.⁵ Bo's view has now been championed by H.

---

3 Thus a plausible reading of the discrepant testimony of Niccoli, Panormita, and Decembrio: see Robinson, ibid., p. 12.

4 Contrast the notice in the margin of O, "hic deest multum: in exemplari dicunt deesse sex paginas" (where one line has been left blank in the text): cf. V's "hic desunt sex pagellae" and L's "deerant in exemplari sex pagellae vetustate consumptae." The manner in which the Hersfeldensis itself marked the lacuna remains deeply controversial: on the problematic evidence provided by the MSS and Decembrio's description, see esp. Murgia, "The Length of the Lacuna," pp. 222ff. On the notice of the lacuna in O, Robinson commented (ibid., p. 14): "I can only suggest that . . . O has borrowed from some member of the Y family, or that the copyist, evidently a scholar, adopted a hearsay report (note his use of *dicunt*)." This is *prima facie* the most reasonable view, given both the actual state of O's text and the similarity between O's "in exemplari . . . sex paginas" and L's "in exemplari sex pagellae": see Barwick (n. 5 below), Murgia, "The Length of the Lacuna," p. 224, and the following discussion.

5 Thus modifying K. Barwick, "Der *Dialogus de oratoribus* des Tacitus," *SB d. sächs. Akad. d. Wissensch. Leipzig*, Phil.-hist. Kl. 101. 4 (Berlin, 1954), pp. 38f., who argued that O showed contamination directly from L. Bo introduced this modification in "Avvaloramento" (p. 112) because of a

Merklin ("'Dialogus'-Probleme," pp. 2270f.). If correct, it would significantly affect (though not "revolutionize," *pace* Merklin) the recension of both the *Dial.* and the *DGR*: **O** would be banished from the apparatus, save where it uniquely offers a true or interesting conjecture, while **W** would by itself represent one branch of the tradition, occupying the position previously held by the hyparchetype **X**. This would not be an unmixed blessing; for in view of its numerous deficiencies, a **W** thus isolated would in general be a less eloquent witness to the archetype than the hyparchetype that can be reconstructed if **OW** are regarded as *gemelli*.

Bo's view, however, is inadequately argued and certainly mistaken. His arguments for the *Dial.* have been criticized by C. E. Murgia, who showed that **O**'s descent from **W** in that work is quite unlikely on several grounds.[6] Before moving on to consider the *DGR* (which Bo did not do), I can here offer some further observations on the character of Bo's argument for the *Dial.*, limiting myself to the question of contamination on which that argument depends.

Barwick's original suggestion that **O** showed contamination from L in the *Dial.* was based primarily on **O**'s description of the lacuna, which does indeed bear a noteworthy resemblance to L's (see n. 4); but Barwick also remarked seven places where a correct and probably conjectural reading in L is found in **O** as well: 5. 5 *factaque* L**O** (for *fataque*), 16. 2 *meas si istud* L, *meas illud* **O**, with *si* written above the line; 17. 1 *Menenium* L, written in the margin of **O** (**O**'s text has *me nimium* with the rest of the MSS); 19. 3 *videretur* L, *videtur* **O**, with *re* written above the line; 21. 5 *eloquentia* L**O** (for *-tiam*), 28. 2 *iam in* L**O** (for *iam*); 30. 1 *notitia*, corrected from *-tiam* in both **O** (by erasure) and L (by deletion of

---

difference between the *inscriptio* to the *Dial.* in **O** and that in L; in his ed. (p. lxxviii), he like Barwick took L itself to be the source; the modification in fact makes no substantial difference in the conduct of Bo's argument. Oddly, in neither of his discussions of contamination does Bo actually refer to Barwick, though elsewhere in the same publications he cites the very page on which Barwick made his suggestion (cf. ed., p. xxxiii n. 5, "Avvaloramento," p. 98 n. 54): both here and below, therefore, I assume Bo's knowledge of Barwick's evidence and argument.

[6] Murgia, "The Length of the Lacuna," pp. 234-36. Murgia's critique is rejected by Merklin, "'Dialogus'-Probleme," p. 2275, in whose own discussion **W**'s alleged descent immediately from the Hersfeldensis plays a pivotal role.

the suspension-stroke for -*m*). Murgia has already observed that these latter places do not present a very compelling set of data: most involve corrections so obvious that they could easily occur independently to more than one competent reader of Latin;[7] by contrast, where more problematic passages are at issue, O contains a number of distinctive readings that are not found in L, and L has an even greater number of distinctive conjectures that are not found in O;[8] accordingly, while O's description of the lacuna may well be derived somehow from L, and while these other readings obviously *could* have entered O from L, the evidence Barwick adduced falls well short of proving extensive contamination of the former from the latter. These observations are all correct; but a further methodological point can also be made, concerning an important difference between the arguments of Barwick and Bo, and a corresponding distinction that should be drawn between the sorts of evidence useful to each.

It is notable, first, that four of the seven passages Barwick cited involve corrections in O, made through erasure or as supplements written above the line and in the margin, apparently in the hand of O's scribe (O's notice of the lacuna is also written in the margin: see n. 4). Plainly, these four do nothing to prove that contamination had taken place in O's *inherited* text, the text that descended (according to Bo) from W to the MS copied by O's scribe. Instead, if these four corrections indicate anything at all about the contamination of O, they rather suggest that the man who wrote O may have entered a few readings from L (or a descendant of L) at some point *after* he had his finished MS before

---

[7] Three do appear in other MSS (5. 5 *factaque*, 16. 2 *meas si*, 28. 2 *iam in*: see at nn. 10, 12 below), and of the rest only O's marginal entry *Menenium* at 17. 1 is at all interesting, insofar as it is less obvious in its immediate context and recalls other places where Pontano shows a penchant for emendations involving personal names: see, e.g., *Dial.* 5. 7 *Eprius Marcellus quam* L (*prius Marcellus quam* ω, *Marcellus prius quam* O), with pp. 23, 120f. (on *DGR* 27. 1 *Otacilius*) and p. 29 (on *DGR* 28. 2 *Mancino*). Note, however, that in each of the latter three places O *differs* from L, and that at 17. 1 O's scribe could himself have introduced the marginal note *Menenium* from 21. 7 *Menenios*.

[8] Murgia, "The Length of the Lacuna," p. 235; for the peculiar readings in L see the lists in A. Gudeman, ed., *P. Cornelii Taciti "Dialogus de oratoribus"*[2] (Leipzig and Berlin, 1914), pp. 118f.

him.⁹ Now such *post eventum* contamination would make very little difference to Barwick's case, for he took O and W to be *gemelli* and was simply seeking evidence to bolster his contention that the description of the lacuna reached O from L (as indeed it may have done): how extensive the contact between the two MSS was, what form it took, at what stage it occurred--whether after O had been written or already in its exemplar--none of these questions would matter to him.¹⁰ All these questions, by contrast, should have mattered a great deal to Bo, who was arguing a very different case: his contention that O was a contaminated *descendant* of W necessarily implies both that the contamination of O was *very* extensive (see below) and that O's base-text--the text written by the scribe as his hand first moved across the page--*already* embodied the results of contamination, whether that contamination was achieved in O's immediate exemplar or in some earlier intermediary between O and W (obviously, if the errors descending to O from W had been removed by contamination only after O was written, we should see the evidence not only in these four places but--by Bo's own count--in several dozen more: see below).¹¹ In short, Bo's thesis that O descends from W should

---

9   For a parallel case in the *DGR* compare the readings from X that entered G only as corrections or variants: see Robinson, diss., pp. 113ff.

10   Though Barwick did not make clear when or how he thought contamination had occurred, one of his statements suggests that he did assume it occurred after O's text had been written ("Der *Dialogus*," p. 38): "Es gibt fünf Stellen, wo [O] . . . zusammen mit [L] allein das Richtige gibt. Dabei hat der Schreiber von [O], mit einer einzigen Ausnahme, die falsche Lesung der übrigen Handschriften zunächst beibehalten, dann aber verbessert," listing 5. 5 *factaque* (i.e., the *einzige Ausnahme*) and the four corrections noted above; he then went on to mention the other two readings (21. 5 *eloquentia*, 28. 2 *iam in*), for which (he thought) L and O are not the only witnesses (on 21. 5, however, see n. 12). Barwick, who was relying on Gudeman's apparatus, did not know that in two of the first five places L and O are *not* alone in giving the correct reading: on 5. 5 *factaque*, see n. 12 below; at 16. 2 *meas si*, the correct *si* also appears in two ζ-MSS reported by Winterbottom.

11   Did Bo perhaps contemplate a third alternative, viz., that O's scribe wrote his MS with both (a descendant of) W and (a descendant of) L open before him, collating the two and correcting the former from the latter as he wrote? It is a further fault of Bo's argument that he nowhere states when and how he supposes the contamination occurred; but it will

have placed upon his argument for contamination demands very different from, and much more stringent than, the demands Barwick's argument had to meet.

Accordingly, were Bo attempting rigorously to demonstrate the sort of contamination actually relevant to his thesis, four of the passages cited by Barwick would be of only questionable utility. Nor would the remaining instances (5. 5, 21. 5, 28. 2) provide him with any firmer ground, since each of these falls squarely into the category noted above, viz., simple corrections of obvious errors: the last of these corrections certainly occurs elsewhere (28. 2 *iam in*, also in H), and at least one of the others apparently does too.[12] Bo's argument would instead require much more extensive and more distinctive evidence even to begin to persuade. Bo, however, apparently did not see the difference between his thesis and Barwick's, or the consequences of that difference for his argument: he merely cites the same seven readings ("Avvaloramento," p. 112), and adds one other, no more compelling (*dicere* for *discere* at 28. 4: "neque *dicere* fas erat quod turpe *dictu* neque *facere* quod inhonestum *factu* videretur").[13] He does not weigh the readings'

---

become plain that his thesis cannot stand whether one suposes the contamination occurred before, during, or after the copying of **O**.

[12] At 5. 5 Winterbottom reports the correct *factaque* also for **M** and two ζ-MSS, against Barwick (= Gudeman) and Bo, who claim it only for **LO** (Bo's claim that the whole phrase *factaque nostra* appears only in **LO**, for *fataque per nostra*, is further contradicted by Winterbottom, who reports the correct *nostra* also for **I**, ζ, and a *corrector nescioquis* in **W**). At 21. 5, however, where Barwick (= Gudeman) attributed the correct *eloquentia* also to **V**, Winterbottom reports that **V** has *eloquentiam*.

[13] The correct *dicere* also occurs in **M** and two ζ-MSS. This instance *is* interesting in at least one respect, though it does not help Bo's argument; for while **O**'s base-text has *dicere*, there is also a suprascript *s*, as though to indicate *discere*. It is unlikely that anyone, faced with *dicere* ... *dictu* ... *facere* ... *factu*, would spontaneously conjecture *discere* here (the original error probably arose mechanically, from anticipation: *dicere faS* > *diScere faS*): the suprascript reading should therefore have a MS source. In that case, there are three alternatives: either **O**'s scribe noted a reading that he found in another MS after he had written his text; or he was reflecting the state of his exemplar, where the alternative reading had already been noted or where *discere* had been corrected to *dicere* with a mark of expunction (**O**'s scribe would then have written suprascript *s* to preserve the memory of his exemplar: cf. Chap. 1 at n. 47); or he saw *discere* in his exemplar, wrote the obvious correction himself, but chose to preserve the

probative value for his own argument, nor does he even indicate (as Barwick had done) that up to half of them may have entered O's text only after it had been written: all are simply attributed to O, with no distinction drawn between base-text and corrections or supplements.

With that, Bo's direct argument for contamination of O from (a descendant of) L effectively ends. He does, it is true, go on to list another forty-odd readings (pp. 112f.), claiming that they too reached O by contamination; but this list, so far from supporting his case, actually undermines it. These places have nothing to do with the distinctive readings of Pontano's MS (to the contrary, they include several places where O does *not* have the singular conjecture found in L); they are merely places where W has peculiar errors (including thirteen omissions) while O transmits the archetypal text found in the other MSS--precisely what O *should* do if it is the *gemellus* of W, but not if it is descended from W. Here Bo seems to have fallen into the fallacy of taking as his premise what it was properly his burden to prove, viz., that O can credibly be regarded as a descendant of W. The results are dizzyingly circular: thus, when Bo claims (p. 113) that O can display these archetypal readings so consistently only as the result of contamination (as opposed to free conjecture), the claim will be true *if and only if* it is already clear that O is descended from W; the claim cannot be used as Bo uses it, as part of his argument to show that O *was* contaminated and so *can* be regarded as a descendant of O. Instead of listing these readings to "prove" O's contamination from (a descendant of) L--which they cannot do-- Bo should have recognized that they tend, rather, to refute his central contention: if contamination of O from (a descendant of) L really had been careful and thorough enough to remove even half these errors of W (a good number of which are scarcely apparent as errors), then the process would certainly have carried along many more of Pontano's unique conjectures than are actually found in O; conversely, if contamination from (a descendant of) L really was as superficial as Bo's only direct evidence shows it would have to have been--even if that evidence is regarded

---

memory of his exemplar with the suprascript *s*. None of these alternatives is obviously more likely than the others, and the relevance of L to the problem is in any case unclear: L originally had *discere*, but the *s* was erased at some (indeterminate) point to produce *dicere*.

uncritically and given its fullest possible value (cf. above)--then an O descended from W would have retained many more of these peculiar errors.

Bo's attempt to demonstrate O's contaminated descent from W in the *Dial.* is not supported by sufficient evidence and is fatally deficient in methodological coherence and rigor. If we turn now to the *DGR*, and subject Bo's thesis to similar scrutiny, a similar conclusion emerges. The possibility that O is descended from W in the *DGR* was addressed already by Robinson; but since he took it to be obvious that neither MS can be derived from the other, his explicit comments are brief (diss., p. 54). His arguments can be supplemented here.

(1) As in the *Dial.*, O often agrees with the other MSS against W, both in error (e.g., 3. 2 *M. Metellum* OY, *M.* recte om. W) and especially in the truth (see (2) below, and cf. Robinson, diss., pp. 47ff., for a full list of W's peculiar readings); and in many of the latter cases--especially those where W has omissions--it is plain that O's text cannot be the product of independent conjecture. At the same time, however, there is no evidence that O's text underwent extensive contamination from any Y-MS--and least of all, that it was contaminated from L or a descendant of L. There are several dozen readings in L that are probably due to Pontano's own correction of the transmitted text that he encountered, and a number of these conjectures are quite distinctive (see Chap. 1, pp. 21-23). Yet from among these many emendations, exactly *two* are also found in O but not in W; and both of them are obvious corrections that occur independently in other MSS: 23.4 *pepercisse* OLUS (where W has *percisse*), 24.3 *cum plurimos* OLDKUCS.[14] Neither the number nor the character of these corrections suggests that anything more than coincidence is at work: plainly, if O

---

[14] Note that in the latter case the archetypal reading was the impossible *cum plurimis*: the correction found in O is based on that archetypal error--an error that O could not have inherited from W, which reads *plurimis* but omits the words *unum et alterum vel cum* that precede it, with half a line left blank, apparently because W's scribe found his exemplar illegible or defective. This, of course, cannot lend comfort to Bo's belief that W's exemplar was the Hersfeldensis, for the correct text is transmitted in the other MSS; neither does it prove (*pace* Robinson, diss., p. 56) that O was copied from the hyparchetype X before the latter suffered damage reflected here in W, since it is not necessary to assume that either O or W was copied directly from the hyparchetype.

represented a text contaminated from **L** or a descendant of **L**, it would share at least *some* of Pontano's distinctive readings (cf., e.g., Robinson, diss., pp. 113ff., on the contamination of **N** from **X**).

(2) In several other places **W** has omissions that are not shared by **O**; among the more interesting examples for our purposes are the following:

> 9. 1 *una atque eadem die* **OY**, *atque eadem* om. **W**
> 9. 3 *namque* vel *nanque* **OY**, *-que* om. **W**
> 10. 5 *altera* **OY**, om. **W**
> 15. 1 *schola* **OY**, om. **W**
> 21. 1 *muneri* **OY**, om. **W**

On Bo's view, the readings of **O** in these places must be the result of contamination, the insertion of text that **O** could not have inherited from **W**. But these places are interesting precisely because the loss of text in **W** is far from obvious: in no case does **W**'s omission disrupt the flow of the passage, in each case the text of **W** is easily intelligible despite the loss. In other words, the ordinary experience of reading or copying would not suggest that anything was amiss: it would require quite careful collation with another MS for **W**'s defect to be spotted and remedied in each case. Yet at the same time we find **O** and **W** sharing such egregious flaws as (e.g.) the yawning incoherence produced by the omission of *cum adversario de iure* at 22. 1 (habent **cett.**), and other instances of singular gibberish--e.g., 14. 3 *libro sed iam* (*libros etiam* **cett.**, recte) and 3. 5 *mutoscedo doceret* (where all the other MSS have one or another version of *multos edoceret* inherited from **Y**: see the discussion ad loc. in Chap. 2). In none of these examples is the obvious corruption addressed in **O**, though a remedy would have been immediately at hand had *any* **Y**-MS been brought to bear. It would be a very strange kind of contamination indeed that provided correction where the error was not noticeable but failed to meet the need where it was so clamant.

If, then, one wishes to believe in the contaminated descent of **O** from **W** in the *DGR*, he must believe the following: contamination took the form of a collation so careful and minute that a number of scarcely apparent omissions were made good; yet this minute collation both failed to address obvious and gross deficiencies that **O** shares uniquely with **W** and failed to impart to **O** *any* of the distinctive readings of the MS that was the source of contamination (see (1) above, and the comments on the *Dial.*). Viewed in this light, the contaminated descent of **O** from **W** is seen to be, not a fact or likelihood that emerges unforced from a disinterested consideration of the evidence, but an implausible a priori construct that Bo must impose on the evidence because it is demanded by his larger thesis, the direct descent of **W** from the Hersfeldensis. The evidence of the *DGR* itself instead squarely supports the usual view: **O** and **W** are *gemelli* descended from the same hyparchetype, whose text is sometimes transmitted more faithfully by **O** than it is by **W**.

(3) The same lesson is provided by the following instances. Here both **O** and **W** show a misunderstanding of the correct, archetypal reading, but **O**'s error is *closer* to the archetype than the false "improvement" or further corruption found in **W**:

> 11. 1 *Latina Siren*] latinas irem **O**, latinas item **W**
> 21. 3 *nunc Iocorum*] nun cio corum **O**, nuntio eorum **W**
> 30. 1 *suscepit eas partes* (vel *-tis*) *atque ita implevit*] suscepit eius partis mores ita implevit **O**, suscepit eius patris mores ita implevit **W**

The errors at 11. 1 and 21. 3 are both ultimately due to the misreading of text in *scriptura continua*, of which **O** and **W** show many other symptoms (cf., e.g., 14. 3 *libro sed iam* **OW**, above; at 21. 3 the letters in **O** are written as shown, with a bit less than a full word-space between the groups): in each place **W** shows a further stage of corruption, with forms (*item, nuntio eorum*) that at least look like Latin in their contexts; and it is particularly clear in the second place that **O** would neither have derived its meaningless text from **W** nor introduced it by contamination (L reads *nunc Iocorum*). It plainly is a more faithful reproduction of the common source of **O** and **W**.[15]

We can draw a similar conclusion from the third example, which is best appreciated if we view the passage in context (30. 1): "... receptusque in Planci oratoris contubernium, cui declamaturo mos erat prius aliquem qui ante diceret excitare, suscepit eas partes atque ita implevit ut Planco silentium imponeret. ..." The texts of **O** and **W** represent the combination of the correct reading, *eas partes atque* (so **Y**), with an interlinear gloss, *eius moris*, which was intended to clarify *eas* by pointing back to *cui ... mos*

---

[15] For several similar examples of **O**'s "greater accuracy in transmitting error" from the common hyparchetype of **OW** in the *Dial.*, see Murgia, "The Length of the Lacuna," p. 235.

erat in the previous clause.[16] The gloss very likely stood in the archetype, where it was correctly ignored by the scribe of hyparchetype **Y** but was conflated with *eas partes* by the scribe of hyparchetype **X**, resulting in the ouster of *atque* and the phrase *eius partis mores*: the latter phrase was then accurately transmitted by **O**; and as in the two places remarked above, **W** produced a further corruption of the hyparchetype's text, with the mechanical (and, in its context, nonsensical) error *patris* for *partis*.[17] It is worth noting, too, that the scribe originally responsible for the error did not simply insert the gloss into the text, to produce a straightforward conflation such as *eas partes eius moris*; rather, he paused long enough to select and combine the pronominal and nominal forms so as to create a new, hybrid phrase. That scribe cannot have been the scribe of **W**, as Bo's thesis would require, for the latter man "copia meccanicamente ciò che ha davanti, senza preoccuparsi del senso o del contesto."[18]

(4) A final example can suffice: 23. 1 *Q. Remmius*] *Remmius* **O**, *Emmius* **W** (*M* littera staturae brevis in spatio praeposit. postea scripta), *al. Q. Remmius* **W**m. Here, following his usual practice at the start of a chapter, the scribe of **W** wrote *Emmius*--that is, the name as it appeared in his exemplar, *minus* the first letter, for which he left a space so that a large capital initial could be entered

---

16 Thus Wessner, rev. of Robinson, diss., p. 541. On intrusive glosses such as this see the discussions of 7. 3 and 25. 4 in Chap. 2.

17 Wessner, ibid., preferred to think that the gloss first appeared in **X**, not the archetype. This alternative is conceivable, though only if the common source of **O** and **W** was not **X** itself, but a copy of **X** in which the conflation arose: if the gloss first appeared in **X**, and if **O** and **W** each descends directly from **X**, then much the same conflation, and the same expulsion of *atque*, would have to have occurred independently twice, once in the line descending to **O**, once in the line descending to **W**--a degree of coincidence that is scarcely believable.

18 Bo, "Avvaloramento," p. 111. **W**'s scribe in fact seems to have been hurrying here, as he neared the end of the text. Though not pinched for space, he began *DGR* 30 in the middle of a line, writing "C. albucius silus" immediately after the last word of chap. 29, without starting a new paragraph and leaving a space for a large initial (so his regular habit: see immediately below); and in the clause preceding the present corruption he almost omitted *ante* by writing *qui diceret*--though he just caught himself, after getting as far as *dic*, then marked the offending letters for deletion and went on his way.

later (on **W**'s regular habits in this regard, see the discussion of 13. 1 *L. Staberius* in Chap. 2); he also noted the correct reading, with the praenominal *Q.*, as a marginal variant (probably fetched from the *index grammaticorum* at the head of the work). Here, as throughout, the space left by the scribe was not filled with the expected large capital; instead, someone subsequently (and bizarrely) entered a small and sketchy capital M, an error apparently prompted either by the name "M. Pomponius Marcellus" at the head of the preceding chapter or by the intrusive recollection of the name "Memmius" from chap. 14. In any case, it is plain that **O**'s *Remmius* cannot be inherited from **W**'s text (*Emmius* or *M Emmius*); equally clearly, it is derived neither from **W**'s marginal variant nor from **L** by contamination, for either of those sources would have provided the *praenomen* that is omitted in the text of **O** and **W** alike (**L** reads *Quintus Reminius* [sic], with a suprascript *h* between *R* and *e*). The obvious conclusion, given all the above: **O**'s text derives from an exemplar that had *Remmius* (period)--the same reading, in other words, that was before **W**'s scribe when he wrote *Emmius* (period).

To sum up: there are a few signs in the *Dial.*, especially in the description of the lacuna, that **O**'s text came into contact with **L**'s at some point--though evidence for anything beyond the most superficial contact is lacking, and such evidence as there is could be taken to show that the contact occurred only after **O** was written; in the *DGR* there is no evidence even of that superficial contact; there is certainly no reason to believe Bo's contention that **O** is a contaminated *descendant* of **W**, for Bo's argument lacks rigor, is supported by no sufficient evidence, and is presented in a way that is virtually self-refuting; there is, on the other hand, every reason to think that the two MSS are what they are commonly taken to be--*gemelli* descended from a common hyparchetype (**X**). It follows that--however one wishes to explain the formal features of **W** noted above (ad init.)--the explanation is not to be found by assuming that **W**'s text is a direct copy of the Hersfeldensis, a notion that can be ruled out on other grounds as well.[19]

---

[19] See the refs. at n. 2 above.

APPENDIX 3

Biblioteca Riccardiana 3595

Biblioteca Riccardiana 3595 (chart., 210 x 140 mm., flyleaves + 124 numbered fol.) is a composite MS, consisting of three segments-- fol. 1-62 + 63-119 + 120-24--which contain the work of nine different hands:[1]

Hand 1, fol. 1^r-7^r: fol. 1^r-1^v, "Oratio de sancta veronica" ("Salve sancta facies nostri redemptoris / in qua inter speties divini splendoris . . .") + fol. 2^r-7^r, "Indulgentiae septem ecclesiarum urbis romae" ("Incipiunt indulgentiae vii eccl(es)ia(rum) romae. Sanctus Silvester papa scribit in cronica sua q(uod) rome fuerunt Mcccccv eccl(es)ie qua(rum) maior pars est destructa . . .")
(fol. 7^v blank)
Hand 2, fol. 8^r-59^r: fol. 8^r-23^v, Suetonius *De grammaticis et rhetoribus* (without title or attribution) + fol. 24^r-58^r, Tacitus *Dialogus de oratoribus* (without title or attribution) + fol. 58^v blank + fol. 59^r, "MAECENAS MARONIS" (= *Eleg. in Maec.* 1. 1-13 *Regis eras*; the rest of the page is blank)
(fol. 59^v-62^v blank)

Hand 3, fol. 63^r: *Probationes pennae* + a version of Livy 1. 16. 7 (without title or attribution: "Romulus ad Iulium proculum in extremis laborans dixit 'abi, nuntia. . .' haec locutus sublimis abiit")
(fol. 63^v blank)
Hand 4, fol. 64^r-96^r: "Caii Plinii Veronei oratoris de viris illustribus libellus foeliciter incipit," with the colophon "Sexti ruffi viri consularis Valentiano Augusto de istoria romana libellus finit / Et ego Alexan-

---

[1] I wish to thank Dr. Maria Prunai Falciani, Director of the Biblioteca Riccardiana, for enabling me to acquire a microfilm of this MS, and esp. for informing me of its composite character, which was not apparent from the microfilm.

der Thomae Blosii filius p(er)scripsi Firmi m⁰ cccc⁰ octuagesimo p⁰ Decimo kln. Februarias")²
(fol. 96ᵛ-98ᵛ blank)
Hand 5, fol. 99ʳ-111ᵛ: fol. 99ʳ-109ᵛ, "CATALICII AD ARTEM METRICAM PERCIPIENDAM BREVISSIME" ("Nosce pedes hii sunt graditur quibus alma Thalia / qui potare cupis Bellerophontis aquas / PEDES quibus frequentius utimur . . .") + fol. 110ʳ-110ᵛ blank + fol. 111ʳ-111ᵛ, remarks on meter, untitled ("Pedes qui metra de quibus dicturi sumus ingrediuntur aliquos dissillabos, aliquos trissyllabos, quadrisyllabos aliquos esse invenio . . .")
(fol. 112ʳ-112ᵛ blank)
Hand 6, fol. 113ʳ-118ᵛ: Untitled, sets of synonymous Latin phrases, each set introduced by "Dicendo"("Dicendo usque ad ultimum vitae c(or)-p(u)s sententiose loquar al(iter) extremo vite corpore (ve)l novissimo vitae victus die sententiose loquar . . .")
(fol. 119ʳ-120ᵛ blank)

Hand 7, fol. 121ʳ: A brief composition, "De coniugali coppula . . ."
(fol. 121ᵛ blank)
Hand 8, fol. 122ʳ: Untitled, a brief composition in the vernacular, "Per non esser piu proliso . . ."
(fol. 122ᵛ blank)
Hand 9, fol. 123ʳ-124ʳ: Untitled, a brief composition, "Quamquam dignas laudes huic pri(n)c(ipi) primus orator . . ."
(fol. fol. 124ᵛ blank)

Since the dated subscription on fol. 96ʳ (Hand 4) occurs in the second segment of this composite MS, it cannot be assumed to provide a precise *terminus ante quem* for the copying of the *DGR* and the *Dial.* in the first (and originally separate) segment, fol. 8ʳ-59ʳ (Hand 2); the latter hand in any case clearly dates to the late 15th century. The texts in this hand are written in a single column of 20 lines / page. The hand is unattractive, spindly in appearance at the beginning of the *DGR* and growing progressively coarser as the scribe's work proceeds; in its spindly phase, the script resembles that of Hands 1 and 5 but is easily distinguished from these by the shape of the lowercase *r*, formed by a short vertical stroke coupled with a very pronounced semicircular stroke, such that the letter can often be mistaken for a *k* or the combination *ic*.³

---

² The *De viris illustribus* is found also in D, Δ, and Univ. Notre Dame 58 (for the last, see Chap. 1, n. 8).

³ A very similar letter-form can be seen in *Catalogo dei manoscritti in scrittura latina datati o databili*, vol. 1: *Biblioteca Nazionale Centrale di*

Both the *DGR* and the *Dial.* begin without indication of title or author and conclude without subscription;[4] the *DGR* also lacks the *indices* of *grammatici* and *rhetores*. A large initial G, the height of four lines, stands at the beginning of the *DGR*. Thereafter, the scribe regularly left a blank square space, the height of two lines, for a large initial to be provided at the start of the biographical chapters (5-24, 26-30) and at several points in the other chapters;[5] but as in the case of W, where a similar pattern is found (see pp. 80f., 145f.), the initials were never provided.[6] The same pattern is found in the *Dial.*, beginning with 1. 1 [ ]*epe ex me requiris* and continuing, passim, throughout.

Neither the *DGR* nor the *Dial.* is consistently punctuated or extensively corrected. In the *DGR*, with which my comments here are primarily concerned, most corrections that occur appear to have been made by a hand other than the scribe's (to judge from the microfilm available to me), and there is reason to think that at least some of this correction had a MS source other than the original exemplar: so, e.g., at the beginning of *DGR* 13, where the archetypal text was already deeply corrupt (see pp. 82-86), the scribe wrote *hero   empturus*, with a space of ca. 9 letters left between the words; *hero* was later changed to *hiera*, and *suo mene* was inserted in the blank space, to produce a text that-- while still scarcely intelligible--is similar to the defective text found in several other MSS (*hiero suo meneaemptus heros*

Roma, a cura di V. Jemolo (Turin, 1971), tav. CLIII (= Vitt. Em. 484, c. 222ʳ, an. 1482), and R. W. Hunt et al., *The Survival of Ancient Literature* (Oxford, 1975), pl. III, text-hand (= Oxon. MS. Add. C. 136, fol. 73aʳ). I am grateful to my colleague W. Braxton Ross for his help on this point.

[4] The word "Τέλος" stands at the end of *DGR* 24, the last of the grammarians' lives, at the bottom of fol. 19ᵛ.

[5] 2. 1 [ ]*Rimus*, 3. 2 [ ]*Elius cognomine*, 4. 1 [ ]*PPellatio*, 25. 1 [ ]*HETORICA*. As in most other MSS, the beginning of the life of M. Epidius (*DGR* 28) is not recognized as such: the text continues without break after the end of the preceding chapter, and no space is left for an initial.

[6] At 13. 1 [ ]*Taberius* and 16. 1 [ ]*Ecilius* a small L and a small C, respectively, were written in the margin, apparently in a later hand. Whatever the source of these notations (cf. next n.), the scribe's exemplar evidently had *C(a)ecilius* (om. Q.) at 16. 1, and probably *L. Taberius* at 13. 1 (cf. p. 81), both errors characteristic of ζ-MSS: see below.

nam&ra : *empturus* **C**, *hiero suo menea emptus heros ramata empturus* **Δ**, *hierausuomene emptus, heros   empturus* **Q**: it is otherwise clear that all three of these MSS are very closely related to Ricc. 3595, see below).[7] If that is the case, it is all the more striking (not to say odd) that so little correction was performed overall, even in places where the text was so plainly corrupt that it was marked by a reader as such.[8] At the beginning of the *DGR* a hand other than the scribe's wrote a few proper names in the margin next to their appearance in the text, but these notations cease after the first few pages. They resume, and are continued more consistently, in the *Dial.*

The texts of the *DGR* and the *Dial.* obviously are derived from the same archetype as the other surviving MSS of both works: thus, e.g., the *DGR* breaks off after 30. 6 *abstinuit cibo* and shows the omission of *velim, cum mihi ille iucundus esse* in the quotation of Cicero at 14. 3;[9] the text of Tacitus includes the major lacuna between *Dial.* 35 and 36, where one and a half lines are left blank, with no comment or notation in text or margin. In the case of the *DGR*, the text--to which I will here give the *siglum* **Z**--can very easily be placed among the *deteriores* of the ζ-family. (Spot-collation of the *Dial.* indicates that it belongs among the corresponding *deteriores* of that text, Winterbottom's ψ-family: cf. p. 7.) Working our way "down" the revised stemma of the *DGR* (p. 32), we find the following:

---

[7] Note also the following corrections, which seem fairly clearly to be in a hand other than the scribe's: 2. 2 *aliorum*] *animos* (**QE**) ex *animorum*, 3. 2 *Stilo*] *histilo* ex *hostilo*, 4. 3 *imbutum* ex *mbutum*, 8. 2 *deterioribus* ex *doctoribus*, 9. 2 *leviter* ex *aliter*, 15. 2 *historicum* ex *historicorum*, 20. 1 *audiit et*] *avide* (**E**; added in a space originally left blank, *ut vid.*), 22. 1 *perseveravit* ex *-bit*, 29. 2 *congiarium* ex *-ius*, 30. 5 *Mediolaneii* ex *Medionaleii*. The corrections at 2. 2, 3. 2, 8. 2, 9. 2, and 20. 1, at least, are likely to have a MS source; cf. also n. 6.

[8] E.g., at 25. 2 *censolium abiebtum* (for *censorium edictum*), crosses were placed above the corrupt words but no correction was made; at 10. 5, where *extent* was omitted after *quamquam paucissimi*, a caret was placed in the text to mark the obvious absence of a verb, and a corresponding caret was placed in the margin, next to a sketchily drawn rectangular box, but no verb was supplied.

[9] It also has all but four of the scores of other errors that already infected the archetype: for the exceptions--6. 2 *simul*, 14. 1 *Memmi*, 16. 3 *Epirota* (om. *et*), 22. 3 *Gallus*--see below.

Appendix 3: Biblioteca Riccardiana 3595   151

1) Z has all but one of the errors that most clearly distinguish the Y-family: 1. 3 *augurandi*, 3. 1 *gener Q.*, 3. 5 *multos edoceret*, 4. 3 *titulos*, 4. 5 *institutionum* (*institionum* Z), 10. 2 *praetextatus nobilis*, 11. 1 om. *P.*, 14. 3 *solicitudo*, 17. 2 *ne quem] neque*, 22. 2 *Tiberium*, 25. 1 *sero] fere*, 25. 2 *uti ei] utsi ei*, 25. 2 *item dixerunt*, 25. 5 *educerent . . . verebantur . . . imposuerunt . . . celarunt*, 25. 5 *recogniti sunt*, 26. 1 *et studiosissimus] cum stud-*, 28. 2 *Nuncino* (*nûcino* Z, cf. p. 29), 28. 2 om. *aureis*. The exception is 25. 2 *Latine*, an error attested also by $W^mN(N^2)G^3$, as opposed to the correct *Latinos* (XN^1G^2Q) and the error *Latine scilicet* (vel *.s.*) found in $GI\beta\gamma$ (hence surely the reading of Y): in view of Z's pronounced tendency to omit text (noted below), it seems most likely that the absence of *scilicet* (or *.s.*) here is the independent result of the same habit.

2) Within Y, Z has all the errors that most clearly distinguish the Γ-family (cf. pp. 12-14): 7. 2 *primum] prius*, 7. 3 *ut hic*, 15. 2 *improbi*, 15. 2 *curconem* (*cûconem* Z), 17. 2 *sextertia centena*, 24. 2 *omnes] se* (cf. also 3. 2 *optimatum*, 13. 1 *empturus*, 17. 3 *parieti] perite*, 20. 1 om. *puerum*, 25. 2 *interiecto] interrupto*).

3) Within Γ, Z has all but one of the errors that most clearly distinguish the γ-family: 1. 2 *aut si quid] at siquidem*, 3. 5 *Gaius] L(a)eneus*, 3. 6 *Siscenius*, 4. 5 om. *scilicet*, 5. 1 *fecitque] ferturque*, 5. 1 *tamen] tum*, 5. 1 *indicatur*, 8. 3 *vulgatosque*, 9. 4 *omni sermone*, 10. 2 *declamantum* (*-ma- tum* Z) 10. 6 *historias* (*in -ias* Z), 11. 3 *medico*, 14. 2 *putem] parente*, 14. 3 *habuero*, 14. 3 *victus] coitus* (*conc(us)* Z, *cintus* C), 17. 3 *publicaret*, 18. 3 *edoceret*, 25. 2 *nova quae] nova* (om. *quae*), 25. 3 *et primo*, 25. 5 *et sic*, 26. 2 *Atratino] acratino* vel *a Cratino*, 26. 2 *subtractoque] subiratoque* (*subimtoque* Z), 28. 1 *docendi*, 30. 5 *excanduisse et* (also in VL, cf. p. 26). Only at 12. 2 *imperfectum* does Z present the correct, archetypal reading, against the peculiar error of γ, *nuper factum* (see below).

4) Within γ, Z has all the errors that most clearly distinguish the ζ-family: 2. 2 *aliorum] animorum*, 3. 4 *aliquid] aliud*, 4. 1 *Corneliusque*, 4. 3 *et grammatistam*, 4. 3 *nam* (om. *-que*), 4. 5 *nihilo] nullo*, 8. 3 *praecipuum] principium*, 10. 3 *Laelium* (om. *Hermam*), 10. 6 *civilique] celeri*, 11. 3 *quem] quam*, 13. 1 *L. Taberius* (ut vid.), 14. 1 *M. Memmio*, 16. 1 om. *Q.*, 16. 2 *ut* (om. *ita*), 17. 1 *exercitandum*, 19. 1 *Libonis] uxoris*, 20. 2 om. *eo*, 22. 1 om. *M.*, 22. 1 *modestissimus*, 22. 2 *civitatem] auctoritatem*, 25. 2 *ostendamus*, 25. 5 *infuit] fuit*, 28. 2 *ab Epidio*, 30. 3 *perorandi] operandi*. Z also

shares the two corrections of archetypal error that are owed to ζ, 14. 1 *Memmi* (*Memmia* ω) and 16. 3 *Epirota* (om. *et*).

The appearance of the authentic reading *imperfectum* at 12. 2 (vs. *nuper factum* γ) is unexpected; but it hardly contradicts the conclusion suggested by the overwhelming preponderance of the evidence, viz., that Z descends from the archetype by way of γ and of γ's offshoot ζ. It should be possible to place Z a bit more precisely within the latter's family. Before turning to that question, however, we should pause here to note the main point of relevance to these *Studies* more generally: Z plainly offers nothing new that an editor of the *DGR* will find useful or interesting. Beyond the two corrections inherited from ζ, Z has only two other improvements on the archetypal text, both of them already known from other MSS (6. 2 *simul*, also in LQUE, and 22. 3 *Gallus*, also in αLQHU; note too the correct spelling at 7. 1 *Scytobrachionis*, also in U). Against these few places can be set not only the scores of inherited errors already noted, but also the scores of other errors that Z seemingly can claim as its own (I have found these errors in no other MS I have collated, and they are not reported in the collations of Robinson and Brugnoli). Notable above all are the more than two dozen singular omissions: 1. 2 *antiquissimi*, 1. 3 *esse*, 3. 1 *multique*, 3. 2 *Praeconinus quod pater eius*, 3. 3 *nondum*] *non*, 3. 3. *morbum incidit*, 3. 4 *ac magis et* (*et* om. T), 3. 5 *vero*, 3. 5 *nummum*, 4. 6 *vero*, 7. 2 *ita ut*] *ita*, 7. 3 *nam*, 7. 3 *esse*, 9. 5 *quo*, 10. 5 *extent*, 10. 6 *et*, 11. 1 *visusque*] *visus*, 14. 2 *iudicaturus sum*] *indicaturus* (sic, om. *sum*), 17. 1 *libertinus*, 22. 1 *et*, 25. 5 *urbani*, 25. 5 *dum retia extraherentur*, 26. 1 *teneo*, 27. 1 *etiam*, 27. 2 *ab*, 29. 2 *et quidem immunia*] *immurii* (sic, om. *et quidem*). To these can be added a like number of singular transpositions or other gross deformations of the transmitted text: 1. 1 *olim* ante *Romae*, 2. 1 *bellum punicum*, 2. 2 *amicorum defunctorum*, 3. 2 *exilium*] *exili vero* (i.e., *vô*), 4. 3 *alicuius*] *ditius*, 4. 6 *Principem*] *principem Romae*, 7. 1 *memoriae singularis*] *singularem memoriae*, 8. 3 *auctoris*] *cunctorum*, 9. 6 *annum aetatis*, 10. 5 *copia*] *gloria copia*, 14. 2 *alter*] *alter alter*, 17. 1 *sed et praemio quod*] *aequales quidem*, 18. 1 *pansam scenam*, 20. 2 *qui eum qui eum*, 24. 2 *emendare*] n· (= *enim*) *claram*, 25. 2 *censolium abiebtum*, 25. 3 *antea*] *c(arm)ina* (per compend.), 25. 4 *et nam*, 25. 4 *per omnes figuras*] *apud omnis*, 25. 5 *aut aut*, 25. 5 *pretioso*] *gratioso*, 26. 2 *pro se de vi*] *de se vi*, 30. 2 *ex eo claro*] *exadatus*, 30. 2 *et tantum non trivialibus*] *eruualibus*, 30. 5 *praeiberent* (corr. *per-*), 30. 6 *contionantis*] *convivantis*. And

Appendix 3: Biblioteca Riccardiana 3595   153

this is to say nothing of the scores of singular errors of a more pedestrian sort.¹⁰

Though Z may be unworthy of citation in an apparatus criticus, it is potentially useful for clarifying the relations among the *deteriores*: I will conclude this report by noting where the potential lies. First, there are the places where Z shares, not only the errors of the ζ-MSS in general (= HUSCΔQ), but also the distinctive errors of one branch of ζ identified by Robinson, viz., θ (= CΔQ

---

¹⁰ The following list presents only the errors that would be most significant in establishing the MS' relation to another book of similar character. Verbal endings suffered especially (the correct form is given in parentheses): 2. 2 *probasset* (*-ent*), *pronuntiabant* (*-bat*), 3. 3 *intercepissent* (*-et*), 3. 4 *scribent* (*-erent*), 3. 5 *constat* (*-et*), 4. 3 *producerent* (*-eretur*), 7. 1 *consequitur* (*-cutus*), 7. 2 *fugerent* (*fungeretur*), 14. 2 *curarem* (*-are*), 20. 1 *putare* (*-ant, -arem* sec. cur.), 22. 1 *argutae* (*-uere*), 22. 2 *futurus* (*-um*), 24. 2 *legerant* (*-at*), *animadverterent* (*-et*), 24. 3 *habent* (*habuit*), *solebant* (*-bat*), 25. 2 *consulit* (*-uit*), *viderent* (*-etur*), 25. 3 *contradicere* (*-et*), 25. 3 *processerunt* (*-rint*), 25. 5 *emeret* (*-ent*), 25. 6 *reperiuntur* (*-entur*), 27. 2 *opinetur* (*-atur*), 28. 2 *praedicabant* (*-bat*). Also noteworthy are the following miscellaneous errors, many clearly derived from misunderstood abbreviations: 2. 1 *crura*, 3. 3 *parte illa*, 4. 2 *eos idem*, 4. 2 *litteratores*] *-tos*, 4. 5 *ipsos*] *ipsis*, 4. 6 *numero* . . . *patronum*, 4. 7 *clara*, 5. 1 *dignatio neque*, 5. 1 *quoque*] *quorum*, 5. 1 *infantiam*, 5. 2 *diem*] *idem*, 7. 1 *tempus*, 7. 1 *natura*] *nam*, 8. 2 *urbem*, 8. 2 *ceteris*] *certis*, 8. 2 *Cumam*, 8. 3 *sedecim* (vel *XVI*)] *VI*, 9. 1 *magistratibus*] *migrantibus*, 9. 5 *ac ne*] *anne*, 9. 6 *prope*] *proprie*, 10. 2 *et inter rhetorum*, 10. 2 *affectione*, 10. 3 *Claudii*, 10. 3 *cognomine*, 10. 5 *genus*, 10. 6 *eum*] *n·*, 10. 6 *Salustium*, 11. 1 *ac fecit*, 11. 3 *villa*] *nulla*, 11. 3 *unicum*] *mimicum*, 14. 1 *retulisset*, 14. 1 *offendit*] *se ostendit*, 14. 3 *quod*] *quae*, 14. 4 *libro et*, 15. 2 *verecunde*, 15. 3 *subiectus* (cf. *subrectus* α), 15. 3 *patria*, 15. 3 *summum*, 16. 1 *gallae*, 16. 2 *nemini*] *memmi*, 16. 3 *perlegere*, 17. 1 *materiam*, 17. 1 *pulchrior et*, 17. 2 *Augusto*] *augo*, 17. 2 *domusque*, 17. 2 *pars*] *par*, 18. 1 *circa*] *curam*, 19. 1 *et* . . . *quo*] *est* . . . *quoque*, 20. 2 *profuit*, 20. 2 *plurimos*] *p(o)p(u)los* (per compend.), 21. 2 *et*] *etiam*, 22. 3 *didicit*] *deducit*, 23. 4 *ut*] *si ut*, 23. 4 *porcum*] *parcum*, 24. 1 *petit*] *praeiit*, 24. 2 *alias*, 24. 2 *fructuum*, 24. 2 *dediti*, 24. 3 *tam*] *tamen*, 24. 4 *minuti*, 25. 2 *vetus*] *utens*, 25. 2 *die toto*, 25. 2 *nostri qui*, 25. 2 *ita revelent*, 25. 3 *causam*, 25. 3 *de gloriae*, 25. 3 *consulibus*] *quos*, 25. 4 *usum*] *suum*, 25. 5 *accedisset*, 25. 5 *unam*] *nam*, 25. 5 *causam*, 25. 5 *adulescens*, 25. 5 *adierunt*] *abi-*, 25. 5 *puer quod* (bis)] *puerque* (bis), 25. 6 *et quorum*] *equorum*, 26. 2 *Cecilius*, 26. 2 *ac*] *et*, 28. 1 *respondit*] *redit*, 29. 1 *cui*] *cum*, 29. 2 *magistrum*] *magnarum*, 29. 2 *tuo*] *modo*, 29. 2 *compotorum*] *comitorum*, 29. 2 *rhetorum*, 29. 2 *materiam*, 30. 1 *aedilitatem*, 30. 1 *patri*, 30. 1 *frageretur* (ut vid.), 30. 1 *quod*] *quam*, 30. 3 *amplissimas*, 30. 3 *ne aliud* (*alium* sec. cur.), 30. 4 *parentem*, 30. 5 *caedis*] *sedis*, 30. 5 *defendente*, 30. 6 *mori*] *mora*, 30. 6 *diu*] *divi*.

or--when Q follows L, from which it was contaminated--CΔ). I can cite the following (Brugnoli's T and E are noted in parentheses where they are reported as sharing the same error: on the significance of T especially, see below): 2. 1 om. *Palati* ZCΔQ(T), 3. 5 *panosagatema* ZCΔ, 4. 6 *statim*] *stanti* ZCΔ (*stante* T; *stanti* also in M), 6. 3 *libellis* ZCΔQ(T), 6. 3 *inscribuntur* ZCΔQ(T), 10. 2 *Ateius*] *Athenis* ZCΔ (E; also in B), 11. 3 *cauliculi*] *calculus* ZCΔQ, 11. 3 *et idem rursus* ZCΔQ(TE), 14. 2 ὀβελίζει] *obeliri* CΔ, *obelin* Z, 14. 3 *Niciae*] *inter nitii* ZCΔ (*inter Niciae* HTE), 15. 1 *eo filiisque*] *eo aliisque* CΔQ, *et aliisque* Z, 16. 1 *Attici*] *Attici Sati* ZCΔQ(TE; *Sati* ω), 17. 3 *hemicyclium*] *hemiculium* C, *hemiculum* Δ, *eniculium* Z, 18. 2 *mimographis* ZCΔQ(TE), 18. 3 *ad Q.*] om. ZCΔQ(T), 21. 4 *componere* om. ZCΔ, 23. 6 *promercalium*] *inde callium* ZCΔ (T; *et inde callium* H, *inde carnium* Q, *perinde callium* S), 24. 4 *nimis*] *minus* ZCΔ, 25. 2 *ei e re*] *ei r.* ZCΔ, 27. 1 *M'. Otacilius Pitholaus*] *Lucius Volcatius* CΔQ, [ ]*Vtius volcatius* Z (with space for the initial, as regularly). These instances are sufficient to make it likely, *prima facie*, that Z too should be classified with the θ-MSS; and there are additional indications that, within this group, Z is particularly close to C: note especially 1. 2 *Latine composuissent praelegebant*] *L- c- Latine p-* ZC(E), 2. 2 *familiaris*] *familiares* ZC (T), 7. 3 *ipsius*] *ipsius impentius* Z, *ipsius impensius* C (T; *impensius* HUΔ), 11. 1 *Sullani*] *Syllam* ZC, 15. 2 *popinonemque*] *et popinonemque* Z, *et pompinonemque* C (*et pompinionemque* T; *et pompinonem* Δ), 20. 1 C.] [ ]*Arcus* Z, *Marcus* C(Q); 22. 1 *ab adversario*] *ad id srº srº* Z, *ad id sarº srº* C(*ad id srº* Δ, *ad id sarº* S), 23. 4 *praesagente* ZC(T), 24. 2 *sicut*] *sic cum* ZC(TE), 25. 2 *recta*] *itam* ZC (*ita* Δ, *item* H, *item iusta* T, *itura* MKU), 30. 1 *atque ita*] *itaque ita* ZC (*itaque* ζ, om. *ita*).

At the same time it is clear that Z must also be very closely related to Brugnoli's T, which has already made its parenthetical appearance a number of times above. I note the following errors that appear to be shared uniquely by the two MSS: 1. 3 *nam quod*] *nam quidem*, 2. 1 om. *in urbem*, 2. 2 *scriptura expositum*] *scripta et positum* (-*tam* T), 2. 2 *legisse se*] *legisset*, 3. 6 *nonnulla*, 3. 6 *hic*] *haec*, 3. 6 *ingressu*] *graessu*, 4. 1 *libello*] *in bello* Z, *in libello* T, 4. 1 *nominemur*, 4. 6 *declarare*, 7. 1 *memoriae singularis*] *singularem m-* Z, *m- singularem* T, 7. 2 *nonnisi nundinis*] *mundis* (om. *nonnisi*), 9. 1 *meruit*] *induit*, 9. 3 *aut*] *at* Z, *ac* T, 9. 4 *naturae*] *ne*, 9. 4 *ut et*] *sed ut*, 10. 1 *est natus*] *natus* (om. *est*), 10. 5 *sic*] *seu*, 11. 1 *licentia*] -*tur* Z, -*ter* T, 13. 2 *recepit*, 14. 2 *de eo legimus*] *de eo colligimus* Z, *de collegimus* T, 14. 3 om. *est*, 15. 2 *scripsisset*] *subscripsisse* Z, *subscripsisset* T, 17. 1 *liber aliquis*] *liberalis*, 17. 2 *acciperet*, 21. 3 om. *Augusto etiam insinuatus est*, 21. 4 *alios*] *animos* Z, *annuos* T, 23. 1 *mulieris*] *militaris*, 23. 7 *dicto quoque*] *dictoque*, 24. 2 *grammatistam*] *-tem* Z, *-ten* T, 25. 3 *ac*] *atque*, 25. 3 *fortuna*] *forma* Z, *forma* corr. ex. *fama* T, 26. 2 *dictasse*] *dictis se* Z, *dictas se* T, 30. 1 om. *contra*, 30. 3 *in ulla locum quam*] *nulla locum que*.[11] Only in the case of ZC is there a pattern of shared error that is at all comparable to this record.[12] The omissions shared by ZT, together with numerous nonsensical errors unlikely to be imported by contamination, show that the relation between the two MSS must be genetic; and since neither MS can be descended from the other, the two must descend from a common source.[13]

What that source may have been, and how it was related to C and the other θ-MSS, I cannot now say. The errors at, e.g., 7. 3 *ipsius*] *impensius* HUΔ, *ipsius impensius* (*-tius*) ZCT or 15. 2 *popinonemque*] *et po(m)pin(i)onemque* ZCT, *et pompinonem* Δ, when

---

[11] Cf. also the following noteworthy errors shared by ZT and one other ζ-MS: 4. 6 om. *remoto* ZTH (spat. ca. 7-8 litt. relict. ZH), 6. 3 *huius cognomen in plerisque*] *in p- h- c-* ZTH, 9. 2 om. *Romam* ZTH, 12. 1 *edidit*] *docebat edidit* Z, *dicebat edidit* TE, 15. 1 *Telluris*] *telluris aedem* ZTE (*-de* E), 25. 2 *qui eo venire*] *qui evenire* ZH, *que evenire* T, 25. 5 *sporta*] *porta* ZT, *porca* H.

[12] I have noticed only the following errors that Z shares with a single other ζ-MS: 16. 3 *nutricula*] *muricula* Z, *miracula* H, 26. 1 *L.* om. ZU, 28. 2 *praecipitatum*] *principatum* ZH.

[13] Z's many singular omissions and transpositions make abundantly clear that neither T nor any other MS so far known can be descended from it. That neither Z nor any other MS descends from T is suggested, in particular, by the following singular errors of the latter: 1. 3 om. *nonnulli*, 2. 2 om. *Vargunteius . . . Vettiusque*, 3. 6 *Iacchus*] *iacobus*, 8. 1 *professione* (om. *in*), 9. 1 om. *dolo*, 9. 3 *persenex*] *personae*, 9. 3 *continentiam continentem*, 9. 3 *acceperat*, 10. 3 *quia fuit sicut*, 11. 3 *cessaret ut dic ductores Bibaculus*, 15. 1 *comes*] *communes*, 17. 1 *Verrius*] *Valerius*, 20. 2 *libertate*, 26. 1 om. *qui*, 28. 1 *consueveris Isaurici esse discipulum sectum sequeretur*. Note also 10. 1 *hunc Capito Ateius notus iuris consultus*] post *fuisse* transp. *Capito Athenis natus iurisconsultus* (om. *hunc*) T, where a corruption shared with Z alone (*Athenis natus*) is worsened by the transposition; similarly 9. 4 *fuit autem naturae acerbae*] *fuit autem ne acerbae* Z, *fuerat etiam ne acerbae* T.

combined with the bulk of the evidence noted in the last two paragraphs, might be thought to point toward:

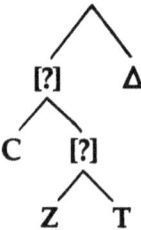

On the other hand, that scheme would not be consistent *prima facie* with, e.g., 14. 3 Niciae] inter Niciae **HTE**, inter nitii **ZCΔ**, 21. 4 *componere* om. **ZCΔ**, 22. 1 *ab adversario*] *ad id sr⁰* **Δ**, *ad id s(a)r⁰ sar⁰* **ZC** (in neither of the latter two instances does Brugnoli report any error in T). Two things, in any case, are clear. The answer to the puzzle will not be simple, and will doubtless need to allow for a significant amount of contamination;[14] and anyone attempting to provide that answer should be prepared to re-examine *all* the progeny of ζ (= 12 of the 26 known MSS, and 2 of the 3 incunabular editions), since the published reports, no matter how thorough, cannot be relied on to provide all the information that will be required.[15] The answer, carefully reached, would clarify our view of this rather untidy sub-basement of the paradosis. Whether the improved view would be worth the candle I leave for others to decide.

---

[14] At 12. 2 *imperfectum*, e.g., it is more likely through contamination than conjecture that this correct, archetypal reading appears in Z, in place of γ's *nuper factum*. It is also plain that any consideration of contamination within this family must start from H and U; on these MSS see Robinson, diss., pp. 156ff.

[15] E.g., several of the errors that H shares with Z, remarked above, are not reported for H by Robinson, full though his accounts of the MSS generally are.

BIBLIOGRAPHY

The bibliography collects the citations for the secondary works mentioned in the text and notes. Standard works of reference (e.g., TLL, articles in RE) are not included.

Acidalius, V. Notae in Taciti Opera (Hanau, 1607)
Adams, J. N. The Latin Sexual Vocabulary (Baltimore, 1982)
Badian, E. "Coo for the Teacher?" LCM 4 (1979): 139-43
Barwick, K. "Der Dialogus de oratoribus des Tacitus," SB d. sächs. Akad. d. Wissensch. Leipzig, Phil-hist. Kl. 101. 4 (Berlin, 1954)
Bauman, R. Lawyers and Politics in the Early Roman Empire (Munich, 1989)
Bickel, E. Diatribe in Senecae philosophi fragmenta, vol. 1 (Leipzig, 1905)
Bione, C. C. Suetoni Tranquilli "De grammaticis et rhetoribus" liber (Palermo, 1939; 2nd ed. 1941)
----------. "Note critiche ed esegetiche a Suetonio De grammaticis et rhetoribus," RFIC 20 (1942): 19-33
Bo, D. Cornelii Taciti "Dialogus de oratoribus" (Turin, 1974)
----------. "Avvaloramento del codice Vindobonense 2960 in relazione al Dialogus de oratoribus di Tacito," AAT 110.2 (1976): 89-116
----------. "Il codice Leidense Perizoniano XVIII Q. 21 in relazione al Dialogus de oratoribus," RIL 110 (1976): 16-40
Bonner, S. F. Education in Ancient Rome (Berkeley, 1977)
----------. "Rhetorica, I: Suetonius De gramm. et rhet. c. 25," CR 61 (1947): 84-86
Bower, E. "Ineptiae and Ioci," Latomus 33 (1974): 523-28
Boyce, G. K. Corpus of the Lararia of Pompeii, MAAR vol. 17 (Rome, 1937)
Brewster, E. H. "On Suetonius De grammaticis 5," CP 10 (1915): 84-87
Brown, P. G. McC. "The Date of Laevius," LCM 5 (1980): 213
Brugnoli, G. C. Suetoni Tranquilli praeter "Caesarum" libros reliquiae, pars prior: "De grammaticis et rhetoribus" (Leipzig, 1960; 2nd ed. 1963; 3rd ed. 1972)
----------. "De IV codicibus libellum Suetonianum 'de grammaticis et rhetoribus' continentibus nuperrime adinventis," GIF 13 (1960): 346-50
----------. Studi Suetoniani (Lecce, 1968)
----------. Studi sulle "Differentiae verborum" (Rome, 1955)
Buckland, W. W. The Roman Law of Slavery (Cambridge, 1908)
Buecheler, F. "Coniectanea," RhM 41 (1886): 10-12
Christes, J. Sklaven und Freigelassene als Grammatiker und Philologen im antiken Rom (Wiesbaden, 1979)
Colker, M. L. "Two Manuscripts of Suetonius' De grammaticis et rhetoribus," Manuscripta 27 (1983): 165-69

Cousin, J. *Etudes sur Quintilien*, 2 vols. (Paris, 1935-36)
----------. rev. of Bione, ed., *REL* 18 (1940): 207-9
Crawford, M. H. *Roman Republican Coinage*, 2 vols. (Cambridge, 1974)
Dahlmann, H. *Cornelius Severus*, Abhandlungen der Akademie der Wissenschaften und der Literatur (Mainz), Geistes- und sozialwissenschaftliche Klasse, Jahrgang 1975, nr. 6 (Mainz, 1975)
----------. rev. of Brugnoli, ed., *Gnomon* 33 [1961]: 796-98
della Corte, F., rev. of Bione, ed., *RFIC* 20 (1942): 136-39
----------. Suetonio: *"Vite di grammatici e di retori"* (Genoa, 1947; 2nd ed. Rome, 1954; 3rd ed. Turin, 1968)
Duncan-Jones, R. P. *Economy of the Roman Empire: Quantitative Studies*[2] (Cambridge, 1982)
Ernout, A., rev. of Robinson, ed., *REL* 4 (1926): 270
Fairweather, J. *Seneca the Elder* (Cambridge, 1981)
Ferraro, V. "La scuola di Orbilio," *RCCM* 9 (1967): 234-38
Graindor, P. *Athènes de Tibère à Trajan* (Cairo, 1931)
Gudeman, A. P. *Cornelii Taciti "Dialogus de oratoribus"*[2] (Leipzig and Berlin, 1914)
Haley, E. W. "Suetonius *Claudius* 24.1 and the Sons of Freemen," *Historia* 35 (1986): 115-21
Helbig, W. *Wandgemälde d. vom Vesuv verschütteten Städte Campaniens* (Leipzig, 1868)
Henriksson, K.-E. *Griechische Büchertitel in der römischen Literatur* (Helsinki, 1956)
Hillscher, A. "Hominum litteratorum Graecorum ante Tiberii mortem in urbe Roma commoratorum historia critica," *Jahrb. f. class. Phil.*, Suppl. 18 (1892): 355-444
Holford-Strevens, L. "Laevius and Melissus," *LCM* 6 (1981): 181-82
----------. *Select Commentary on Aulus Gellius Book 2* (D. Phil. diss. Oxford, 1971)
Housman, A. E. *The Classical Papers of A. E. Housman*, ed. J. Diggle and F. R.D. Goodyear, 3 vols. (Cambridge, 1972)
----------. "Praefanda," *Hermes* 66 (1931): 402-12
Howard, A. A., and C. N. Jackson, *Index verborum C. Suetoni Tranquilli* (Cambridge, Mass., 1922)
Ihm, M. "Zu Ueberlieferung und Textkritik von Suetons Schrift *De grammaticis et rhetoribus*," *RhM* 61 (1906): 543-53
Kajanto, I. *The Latin Cognomina* (Helsinki, 1965)
Kaster, R. A. *Guardians of Language: The Grammarian and Society in Late Antiquity* (Berkeley and Los Angeles, 1988)
----------. *The Tradition of the Text of the "Aeneid" in the Ninth Century* (New York, 1990)
Killeen, J. F. "Suetonius *De gramm*. ix," *WS* 3 (1969): 233-34
Kinsey, T. E. "Should Appuleius be Sent to Cos? (Suetonius, *de gramm*. 3)," *LCM* 4 (1979): 79
Konrad, C. F. "Cotta off Mellaria and the Identities of Fufidius," *CP* 84 (1989): 119-29

Lammert, L. "Laevius Melissus?" *Hermes* 62 (1927): 251-53
Lausberg, L. *Handbuch der literarischen Rhetorik*³ (Stuttgart, 1990)
Lebek, W. D. "Eine pollionische Bemerkung Suet. *Gramm.* 10,1 (Rob.) und der Name des Ateius Philologus," *Hermes* 98 (1970): 127-28
----------. "*Festinare* (Suet. *gramm.* 23, 6; *CIL* IV, 4758; Hor. *Epist.* 1, 1, 85)," *ZPE* 45 (1982): 53-57
----------. *Verba Prisca: Die Anfänge des Archaisierens in der lateinischen Beredsamkeit und Geschichtsschreibung* (Göttingen, 1970)
Lewis, R. G. "Pompeius' Freedman Biographer: Suetonius, *De Gramm. et Rhet.* 27 (3)," *CR* 16 (1966): 271-73
Lynch, J. P. *Aristotle's School: A Study of a Greek Educational Institution* (Berkeley and Los Angeles, 1972)
Mejer, J. *Diogenes Laertius and His Hellenistic Background* (Wiesbaden, 1978)
Mercklin, L. "Zu Suetonius *de grammaticis* c. 10," *Philol.* 19 (1863): 158-59
Merklin, H. "Probleme des 'Dialogus de oratoribus,'" *A&A* 34 (1988): 170-89
----------. "'Dialogus'-Probleme in der neueren Forschung: Ueberlieferungsgeschichte, Echtheitsbeweis und Umfang der Lücke," *ANRW* 2:33.3 (Berlin and New York, 1991), pp. 2255-83
Murgia, C. E. "The Length of the Lacuna in Tacitus' *Dialogus*," *CSCA* 12 (1979): 221-40
----------. "The Minor Works of Tacitus: A Study in Textual Criticism," *CP* 72 (1977): 323-43
Murgia, C. E. and R. H. Rodgers, "A Tale of Two Manuscripts," *CP* 79 (1984): 145-53
Nicolet, C. *L'ordre équestre à l'époque républicaine (312-43 av. J.-C.)*, 2 vols. (Paris, 1966-74)
Osann, F. *C. Suetonii Tranquilli "De grammaticis et rhetoribus" libelli* (Gissen, 1854)
Perret, J. *Recherches sur le texte de la "Germanie"* (Paris, 1950)
Pfeiffer, R. *History of Classical Scholarship* (Oxford, 1968)
Rawson, E. *Intellectual Life in the Late Roman Republic* (Baltimore, 1985)
----------. "M. Aeficius Calvinus and His *Grammaticus* (Suetonius, *de gramm.* 3)," *LCM* 4 (1979): 53-58
Reifferscheid, A. *C. Suetoni Tranquilli praeter "Caesarum" libros reliquiae* (Leipzig, 1860)
Reynolds, L. D., ed., *Texts and Transmission: A Survey of the Latin Classics* (Oxford, 1983)
Ritschl, F. *Parerga zu Plautus und Terenz, I* (Leipzig, 1845)
Robathan, D. "Another Fifteenth-Century Manuscript of the *Germania*," *AJP* 71 (1950): 225-38
Robinson, R. P. *C. Suetoni Tranquilli "De grammaticis et rhetoribus"* (Paris, 1925)
----------. *De fragmenti Suetoniani "De grammaticis et rhetoribus" codicum nexu et fide* (Urbana, 1920)
----------. *The "Germania" of Tacitus* (Middletown, Conn., 1935)
Römer, F. "Kritischer Problem- und Forschungsbericht zur Ueberlieferung

der taciteischen Schriften," *ANRW* 2:33.3 (Berlin and New York, 1991), pp. 2299-339

Rolfe, J. C. *Suetonius*, 2 vols. (Cambridge, Mass., and London, 1914)

Roth, C. L. *C. Suetoni Tranquilli quae supersunt omnia* (Leipzig, 1858)

Rubenstein, N. "An Unknown Letter of Jacopo di Poggio Bracciolini on Discoveries of Classical Texts," *IMU* 1 (1958): 383-400

Saller, R. P. "Anecdotes as Historical Evidence for the Principate," *G&R* 27 (1980): 69-83

Sauerwein, I. *Die leges sumptuariae als römische Massnahme gegen den Sittenverfall* (Diss. Hamburg, 1970)

Schaps, D. "The Found and Lost Manuscripts of Tacitus' *Agricola*," *CP* 74 (1979): 28-42

Scheuer, F. "De Tacitei de Oratoribus Dialogi Codicum Nexu e Fide," *Breslauer philologische Abhandlungen* 6. 1 (Breslau, 1891)

Sirks, B. "Juridical Rationality in Rhetorics," *Atti del III Seminario Romanistico Gardesano (22-25 ottobre 1985)* (Milan, 1988), pp. 333-59

Solin, H. *Beiträge zur Kenntnis der griechischen Personennamen in Rom, I* (Helsinki, 1971)

----------. *Die griechischen Personennamen in Rom: Ein Namenbuch*, 3 vols. (Berlin and New York, 1982)

Spann, P. O. *Quintus Sertorius and the Legacy of Sulla* (Fayetteville, 1987)

Stegemann, W. "Die ältere griechische Bezeichnung für rhetorische Kontroversen," *PhW* 57 (1937): 509-12

----------. rev. of Bione, ed., *PhW* 61 (1941): 343-46

Stok, F. "Le vicende dei codici Hersfeldensi," *MAL* 28 (1984-86): 277-319

Sumner, G. V. "Varrones Murenae," *HSCP* 82 (1978): 187-95

Svoronos, J., and B. V. Head, *The Illustrations of the "Historia Nummorum"* (Chicago, 1968)

Till, R. *Handschriftliche Untersuchungen zu Tacitus "Agricola" und "Germania"* (Berlin and Dahlem, 1943)

Treggiari, S. "Pompeius' Freedman Biographer Again," *CR* 19 [1969]: 264-66

----------. *Roman Freedmen during the Late Republic* (Oxford, 1969)

Tross, L. *C. Cornelii Taciti "De origine, situ, moribus ac populis Germanorum" libellus . . . Accesserunt "Dialogus de oratoribus" et Suetonii "De viris illustribus" libellus* (Hammone, 1841)

Ullman, B. L. "Pontano's Handwriting and the Leiden Manuscript of Tacitus and Suetonius," *IMU* 2 (1959): 309-35

Vahlen, J. *De Verrio Flacco et Suetonii libello "De grammaticis"* (Berlin, 1877)

----------. *Opuscula Academica*, 2 vols. (Leipzig, 1907-8)

Verdière, R., rev. of Brugnoli, ed., *Latomus* 19 (1960): 800-801

Watson, A. *The Law of Persons in the Later Roman Republic* (Oxford, 1967)

Watt, W. S. "Facessat Mutusca," *LCM* 4 (1979): 167

Wessner, P., rev. of Robinson, diss., *PhW* 43 (1923): 511-16, 536-42

----------. rev. of Robinson, ed., *PhW* 46 (1926): 1224-30

Wiedemann, T., rev. of Christes, *Sklaven, CR* 32 (1982): 75-76

Winterbottom, M. "The Manuscript Tradition of Tacitus' *Germania*," *CP*

70 (1975): 1-7
----------. *The Minor Declamations Ascribed to Quintilian* (Berlin and New York, 1984)
----------. "Suetonius (*De grammaticis et rhetoribus*)," in Reynolds, *Texts and Transmission,* pp. 404-5
----------. "Tacitus (*Minor Works*)," ibid., pp. 410-11
----------. "The Transmission of Tacitus' *Dialogus,*" *Philol.* 116 (1972): 114-28
Wissowa, G. *Taciti "Dialogus de Oratoribus" et "Germania," Suetoni "De Viris Illustribus" Fragmentum: Codex Leidensis Perizonianus phototypice editus* (Leiden, 1907)

INDEX LOCORUM

The index includes only the passages that are at the center of discussion in Chapters 1 and 2 and the Appendixes. It does not include all the texts cited in the those discussions.

Cassius Dio
   57. 17. 1-3: 100-102

Cicero
   Att. 12. 26. 2: 88

Horace
   Serm. 1. 10. 22: 121

Laevius
   FPL frag. 23. 1: 43

Livy
   21. 14. 3: 66

Macrobius
   Sat. 2. 2. 13: 121
      2. 6. 4: 67f.

Pliny the Elder
   HN 3 index: 70f.
      7. 128: 42
      14. 49-52: 105, 108
      35. 199: 85f.

Plutarch
   Sull. 14. 3: 71

Seneca (philosophus)
   Ben. 2. 13. 2: 66

Seneca (rhetor)
   Suas. 2. 12-13: 100-102

Suetonius
   DGR 1. 2: 23
      1. 3: 38-40
      3. 3: 40f.
      3. 5: 21 n. 33, 23f., 41-47, 47-52
      3. 6: 52
      4. 1: 25, 97
      4. 6: 21, 52-54
      5. 1: 54-59
      6. 2: 60-62
      7. 1: 25
      7. 3: 13, 62-64
      8. 3: 64
      9. 3: 65f.
      9. 4: 66f.
      9. 5: 67-70
      10. 1: 70f.
      10. 2: 71-73, 89
      10. 3: 73-77
      10. 4: 20
      10. 6: 77f.
      11. 1: 144
      11. 3: 24, 78-80
      13. 1: 80-87, 149
      14. 1: 87
      14. 2: 27
      14. 3: 88

Suetonius
  DGR 15. 2: 13, 88-91
      15. 3: 91-93
      16. 1: 28
      16. 2: 28f.
      16. 3: 93-95
      17. 2: 13
      17. 3: 20
      18. 3: 24f.
      21. 3: 144
      21. 4: 44, 98f.
      22. 1: 99-102
      22. 2: 20, 102f.
      23. 1: 145f.
      23. 4: 103f., 104f., 142
      23. 6: 105-8
      23. 7: 95-97
      24. 1: 109f.
      24. 2: 13, 110f.
      24. 3: 20, 142
      25. 2: 23
      25. 4: 20, 111-14
      25. 5: 23, 26, 114-17, 117-20
      27. 1: 23, 120-24
      28. 1: 124-26
      28. 2: 29, 126f.
      29. 1: 127f.
      30. 1: 144f.
      30. 2: 128-30
      30. 5: 26
  Jul. 75. 5: 121

Tacitus
  Dial. 5. 5: 137-40
        16. 2: 137-40
        17. 1: 137-40
        19. 3: 137-40
        21. 5: 137-40
        25. 4: 9f.
        28. 2: 137-40
        28. 4: 140
        30. 1: 137-40
        31. 7: 8f.
        35-36: 136, 137, 138, 150

Vergil
  Aen. 4. 1-600: 35f.

www.ingramcontent.com/pod-product-compliance
Ingram Content Group UK Ltd.
Pitfield, Milton Keynes, MK11 3LW, UK
UKHW041428180426
11947UKWH00007B/348